Graceful Leadership

Inspiring hope, creativity
and resilience in times of
peace and crisis

Will Parks

Graceful Leadership

ISBN 978-1-915483-43-0

eISBN 978-1-915483-44-7

Published in 2025 by Right Book Press

Manufactured by

Sue Richardson Associates Ltd.

Studio 6,

9, Marsh Street

Bristol BS1 4AA

info@therightbookcompany.com

EU Safety Representative

euComply OÜ

Parnu mnt 139b-14

11317 Tallinn

Estonia

hello@eucompliancepartner.com

+33 756 90241

© Will Parks

Disclaimer: The information in this book expresses my personal views and opinions and does not necessarily represent the position or views of any particular organisation. Designations employed and the presentation of the material in this book do not imply the expression of any opinion whatsoever concerning the legal status of any country, territory, city or area, or of its authorities, or concerning the delimitation of its frontiers or boundaries. Reference to any individual, organisation, brand, company, product or service does not imply that they are endorsed or recommended in preference to others of a similar nature that are not mentioned. Reference to any organisation's website or publication does not imply endorsement or responsibility for the accuracy of the information contained therein or of the content and views expressed. Information on URLs and links to websites contained in the book are provided for the convenience of the reader and are correct at the time of publication. All reasonable precautions have been taken to verify the information contained in this book. However, the book is being published without a warranty of any kind, either expressed or implied. The responsibility for the interpretation and use of the material lies with the reader. This book does not substitute for the advice of physicians or other health specialists. The reader should consult appropriate professionals before adopting practices described in the book or making any inferences from it.

The author's proceeds from this book will go to The Alfred Foundation and UNICEF Australia.

'This will challenge your thinking about what it means to lead. Will Parks reveals how leaders can ennoble, engage and empower followers as a means of achieving sustainable outcomes. Told with passion and purpose, this book provides a window into how to bring people together for common good.'

   John Baldoni, member of 100 Coaches and author of many books on leadership, including *Grace Under Pressure*

'This book is an appeal to the best in us, to be a kind and thoughtful human as well as an effective leader. Will Parks has integrated research from experts with his humanitarian work into a framework for effective, graceful leadership. Read it and practise it – the people around you will appreciate it!'

   Prof. Richard Boyatzis, academic, executive coach, co-author of *Primal Leadership* and author of *The Science of Change*

'Will Parks beautifully captures the essence of compassionate and empathetic leadership needed in today's challenging world. Through his personal stories, global experiences and reflections on humanitarian leadership, he offers a unique perspective on what it means to lead with grace. This book encourages us to lead not through authority but through humanity.'

   Prof. Deborah Crowe, academic, leadership coach and author of *The Heart-Centered Leadership Playbook*

'Too much of the leadership we have experienced, either first hand or indirectly, is the opposite of graceful. In this book, Will Parks beautifully weaves in his own story of leading with grace to define what it is together with practical ways to help us become more graceful. I will be embodying more grace in my leadership as a result of reading.'

   Paul Hargreaves, chief empowerment officer, Cotswold Fayre & Flourish, and author of *Forces for Good* and *The Fourth Bottom Line*

'Will Parks captures the very essence of leadership in this important book. It is a call to action, a call to lead with empathy, compassion and care, a call to lead with grace. A book for our times.'

   Steven Hargreaves, founder and director of The
   Compassionate Leadership Company and author of
   The Compassionate Leader's Playbook

'Drawing on the wisdom of the world's top leadership gurus and the author's personal experience of working with UNICEF in several challenging assignments, this book makes a compelling case that leading with grace is the most relevant trend of leadership development of our times.'

   Kul Gautam, former UNICEF deputy executive director
   and assistant secretary-general of the United Nations, and
   author of *Global Citizen from Gulmi*

'Graceful leadership is essential in today's world of complexity and crisis. This book provides practical wisdom and actionable practices that any leader can apply to create lasting, positive impact.'

   Rasmus Hougaard, founder and managing partner of
   Potential Project and, with Jacqueline Carter, author of
   Compassionate Leadership

'A thoroughly researched and inspiring guide to leadership in international development and humanitarian work. Incorporating practical examples from Will Parks's career with UNICEF, it is hugely relevant to any complex environment where the stakes are high.'

   Chris Whitehead, director of Damflask Consulting Ltd and
   author of *Compassionate Leadership*

'Grounded in experience from three decades at UNICEF, this book articulates a compelling vision for graceful leadership and is a helpful companion for those working across the humanitarian sector and beyond.'

Prof. Amy Bradley, academic and author of *The Human Moment* and *Running on Empty*

'This is a powerful, moving, practical account of how to lead in a world of uncertainty. Drawing from research and the author's own experiences, this book will pull you in from the very first pages and help you become a leader that helps people thrive.'

Prof. Amy C. Edmondson, academic and author of *The Fearless Organization* and *Right Kind of Wrong*

'A comprehensive and beautifully written guide for current and future leaders. Using personal stories and wisdom from experts, Will Parks shows us how to move from old-style command and control to serving the world by leading through compassion and coaching. You will want to keep this book nearby as it is packed with pragmatic practices and tools that you'll refer back to again and again.'

Cindy Wigglesworth, founder and president of Deep Change, Inc., and author of *SQ21*

'An inspirational read for all leaders. It takes us on a journey of understanding how we can go from a "command and control" way of influencing others, to a more compassionate way of leading. Combining the author's authentic journey, deep research and observations, along with examples and thoughtful reflective questioning, this is a guide to help us embody grace through our leadership.'

Sarah Higgins, leadership coach and author of *Power of Love Leadership*

'I am so thrilled to endorse this book and Will Parks as he dares to bring grace into the conversation about how we lead. He shares incredible stories through his career with UNICEF that open your heart and plant the seed of what grace is and how to evoke it within your inner and outer worlds.'

Alexsys Thompson, executive leadership coach, author of *The Power of a Graceful Leader*, creator of Gratitude 540 Journal Series and co-creator of the 'Do Love' movement

'Our world badly needs the graceful leadership that Will Parks describes so lovingly and practically. This book demonstrates how leaders, when they blend compassion with coaching, can inspire teams to achieve amazing results even when against the odds.'

Clare Norman, Master Certified Coach, mentor coach, coaching supervisor and author of *The Transformational Coach* and *Cultivating Coachability*

Contents

Graceful leadership toolbox

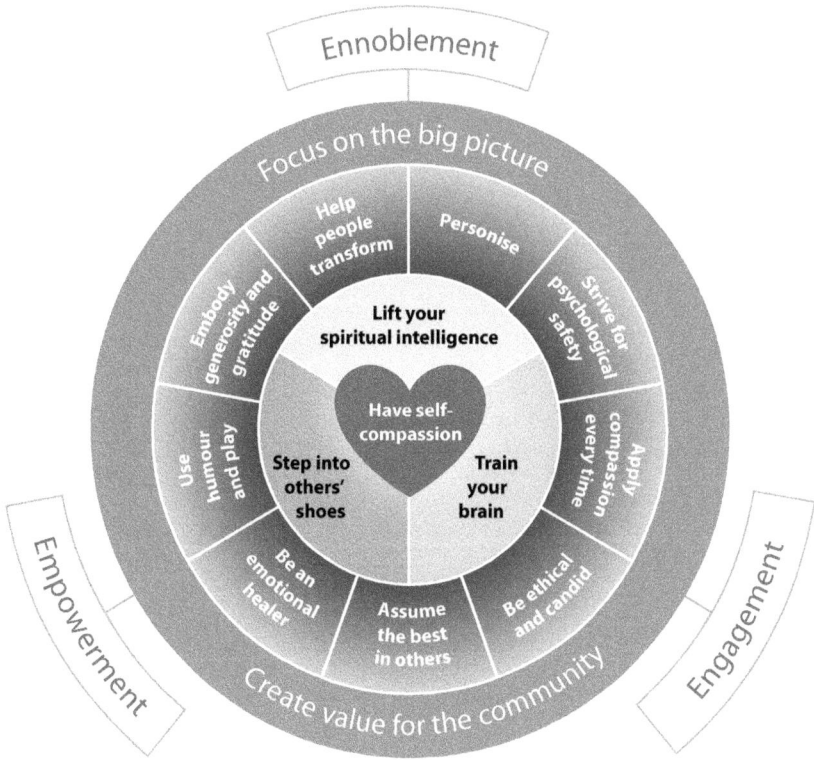

Three aspirations and 15 practices of graceful leadership

The beginning

> I am of the opinion that my life belongs to the whole community and as long as I live, it is my privilege to do for it what I can. I want to be thoroughly used up when I die, for the harder I work, the more I live. I rejoice in life for its own sake. Life is no brief candle to me. It is a sort of splendid torch which I have got hold of for the moment and I want to make it burn as brightly as possible before handing it on to future generations.
> – George Bernard Shaw, playwright, activist and winner of the Nobel Prize for Literature.

For me, this short passage from George Bernard Shaw's 1903 letter explaining his play *Man and Superman* to a friend, the theatre critic Arthur Bingham Walkley, says it all. The words continue to stir. They helped me to distil my own life purpose typed on a slip of paper that, now dog-eared, sits within the frame of a small black-and-white photo of myself as a young boy standing happily beside a pedal car I would 'drive' for hours around my family's garden.

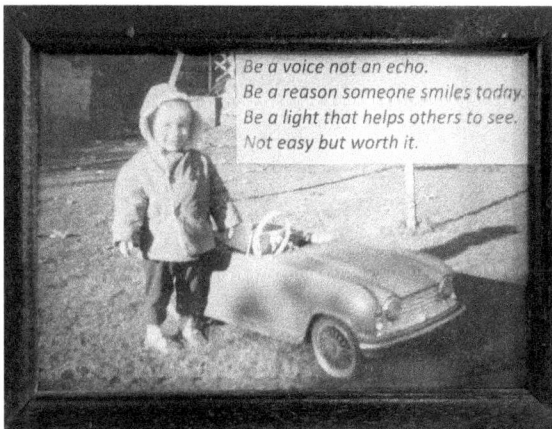

I later learned that this Shaw quote was also a favourite of James P or 'Jim' Grant, a visionary, compassionate leader of the United Nations International Children's Emergency Fund (UNICEF) between 1980 and 1995 (Jolly 2001).* Jim ignited a 'child survival revolution' across the world that not only redefined international development but also saved perhaps more lives than were destroyed by Hitler, Mao and Stalin put together (Fifield 2015).

I was 16 years old, studying at Wellington College in the United Kingdom, when I first learned about Jim. From 1984 onwards, I dreamt of working for UNICEF.

In November 2016, we held a school reunion in London entitled 'Thirty Years On'. My classmates described their varied careers – community leaders, teachers, lecturers, artists, musicians, engineers, bankers, stockbrokers, mortgage lenders, executives, volunteers, consultants, armed forces personnel, nurses, doctors, politicians, lawyers and so on. 'What've you been up to, Will?' many asked, shouting above the excited din of the evening. 'I'm working with UNICEF,' I replied. 'Wow, that's what you always said you'd do!' Each of them could recall my boyhood dream.

I might have had the wonderful opportunity to meet Jim Grant in June 1995 when a poster presentation that I'd developed with a fellow Queensland University student (thanks Vicki!) was accepted for display at the ChildHealth 2000 World Congress in Vancouver, Canada. But Jim succumbed to cancer on 28 January that year, a day before my 27th birthday and just 11 days before my father tragically died of a heart attack. Oh, Dad… Almost a decade later, 28 January was to be the birthday of Oliver, my second son.

So, although he inspired my career, I sadly never met Jim Grant. And I never met the other graceful soul who launched my career.

September 1992: I was a tutor at the University of Durham's anthropology department and volunteer for

---

* While the 'UNICEF' acronym has been retained, the agency is now called the United Nations Children's Fund.

UNICEF UK. Motivated by a 1987 visit to the gentle people and the breath-giving, breathtaking rainforests of eastern Papua New Guinea, I'd become fascinated by ethnopharmacology – the study of indigenous medical systems and their physiological potential to help improve global health. The late Professor Norman Farnsworth, then at the University of Illinois, was one of the field's leading lights. I posted a handwritten letter to him enquiring if there was any chance of being part of his research endeavour. Though no reply came, I realised later that he had considerately kept my correspondence.

February 1993: I had just turned 25. I was standing at the department's reception desk when the phone rang. 'Hold on. He's right beside me.' The receptionist handed the call to me. On the other end of the line was the chargé d'affaires for Solomon Islands. 'Hello Will! Professor Farnsworth passed on your name to us. Would you be willing to help us assess whether a biodiversity institute can be set up here to research traditional medicine and to find alternatives to logging our rainforests?'

With this out-of-the-blue 'Yes!' from the Solomon Islands' government, my leadership journey in international development began. So, bless you, Professor Farnsworth. Although you sadly left us in 2011, I hope that you can sense my eternal gratitude.

From that first consultancy in Solomon Islands in 1993, the past three decades, during most of which I was with UNICEF, gifted me the privilege of working with the people of another 40 nations: Afghanistan, Australia, Bangladesh, Bhutan, Brazil, Cambodia, China, Cook Islands, Costa Rica, Cuba, Dominican Republic, Ethiopia, Federated States of Micronesia, Fiji Islands, India, Indonesia, Iran, Iraq, Laos, Malaysia, Marshall Islands, Myanmar, Nauru, Nepal, Nicaragua, Niue, Palau, Papua New Guinea, Philippines, Samoa, South Africa, Sri Lanka, Sudan, Tanzania, Thailand, Timor-Leste, Tonga, Tunisia, United Kingdom and Vanuatu.

In assisting communities, governments, civil societies, academia, businesses, media, religious authorities and international agencies, I hope that in some small way I've improved the lives of children and their families in these countries during times of natural disasters, epidemics, financial downturns and wars as well as in times of relative calm, if we can call that 'peace'. From child survival to youth empowerment, from sustainable development to financial crises, from tsunamis, floods and earthquakes to economic sanctions, from armed conflicts to Covid-19, the following pages are my humble attempt to distil what I have seen of and learned about leadership along the way.

About this book

This book is divided into two parts. Each part tries to answer core questions about leadership, questions that I believe are of pressing relevance right now and likely will remain so.

In Part 1, I explore *what graceful leadership means and why it matters so much*. I define key terms and present compelling evidence of the benefits of graceful leadership gathered from around the world through my encounters with individuals who led and lead with grace and from different types of organisations, profit to non-profit, government to non-government.

In Part 2, I examine *how to embody graceful leadership each day*. I offer 15 mutually reinforcing practices that are proven to unleash talent, create joy and transform performance – practices that can help you to become and remain a graceful leader regardless of your position in life or your job title.

I present short stories drawn from my own leadership journey towards grace (I'm still travelling) to illustrate key points. I've combined ethnography, action research and participant observation to document my experiences over the years.

In several special sections entitled 'What graceful leaders say', I share the thoughts and experiences of a small sample of leaders I've worked with or met and later interviewed for this book: Dr Mohamed Ag Ayoya, Ugochi Daniels, Peter Hawkins, Hamida Lasseko and Gillian Mellsop. Their biographies can be found at the end of the book. Other exceptional individuals are mentioned along the way.

I also cite the many scholars, leaders and coaches who have deepened my realisation of what leadership is, can be and indeed should be. Finally, I've included a toolbox containing examples of reflective questions to use in various leadership situations and some other handy resources.

This book is for aspiring, emerging and established leaders of governmental, non-profit and for-profit organisations; humanitarian workers; sustainable development professionals; human resource managers; organisational change specialists; leadership scholars; social change practitioners; as well as team and one-on-one coaches and mentors. But there are others, in families and communities, who might also browse through these pages.

Writing this book was enlightening and yet humbling because it contains advice that I wish I'd sought 30 years ago.

I loved playing rugby (the version with 15 players per team). In September 1988, soon after I began my biology degree at the UK's University of Southampton, I joined Havant Rugby Club. There I experienced the mindful coaching of the compassionately tough Welshman Brian Powell – also the Royal Navy's rugby coach at the time. He would urge before every game, 'Billy Whizz,' as I was nicknamed by the club, 'leave everything on the field. Crawl off, bleeding if needs be, but with nothing left to give.' I gave it my all. Brian's words stuck with me, and I've tried to do the same in the pages that follow.

Part 1

What is graceful leadership? And why does it matter so much?

The global community is confronted by unprecedented volatility, uncertainty, complexity, ambiguity and hyperconnectivity (VUCAH). A once-in-a-century pandemic has crippled societies and unravelled economies, even as conflicts and disasters proliferate. The desire for individual gain continues to supersede commitment to people, our planet and collective prosperity.

Some even talk about a shift away from singular crises (natural or human-made disasters of one type occurring in one place, at one time) to the spread of simultaneous catastrophes, of different types in different places but so interlinked, partly through our hyperconnectivity, that their impacts become mutually amplified. We have entered the era of the *polycrisis*, even as the 'fourth industrial revolution' emerges with human interaction and ever-advancing technology becoming increasingly enmeshed.

The Collins Dictionary defines polycrisis as 'the simultaneous occurrence of several catastrophic events' and the Cambridge Dictionary as 'a time of great disagreement, confusion or suffering that is caused by many different problems happening at the same time so they together have a very big effect'. For historian and economist Professor Adam Tooze, the frequent convergence of forces originating from economics, politics, geopolitics and the natural environment presents us with the experience of an apparent collage of colliding crises: climate change, biodiversity loss, pollution, poverty, inequality, pandemics, increasing rates of non-communicable disease and mental ill health, food and fuel price spikes, global supply chain interruptions, financial downturns, inflation, increasing xenophobia, decreasing international cooperation and multiple wars, to name just a few (Tooze 2023).

And there are others who have begun to talk about the advent of a *permacrisis* – an age in which we seem to lurch from one crisis or even one polycrisis to the next without ever recovering from or stabilising previous chaos. The Collins Dictionary defines permacrisis as 'an extended period of insecurity and instability' and the Cambridge Dictionary as 'a long period of great difficulty, confusion or suffering that seems to have no end'.

Perhaps at the heart of this state of potential permacrisis are ineffectual leadership approaches to economic growth, environmental management and governance (Brown et al 2023). Polycrisis or not, permacrisis or not, the crystal-clear fact is that the very essence of humanity is being tested – relentlessly, and largely by and because of humans.

As I thought about the title for this book, I was tempted to add 'in times of peace and permacrisis'. There was the allure of alliteration – but that wouldn't have made much sense. If peace is a state of harmony, tranquillity, no disturbance, no disorder, no hostility and no conflict, then there can never be peace if we are ensnared within a permacrisis.

So, what about 'peace and polycrisis', which would make more sense (and still alliterate!)? But the optimist in me firmly believes that we can collectively emerge from this dark period with great solutions – yes, even to polycrises. While some disasters are unavoidable, we can build more resilience in ourselves, our families, communities, systems, organisations, industries, institutions and societies to be more responsive to and improve how we handle shocks. We can also better predict and prevent many adversities plus get smarter at minimising the impacts of interconnections between crises. We can take the 'poly' out of 'polycrisis'. And yes, all this *without* abrasive nationalism. Finally, lest we forget, humans have shown we can courageously create periods of peace without resorting to arms. Why? How? I think *graceful leadership* is one of the reasons.

In the first part of this book, I outline what graceful leadership means to me, highlighting authors and researchers who have shaped my perspective and turning to leaders I've encountered to seek their views. I define key terms: grace, compassion, kindness, courage and coaching. This is followed by a story about leading humanitarian work during an armed conflict. I then examine why graceful leadership matters so much, providing evidence of its benefits for individuals, teams and organisations as well as for society at large.

But let me begin with what unfolded one morning back in 2007.

Chapter 1

The Pacific Ring of Fire

Solomon Islands, Monday 2 April 2007

Without looking across or being in an ocean, you can still sense its power. Perhaps you've stood, trousers, dress or sarong rolled up above the knees, bare feet nestled within that zone of a sandy beach where graceful waves are expending the last of their energy. And when the next wavelet froths across your ankles and gently retreats, you can feel the ocean's pull as your toes sink deeper into the wet sand...

I'm honoured to know these sincere people, their azure sea and their lush green forests. Between 1995 and 1996, I conducted child survival research based out of Chubikopi village on the island of Marovo in the New Georgia group of Solomon Islands. And I'd returned to the Western Solomons a few times since, including to the fishing town of Gizo, the Western Province's capital on Ghizo Island.

The nation state of Solomon Islands stretches over 1.34 million square kilometres of ocean, from Papua New Guinea's island of Bougainville in the north-west to Vanuatu in the south-east. This is the Pacific Ring of Fire, one of the most seismically active areas of the planet. There are frequent, tsunami-generating earthquakes and volcanic eruptions due to the rapid and complicated convergence of the Pacific tectonic plate with the Australian plate and numerous microplates. Since 1950, natural disasters have directly affected more than 3.4 million people and led to more than 1,700 reported deaths in the Pacific (not including Papua New Guinea). In the 1990s, for example, reported natural disasters cost the region US$4.6 billion, in real 2023 figures (Bettencourt et al 2006).

But this Monday morning was another beauty. The sea was calm. Men and women were returning from their pre-sunrise fishing. Families were preparing or eating breakfast, gathered around smoky kitchen fires. Slow-roasted fish and sweet potato have an enticing scent. Teachers and some children were already on their way to school, paddling wooden canoes or crossing the sea channels between islets in their outboard engine-powered skiffs. It was supposed to be just another day.

At 7.39 am local time some 45 km south-south-east of Ghizo Island and about 345 km north-west of the nation's capital, Honiara, tectonic plates wrestled 10,000 metres beneath the ocean's surface, triggering an 8.1 Richter earthquake that rocked Western and Choiseul Provinces. It was the largest quake experienced in Solomon Islands since 1900.

Residents in Gizo recall more than one minute of violent shaking so fierce that many were thrown and then pinned to the ground while palm trees thrashed back and forth, their multi-fingered leaves brushing the sand. Tremors were felt as far as Honiara.

The Pacific Warning Centre in Honolulu issued a tsunami alert, soon expanded beyond Solomon Islands to include Papua New Guinea, Vanuatu, Nauru, New Caledonia, Fiji, Chuuk, Pohnpei, Kosrae, Indonesia, Tuvalu, Kiribati, Marshall Islands, north-eastern Australia, Kermadec Islands and mainland New Zealand. But for the Western Province, a multiple-wave tsunami beat the warning. No sooner had the massive shaking stopped than the ocean retreated, exposing the sea floor along coastlines, inlets and lagoons. Ancestral knowledge of tsunamis triggered many islanders to spontaneously self-evacuate, running as fast as they could to higher ground.

Within just 360 seconds of the earthquake, those in the New Georgia island group were confronted by a sequence of sinister tsunamis racing back towards them. Some described it as an onslaught of huge tidal surges, rushing in, one after the other. Many had no time to run. Ghizo, Noro and Taro Islands were badly hit. In some places, 5 m walls of salt water rampaged across coastal lowlands. On Ghizo Island, the waves reached almost 6 m above sea level before relinquishing their overland progression. In Gizo Town, several children and adults were engulfed and swept out to sea. Parts of the town were inundated, the sea advancing up to 70 m inland. Buildings and homes were broken, many completely flattened. Large fishing vessels and ferry boats were lifted indifferently and dumped into the centre of town. Road vehicles were scattered, power and communication lines wrecked, the airport damaged, coastal roads washed away and the hospital rendered instantly inoperative.

The multiple tsunamis kept moving, reaching Choiseul Island's south coast less than 30 minutes after the quake. Waves of up to 10 m swept through the village of Sasamunga, penetrating up to half a kilometre inland and destroying at least 300 houses. Choiseul Province's hospital and health centres were lost. Destructive waves struck parts of Vella La Vella, Kolombangara, Simbo, Shortlands, Munda, Mono and Ranongga – large areas of the latter island were raised over 3 m due to the geological uplift associated with the earthquake. Even eastern Papua New Guinea experienced the tsunamis' multiple impacts.

Sadly, large-scale natural calamities continue across the globe. But what happened that April morning was the worst humanitarian disaster in this part of the South Pacific since the Second World War. Fifty-two precious souls were lost, 24 of them children under 10 years of age. Almost all were overwhelmed by the waves. Several adults drowned trying to save their loved ones. Two died in landslides (more than 1,000 landslides were triggered). Forty were injured. An estimated

9,000 people were internally displaced to more than 130 spontaneously erected camps. Some 6,000 needed temporary food supplies. More than 3,250 houses were ruined and a further 3,047 damaged. Thousands of families lost *all* their possessions. More than 200 schools were destroyed, interrupting the schooling of some 18,000 students for many months. The two main referral hospitals in the vicinity (Gizo and Taro) and several health facilities were damaged. In all, more than 36,500 people (equivalent to the nation state of Monaco) living in 304 coastal communities were affected. Infrastructure damage was estimated to be US$134 million (in real 2023 figures). And destruction of fragile coral reefs, scattered throughout the area, would have long-lasting effects on fish stocks.

Coastal damage in Solomon Islands from the 2 April 2007 tsunami.
Photo: Australian Agency for International Development (AusAID).

The diversity and scale of these impacts coupled with the remoteness of the affected populations exponentially increased the complexities of planning and delivering humanitarian aid. Alongside other United Nations agencies, international, national and faith-based non-government organisations

(NGOs) including Save the Children Fund Australia, World Vision, Caritas Solomon Islands, Oxfam and the National Red Cross supported by the International Federation of Red Cross/Red Crescent and the French Red Cross, UNICEF played a significant role in the immediate response.

We already had a small team of social sector specialists based in Honiara who were reinforced by the immediate deployment of an emergency response team composed of experienced humanitarians mobilised from our international emergency roster as well as UNICEF emergency professionals hand-picked from our offices in Bangladesh, Indonesia, Myanmar, Pakistan, Papua New Guinea, Philippines and Timor-Leste as well as from our regional office based in Thailand.

I had officially joined UNICEF just a month before, as the new Pacific chief of policy, advocacy, planning and evaluation. Based at the UNICEF sub-regional office in Suva, Fiji, over the next few days and nights I joined numerous conference calls with our colleagues in Honiara as well as with those who had already moved to Gizo as we scrambled to obtain information, deliver pre-positioned emergency supplies and mobilise additional support.

Tim Sutton was the deputy representative (or second in charge) of UNICEF Pacific at the time. Tim's workstation in the UNICEF Pacific office on Suva's Victoria Parade was adjacent to mine. Within a few days of my arrival, I started what became a morning ritual of poking my head around his door and asking Tim, 'How ya going?' To which he would always reply, 'Oh, mate, like a box of fluffy ducklings!' Of course, you may disagree but I don't know if there's a better way to describe soft, graceful yet unbridled positive energy that spreads warmth and uplifts the spirit. That's just sheer joy, the heartbeat of effective leadership – Tim personifies exactly that. He tasked me with deploying to the Western Solomons to lead the coordination of rapid consultations with affected communities, officiating government counterparts and partners to develop an emergency management plan (EMP) with the dual aims of aligning

UNICEF's response with critical needs and synchronising with the efforts of other partners.

I soon found myself back in Gizo to help our emergency response team led by the highly experienced Bob Koepp who, by then, had established a small coordination office. UNICEF was the only UN agency to set up field presence in the disaster zone from which we helped to facilitate the work of many other organisations.

My heart was truly broken to see these familiar communities and islands so devastated. I didn't disclose it at the time but this tragedy was deeply personal. Bob and I started gathering first-hand insights as to what had already been done and what more needed to be done to help children, their families, communities and government service providers. What do you see as the top three immediate priorities? And what if we jump forward three months? How about when we reach six months from today? What are our options to ensure the quickest recovery? What else do you have in mind? What do we not know now that you think we must know now? What would a successful response look like? And so on...

My curiosity was in full flow. And then, after each question, I would listen in stillness, intently absorbing *the wisdom* – the wisdom of children, parents, family members, community and religious leaders, local authorities, senior government officials, other UN agencies, NGOs, development partners and, of course, the UNICEF team itself.

I was lucky enough to speak fluent *Pijin* or Pidgin English, the *lingua franca* of Solomon Islands, as well as a fair amount of Marovo and some Roviana (two languages indigenous to New Georgia) learned 12 years earlier. My inner energy was devoted to remaining calm, meticulously documenting and offering a healer's heart and ears to everyone as they shared their stories of distress, concern and hope. What we were told became UNICEF Pacific's EMP, which was to rapidly inject technical and material resources to provide for the crucial health, nutrition, safe water, safe sanitation and protection needs of all affected children and adolescents, including those with disabilities, as well as to re-establish front-line services for these same urgent needs. I invited everyone involved to set their own benchmarks of what 'success' would look like at ten weeks and at six months.

We were assisted through gracious support from the governments of Japan and Spain, the UNICEF USA Mercury Fund, as well as from UNICEF National Committees based in Australia, Japan, New Zealand and the USA. We received additional finances from UNICEF's Global Thematic Humanitarian Funds for both education and emergencies. We also diverted what UNICEF calls regular resources (or RR) away from earlier intended uses to the emergency response. (These are global finances voluntarily contributed to UNICEF by governments, philanthropists, businesses, other institutions, funds and foundations, as well as the general public, and distributed each year to country-level UNICEF operations. RR funds can be used without restrictions for children wherever and whenever the need is greatest. Because of their flexibility, they are the best type of contributions that, through UNICEF, the world's children can receive.)

Within four days of the onset of the emergency, helped by the government of Solomon Islands, NGOs and the military forces of Australia, New Zealand, Papua New Guinea and the USA, UNICEF moved emergency medical supplies for up to 10,000 people, hundreds of tarpaulins and dozens of school-in-a-box kits, already pre-positioned in Honiara, to affected areas in the Western Solomons. These kits, designed for use almost anywhere in the world, are portable classrooms stored in a lockable metal box containing enough school supplies and materials for up to three months for one teacher and 40 students aged six years and over.

Within three weeks, with the help of our partners, UNICEF had procured and then distributed numerous tents for families and schools (the latter to create temporary classrooms), thousands of oral rehydration solution sachets to treat dehydration caused by diarrhoea, Vitalita packets (a multiple-micronutrient powder to add to food), as well as hygiene kits and packets of soap, hundreds of family water storage containers, dozens of bladders for community water storage, rehabilitation hardware for water and sanitation systems, clinical medical equipment, boats, recreation kits (metal boxes containing games equipment to cater for 90 children playing simultaneously), Kindy Kits for young children (containing colourful building blocks and wooden toys), sports gear, musical instruments for young people and wind-up radios – compact radios that don't need batteries or access to an electrical outlet, just several turns of a crank handle on the radio's side to generate enough internal power to listen to news, music and other radio broadcasts.

Within eight weeks of the disaster, UNICEF and our partners had helped the Solomon Islands Ministry of Health and Medical Services to re-establish essential healthcare services in Western and Choiseul Provinces. Widespread immunisation, vitamin A supplementation, temporary medical clinics and provision of vital nutrition advice for children and pregnant women, as well as surveillance of communicable disease outbreaks, were up and running. Further guidance was relayed to the many temporary camps and villages by teams of specially trained local health promoters, backed by local radio announcements. UNICEF managed to provide safe water to camps and rehabilitate essential water supplies in affected villages, but ensuring safe sanitation proved much harder, since many families had never used latrines before, preferring to use the sea instead. Nevertheless, we persevered while intensifying our efforts to promote hand washing with soap.

Ten weeks into our response, Save the Children, World Vision and UNICEF had united to support the Ministry of Education and Human Resource Development to set up 94 play-safe areas that permitted 6,500 children across the two provinces to laugh and have fun together. In the chaotic aftermath of emergencies, we can often overlook the intense healing power of children being free to be... well, just children.

Heartbreakingly, the mental and social upheavals of such

calamities always heighten the risks of child- and women-targeted violence. So, UNICEF and partners assisted the Social Welfare Division of the Ministry of Health and Medical Services to train 105 community welfare volunteers from all affected islands to raise awareness about preventing as well as reporting any case of physical or sexual abuse to local authorities.

Finally, many of the damaged houses and public buildings contained asbestos. After an assessment by the World Health Organization, UNICEF mobilised young people from the affected locations to design hand-painted warning signs and to learn how to advise their own communities about the dangers of asbestos while local authorities conducted a clean-up and disposal campaign.

These were just some of the interventions scripted into UNICEF's emergency management plan. But I was not done. I called for one more intervention, which I realised later was rarely practised. At least, back then. I noted earlier that UNICEF and all our partners had established EMP 'success' targets at ten weeks and at six months from the emergency's onset. As we neared the completion of ten weeks, I trained and coached a small team – although I didn't call it coaching at that time – to organise and conduct a rapid, population-based survey to measure whether our ten-week targets had indeed been reached (Miskelly et al 2009). The survey demonstrated that many interventions were succeeding but several lagged behind, giving us much-needed evidence and motivation to strive faster, better and further. And we kept on monitoring, evaluating and refining our collective efforts (Legu et al 2008).

Now breathe, *deeply*, for six seconds in… *slowly*, for six seconds out… Be compassionate, always. Heal emotions, in yourself and others. Be curious and remain so. Listen to everyone, with authentic attention. Strengthen key relationships and expand vital partnerships by building trust and giving respect. Be bold, but in being so, hold yourself and others accountable. Stay humble and remain honest at all times. Assume the best in others. Tap into their talents and wisdom. Use crucial moments to coach as much as you can. Be generous in appreciating others. Give back to the community. Always focus on the bigger picture. Embrace volatility, uncertainty and complexity. Suspend premature judgements. Stay agile and be prepared to adapt. Remain calm and resilient… These were just some of the graceful leadership lessons that I gleaned from that first year with UNICEF. I would go on to learn more.

The extent of damage on that Monday and the sheer logistics of recovery meant that even two years on, UNICEF was still assisting school reconstruction in the Western Province. Our teams, therefore, were present when, on 4 January 2010, two earthquakes measuring 7.2 and 6.5 on the Richter scale struck back to back around 88 km south-south-east of Ghizo Island, generating a tsunami that hit the southern and northern coasts of Rendova and Tetepare Islands. Some 8,000 people were living in the affected areas and required help. We were there. UNICEF responded.

This is the *Pacific* Ring of Fire but – and forgive me for dramatically extrapolating – it seems to me that the world has become a *metaphoric* Ring of Fire. We are now studying in schools (if we have access) and working in jobs (if we have employment) where criticism, blame, complaining and cynicism might be rampant, and appreciation, gratitude, positivity and kindness are rarities; inundated by advertising that tells us we're neither beautiful nor stylish enough; living in the daily presence of pollution, discrimination, violence and other harmful social norms; bombarded by grim news cycles that remind us of how fragile we are and how much we have to fear; exposed to constant human-made conflicts; shocked by frequent natural disasters; regularly jolted by economic downturns; and disrupted by global calamities, with climate change, biodiversity loss, financial crises and pandemics being just some of the more complex examples. Is World War Three on the cards?

All the while, most of us are seeking leaders in our communities, organisations and societies who can help us navigate through and overcome these challenges – leaders who truly care about us and our planet, not themselves.

Leadership is an incredible responsibility, a humbling call to duty. Over the years, during peace and crisis, I have quietly witnessed and sometimes painfully realised that should humanity require leadership *at all* then let it be *graceful*. This book offers insights into what graceful leadership is and the tremendous benefits it brings in periods of relative calm and, even more so, in times of catastrophe.

Chapter 2

Graceful leadership

To describe 'graceful' leadership, it is perhaps easier to picture someone with whom you might have worked, heard of, seen in action or read about who personifies 'disgraceful' leadership.

Disgraceful leadership

Self-absorbed, egotistical, selfish, uninterested in others, inattentive, unempathetic, dismissive, interruptive, obstructive, insensitive, intolerant, self-opinionated, a know-it-all, biased, unappreciative, exhibitionistic, incurious, controlling, forcing their own narrow solutions, micromanaging, manipulative, disinterested in diverse opinions, unforgiving, authoritarian, top-down, hyper-masculine, untrusting, cynical, disempowering, disrespectful, belittling, impolite, intimidating, judgemental, unfair, discriminatory, inconsistent, inauthentic, sarcastic, dishonest, sycophantic, unethical, scared of failure, blame-seeking, credit-stealing, rude, short-tempered, vindictive, confrontational, aggressive, abusive... I could go on.

Yes, I accept that leaders with these types of character-istics can be visionary, audacious, charismatic and produce short-term results (though these are usually self-serving). But tragically, these fear-based leaders also mistreat fellow humans and damage our planet.

It was ground-breaking research led by Stanford University professor Jim Collins and described in his classic organisational management book *Good to Great* (2001) which helped to shift our notion of what great leadership really entails. Jim and his research team analysed 1,435 companies with strong track records across 40 years and identified 11 that had become 'great' according to a set of rigorously designed performance markers. Were all the leaders of these 11 awesome companies big-personality celebrities?

Well, the leaders of all these 'good to great' companies did have certain characteristics in common but it wasn't magnetism or fame. First, these successful leaders all tended to be deeply humble, some even introverted. And second, they all had an unrelenting desire for success, not for themselves, but for their teams and companies.

The disturbing reality, however, is that most of us have grown up witnessing the ungracious faces of leadership. We may even have followed such leaders on so-called reality TV or on social media. Should we ourselves be blessed enough to be granted leadership positions whether in families, communities, organisations, companies or even countries, if not extremely *mindful* we may misguidedly assume that this disgraceful leadership style is *the* way to lead. After all, we are emerging or perhaps better to say 'awakening' from a long period (1911–2011) known as the 'management century' throughout most of which autocratic, command-and-control, top-down leadership was the 'favoured' model (Kiechel 2012).

In his foreword to the phenomenal *Awakening Compassion at Work* (2017), beautifully written by Dr Monica Worline and Professor Jane Dutton, Raj Sisodia (F W Olin distinguished professor of global business and co-founder of Conscious Capitalism) grimly surmises, 'Human beings have extraordinary, almost divine capacities. Yet the vast majority of people never get to realise that potential because they are embedded in organisational systems that fail to promote human flourishing. As the expression goes, most people die with their music still inside them.'

From command and controlling to compassion and coaching

In workforces across the globe, different cultures, gender identities and generations are mixing more and more – Baby Boomers alongside Gen Xers, Millennials (Gen Y) and Generation Z – redefining what leadership should be. Nowadays, people desire and indeed expect leaders and colleagues to be considerate, humble and humane, and to prize the special traits and intrinsic talents each person brings to the team and organisation. Gallup's extensive research shows that the world wants leaders who *care for and coach us to be better versions of ourselves* (Clifton & Harter 2019). As we shall see, some are calling this 'graceful leadership' and I believe it has never been more important.

Graceful leadership – leadership that blends compassion with coaching – falls into the well-researched and proven *affiliative* or *servant leadership* approach in which leaders are not self-centred but instead are *other-centred*, attending to their followers' needs (not wants) with empathy and kindness. Such leaders put followers *first*, nurturing them to reach their full potential but always doing so with the highest levels of ethics and integrity so that the greater good of the organisation, community or society at large is also served (Dhiman & Roberts 2023).

At its core, graceful leadership blends profound empathy with the skills and daily habits of caring for and coaching others towards three interrelated leadership aspirations:

Ennoblement: Making all team members feel significant, treasured and dignified, elevating their own sense of worth, excellence and innate qualities as a human being.

Engagement: Establishing the emotional connection of members toward their team or organisation that excites them to eagerly step forward, innovate, learn and go that extra mile without being asked; they become intrinsically motivated.

Empowerment: Creating the conditions that enable team members to become more confident in self-determination and in making independent decisions.

The foundations of graceful leadership

I'm by no means the originator of the expression 'graceful leadership'. There are elements of it in the work of all those I've referenced or quoted so far. And my own leadership journey has been guided by the writings of Stephen Covey (*Principle Centered Leadership*, 1989), Peter Drucker (*Managing in the Next Society*, 2002), Daniel Goleman (*Emotional Intelligence*, 2005), John Maxwell (*The 5 Levels of Leadership*, 2011), and Brené Brown (*Dare to Lead*, 2018) who all touch upon most of the practices I associate with graceful leaders.

Along the way I also came to learn that the graceful foundations for modern theories of leadership and management were laid by Mary Parker Follett (1868–1933), an American social worker, management consultant and organisational behaviour pioneer. Peter Drucker labelled her 'the brightest star in the management firmament' (Drucker 1995). She was an outstanding expert in the founding days of classical management theory yet following her death, Mary's ideas largely vanished from organisational and management circles until they were 'rediscovered' some 40 years later.

Mary speculated that power sharing and collaborative decision making between managers and employees led to better business solutions. She advocated for flatter organisational structures, informal networks and lateral processes, advancing the idea of 'reciprocal relationships'. She coined the term 'co-active power' to explain her concept of 'power with' rather than 'power over'. Mary was highly critical of micromanagement or overmanaging employees, labelling it as 'bossism' in her 1926 essay 'The Giving of Orders' (Metcalf & Urwick 1940). Of the many passages that one could quote from her work, two resonate strongly with me across the century since Mary wrote them:

Leadership is not defined by the exercise of power but by the capacity to increase the sense of power among those led. The most essential work of the leader is to create more leaders.
The Creative Experience (1924)

...tenacity, sincerity, fair dealings with all, steadfastness of purpose, depth of conviction, control of temper, tact, steadiness in stormy periods, ability to meet emergencies, power to draw forth and develop latent possibilities of others...
The Essentials of Leadership (1949)

Besides those authors and researchers I've referred to already, my comprehension of leading with grace has also been enhanced by the writing of, among others, the following:

✦ Richard Boyatzis and Annie McKee (*Resonant Leadership*, 2005)
✦ Dev Patnaik (*Wired to Care*, 2009)
✦ Manley Hopkinson (*Compassionate Leadership*, 2014)
✦ Bob Chapman and Raj Sisodia (*Everybody Matters*, 2015)
✦ Donn Sorensen with Vaughn Kohler (*Big-Hearted Leadership*, 2016)
✦ Cheryl Bachelder (*Dare to Serve*, 2018)
✦ Gay Haskins and co-authors (*Kindness in Leadership*, 2018)
✦ Chris Whitehead (*Compassionate Leadership*, 2019)
✦ Amy Bradley (*The Human Moment*, 2020)
✦ Sarah Higgins (*Power of Love Leadership*, 2020)
✦ Paul Axtell (*Compassionate Leadership*, 2021)
✦ Paul Hargreaves (*The Fourth Bottom Line*, 2021)
✦ Steve Hargreaves (*The Compassionate Leader's Playbook*, 2021)
✦ Joan Van den Brink (*The Three Companions*, 2021)
✦ Michael West (*Compassionate Leadership*, 2021)
✦ Rasmus Hougaard and Jacqueline Carter (*Compassionate Leadership*, 2022)
✦ Karyn Ross (*The Kind Leader*, 2022)
✦ Donato Tramuto with Tami Corwin (*The Double Bottom Line*, 2022)
✦ Kirstie Papworth (*Compassionate Leadership*, 2023).

And specifically in relation to graceful leadership, my personal reflections have been more recently inspired by:

✦ John Baldoni (*GRACE: A leader's guide to a better us*, 2019)
✦ Jessica Cabeen (*Lead with Grace*, 2019)
✦ Alexsys Thompson (*The Power of a Graceful Leader*, 2020)
✦ Heather Younger (*The Art of Caring Leadership*, 2021)
✦ Katelyn Brush (*Heart-Centered Leadership*, 2022)
✦ Gary Burnison (*The Five Graces of Life and Leadership*, 2022)
✦ Deborah Crowe (*The Heart-Centered Leadership Playbook*, 2023).

The above represent only the major books, not the many academic articles, websites, dissertations, podcasts, blogs and so on that have been produced on leading with grace through compassion and coaching.

Why yet another leadership book?

'If there's already so much literature and resources on leadership associated with grace, compassion, empathy, kindness, care and coaching,' you might be asking, 'why another book?' Fantastic question! Let me offer three reasons why I wrote this book.

First, while research on and writing about these more nurturing, serving dimensions of leadership are indeed accumulating – and though I have no evidence to support this hunch, I sense this accumulation is occurring at an exponential rate, given that there are such pressing needs – the command-and-control approach to leadership still largely prevails. So I felt it important to add my voice to the rising global call for an alternative form of leadership.

Second, much of what has been shared by leadership authors and researchers draws upon the 'for-profit' world – stories and analyses on businesses of all sizes. While there are some excellent commentaries and studies, particularly in the field of healthcare, less has been written about leadership in 'non-profit' spheres (Gautam 2018; Tripathi et al 2023). To my knowledge, this is one of just a handful of books to consider graceful aspects of leadership specifically within the field of international development and humanitarian work. I hope it encourages more studies of and writings about leadership in this vital field of humane endeavour.

Third, I felt the time was right to try to distil my real-world experiences as well as the flourishing literature produced to date into a set of proven and practical habits for leading with grace. Just as I did not invent this label neither do I claim to be a graceful leader – simply a student of how compassion and coaching can make a difference in leadership. *I remain a work in progress.*

For now, my life journey and research for this book suggest that this leadership style sits at the vibrant confluence of many cutting-edge disciplines, topics and research agendas – for instance, positive psychology, neuroscience, behavioural science, emotional and spiritual intelligences, psychological safety, management science, organisational compassion, emotional healing, humour in leadership, appreciative enquiry, team coaching, organisational change and societal transformation – and, crucially, it is being constantly enhanced by an assortment of reflective practices including mindfulness, meditation and yoga. Leading with grace .– leading through compassion and coaching – is part of a leadership movement that's not only coming of age but is also very much needed for this age and, I suspect, ages yet to come.

But before we examine this any further, let's get 'definitional'.

What is grace?

Grace is an inclination to promote others' interests, to treat them with big-heartedness and admiration, to assist them with kindness and, ultimately, to work for the 'greater good' (Thomas & Rowland 2014).

What graceful leaders say

Mohamed: 'When I hear grace, I hear empathy, I hear openness, I hear kindness. How would I call it? It's not sophisticated. I hear somebody civilised, elegant. I hear very soft kinds of behaviours that are all gentle and opening you to others. You know it's no barrier. It's putting away any kind of barrier that can be put between you and the rest.'

Gillian: 'Treating everyone the same and being courteous with everybody. That breeds a sense of goodwill in your interactions with everyone. And also, in your leadership with other organisations, be it with government, donors, other UN agencies, by being graceful with all your partners. That can also bring honour to the team. And how you behave is a window on your organisation, your team, with the outside world.'

Hamida: 'I associate grace with good leadership that reaches the ultimate goal of where you want all the people you lead to be – with this grace in them. So, I take grace very spiritually, but at the same time I like putting my heart into leadership. Maybe because we have a mandate on children, a beautiful mandate that I love, I combine all of this and find that grace comes very much if you are a good leader. You are able to get what you want to be done not only in a very responsible way but also in a very positive way through the people you are leading. Grace is two-way. Grace comes back to you.'

Peter: 'It's Nelson Mandela – our greatest leader. I mean, how graceful could you be? How generous and humble can you be and yet you lead the world into a completely different domain? An amazing person. A leader walks into a room. When a dictator walks into that room, it's like a punch. People are fearful that this person has come in. Or do you walk into that room gracefully and you get integrated into that room? The room brings you in and embraces you. That, to me, is what grace is about. Coordination is the greatest skill you need. And grace, in this sense, is paramount, because coordination requires patience. It requires genuinely reaching out to people to come forward and think. Grace and patience are not synonymous, they're slightly different, but the two go very closely together.'

Ugochi: 'So, one [aspect] is *inner peace. One is conviction. And there's a gentleness there. And then there's certainty. It means that you're not threatened because you have inner peace. And then conviction stemming from the fact that I'm grounded. I'm calm. It's recognising that you don't have to humiliate, you don't have to denigrate. You don't have to put down. You don't have to make others feel small. You don't have to assert your authority. You can convince, influence, persuade, motivate with grace. Let's say you're in a meeting and a team member is trying to convey that they know more than you on the subject. I'm not the expert on all things, and I can very gracefully appreciate this person's knowledge. I'm comfortable enough in my own value and not threatened by this colleague who initially was being a bit obnoxious. I've diffused the tension hopefully very gracefully because I'm not threatened.'*

What is compassion?

Compassion is to feel both *with* and *for* others and then to act with kindness based upon these feelings; to possess deep empathy (and authentic sympathy when situations demand) and then be highly responsive. Compassion goes beyond empathy. Empathy is human connection. Compassion is humane action. Empathy is an *emotion* whereas compassion is an *intention*. Empathy can sometimes be impulsive, divisive, inert, draining (Bloom 2016). Compassion is always deliberate, unifying, active, regenerative.

The good news is that we all possess compassion; it is deeply rooted in our human psyche. And the even better news is that to help its emergence, compassion can be *learned*. For example, within the Eastern traditions – especially Mahayana Buddhism – exercises and mental practices are used to train the mind in compassion. Compassion can also grow after experiencing considerate behaviours. Leaders can demonstrate compassion by being kind, while those being led in such a way can themselves learn to be compassionate to others.

Compassion is grace expressed. It manifests when you embrace the dignity of others and place their needs above your own.

I disagree with the proposition that compassion is triggered only when one witnesses the suffering of others. I've learned that expressing compassion can be a much more *omnipresent* practice. For me, like coaching, compassion is an embodied mindset – how you consistently demonstrate kind commitment to others, in good times and in bad, in peace and crisis.

Buddhist tradition describes three compassionate leadership styles:

+ Trailblazers who forge new paths and set examples so that others can follow.
+ Ferry folk who care for those in the boat and try to make each crossing smooth.
+ Shepherds who prioritise the flock's safety above their own.

Three approaches – but all focus on the wellbeing of followers (Dalai Lama & Hougaard 2019). I use compassion to describe the combination of having empathy and then acting with kindness. If this was a formula, it might look something like this…

TO BE COMPASSIONATE = EMPATHISE → ACT WITH KINDNESS

What graceful leaders say

Mohamed: *'Compassion is really feeling for others. Putting yourself in others' shoes. And then being there and treating them the way you would like to be treated, if you were indeed them, or if you are in their shoes. Compassion for me also means I'm here for you genuinely, without any kind of thought of getting anything else from you. It's just heart. An open, genuine, attitude to help, to support, to listen and to feel for you.'*

Hamida: *'Like the way I show my concern when we have a staff member, for example, who has lost a close family member. Or we have a staff member who for some reason had a major issue and that issue is affecting their ability to deliver what they are supposed* to deliver. So, looking into that and sympathising with that person without compromising what I'm supposed to do as a leader. Because I've worked in hardship areas on a number of occasions, maybe that's why I take compassion much more seriously. Because you're dealing with a lot of issues that you're concerned about, and which have impacts on what you are expecting your team to deliver.'

Peter: 'It's about bringing people in, listening to them, feeling for them. How are they? If you don't put people first, then your primary vehicle for achievement has gone. Leadership is about people. It's the compassion and energy that you give each other. But if you miss out the people in the middle, you ain't going to go anywhere. And other people that you're working with, if they don't show compassion, I think you're never going to get there. So, when you walk into a room and you're chairing a meeting, the first thing you've got to do is make them feel part of what the solution is. And that to me is about compassion.'

Ugochi: 'I always think of the goodwill trust. I want to have many goodwill accounts in different trusts. And each trust is a different person. Because the thing about compassion is how it's received by the other person and it's almost directly proportional to the level of trust that they have in you and the connection that they feel in your being compassionate. I always try and establish a personal connection and I'm always trying to increase, to grow my goodwill trust account with colleagues. It's not so much about what you say but what you're able to convey. It's what your body language communicates. It's what your tone of voice communicates as well.'

Gillian: 'It's having concern for everyone you're working with. Obviously, people at different times of their lives are going through different misfortunes, and may be suffering from bad health or difficult family situations. It's about looking at a situation from the other's perspective, what's best for them that will enable them to continue to be a productive, happy member of the team. So, I think it is looking out for your team. It's also looking out for your peers. You know, you might find another representative who is going through a hard time. And you can say, "Look, I'm very happy anytime you want to have a call, and we can just talk things through." And maybe it's time for someone to move on, being compassionate in support. And when you've got non-performance, you can deal with that in a compassionate way.'

What is kindness?

Kindness can be defined as an act or acts that link one's compassion and empathy for others to create a positive outcome for them, *without expecting anything in return* – bravely, actively, frequently demonstrating sincere goodwill to others.

Those who are regularly kind to others enjoy better health and live longer than those who show less kindness (Curry et al 2018). This is partly because kindness releases at least three neurochemicals from our brain into our blood: serotonin (which improves our mood, builds our confidence and helps us to feel cherished as well as to respect others); oxytocin (which helps us to bond with and develop trust in others, reduces stress, increases our motivation and sharpens our cognition to unravel complexity); and endorphins (which increase our perseverance and endurance, and make us more resilient to tension and anxiety). These neurochemicals deliver hidden benefits to our heart, mental health and immune system. At the same time, again without us noticing, these neurochemicals dampen our unhealthy, often ego-driven, impulses (eg predisposition to react with anger or be highly critical of others) and harmful addictions (eg life–work imbalance, perfectionist tendencies, excessive alcohol consumption to cope with stress, etc).

What graceful leaders say

Ugochi: 'Kindness demonstrates that you see people and value people and that you're ready to invest in caring. And acts of kindness are even sometimes just a smile. It's not from big things that I've done – it's these little acts of kindness that have built up and up. You must invest in people. Kindness is an investment, and I don't mean investment because you want to get something. I don't mean it in a transactional sense but because I know this is more important to my team gelling and performing than many other things that I can't give. I can't give cash bonuses. I can't give vacations – you know, a holiday cruise for a vacation. But I can show that I care and that I'm invested.'

Peter: 'Trust and respect, those are the two most important. If you don't develop an atmosphere of trust or respect, you will never get leadership of a team. That's not an individual's trust. The team has to trust each other, to respect each other. So, you have to work on trust, and kindness comes as a result of that. You see, I could be kind to you yet not respect you; kind to you but not trust you. And that's a hollow honour. You must earn respect, but the only way you can do that is by giving respect. A bad leader does not respect you. You feel it. How many of the poor leaders do you hear say, "This is how I'm going to do this. This is what I want to see happen." You know, once you state the "I", you're not respecting the "us".'

Gillian: 'It's putting yourself in other people's shoes. I think it's also being authentic to yourself because that enables you, when you're feeling comfortable with yourself, to be kind to others and to offer care and support when people need it. When there are some tough decisions to be made that maybe this person is not the right person for this job, you can say that to them. It's never going to be easy, but you can bring kindness into how you have that discussion with someone on difficult issues. And when someone's not performing, not behaving well, not living by the UN's values, you do need to have those conversations. And sometimes it's being kind to make that effort. Because often it would be easier not to do it.'

Mohamed: 'For me, kindness in leadership is really being there. I mean genuinely, honestly and actively being there for others – learning to understand them, trying to support them as much as you can, as much as they need it, and breaking barriers that can be there because of hierarchy or any other reason. At the end of the day, I'm a strong believer that we're all equal and we're all the same. The only thing in life is that you know there needs to be a leader. There needs to be a manager. That there needs to be a specialist. But we are one team and none of us is better or is higher or is the "boss", as some people like to say. I think that kind of attitude puts kindness away and it should not be happening.'

Hamida: 'I take kindness in relation to leadership in terms of really being considerate. Because some people may confuse kindness with maybe favour. Kindness goes together with being compassionate, but it is much more about being considerate. And I think in leadership we need to be more and more considerate without compromising on what goal we have. You can still reach your goal without being unnecessarily harsh and hard on people. And if there are times you have to apply pressure, you can still apply pressure in a kind way. For me, I think the results of applying that pressure in a kind way actually gives you better results and more results than even when you are putting pressure in a very harsh and very hard way.'

What is courage?

I believe that to become and remain a graceful leader, you must have *courage* – grace under pressure. (A definition of 'courage' attributed to Ernest Hemingway during a 1929 interview with *The New Yorker*'s Dorothy Parker – see Monteiro 1990.)

What graceful leaders say

Ugochi: 'For me, it's about the courage to speak up for those who can't speak or whose voices aren't at the table and who, many times, are inconvenienced in the course of whatever is being discussed. So, as an example, I was in Afghanistan meeting with the head of the Ministry of Migration. There was a bit of sensing each other out for the first 15–20 minutes and then I said to myself, "Ugo, you're not going to have this conversation and not bring up the issue of women and girls." So, I said to the minister, "We're not going to get the results if we don't engage women and girls and have access to women and girls." Of course, he didn't say, "Absolutely, we fully agree with you." But what he did say was that the issues that I was speaking about were relevant for everyone and they needed a strategy that could serve the whole population. Fair enough. I don't want to applaud myself and say I was courageous in bringing it up because I think it's the minimum that was expected of me. I did it as much for the new government leadership as for my colleagues who were with me. I wanted to show my colleagues that we can stick to our principles without being confrontational. So, it's the courage to do the right thing and speak truth to power. Because courage is not a raging lion. In fact, many times it's a very soft but very clear voice on an issue, typically on behalf of someone who's not in the room that you as a leader have access to.'

Hamida: 'A few years back when I came here [South Sudan], I had to cut about 150 staff posts. So, you can imagine the courage that I needed to even face these staff, despite the fact it was very consultative, they knew everything. Everything was on the table. But still I needed that courage to be able to sit with these staff, to face them, to talk to them. There are times when there are tough questions and everybody expects you, as a leader, to have an answer. You don't have an answer for everything, but people are expecting you to come up with the answers. It is in these moments when you really need to have that energy and that spirit of being brave, the positive aspect of being brave.'

Mohamed: 'Courage is standing for the people you serve and sacrificing yourself, exposing yourself, your life, your wellbeing sometimes to serve them. For me, that's courage. Courage is also not letting yourself get into inappropriate behaviours, anything that can affect your integrity. We work in a world where you can easily be thrown by unethical issues that can carry any human away. Resisting that is courage because as a leader you will be tested and you may be tempted but you have to resist. You have to have the courage to resist getting into those kinds of things.'

Peter: 'Courage has a spectrum to it and it's a beautiful word. It shows that someone goes beyond their comfort zone. But it tends to have this machoism about it but it's not about that. It's about making those small decisions that take you out of your comfort zone. And it's *very internal. Courage without accountability, anyone can do that. It's those small steps that you take that move you out of your comfort zone, that allow you to achieve more than the sum of its parts.'*

Gillian: 'Leadership that is courageous is being willing to speak out on difficult issues and particularly child rights, human rights issues, when the environment in which you're working is not supporting you. For example, when I was in Nepal, we had a very complex issue around international adoption. It was completely unregulated. And I spoke out and said, "No, we need to bring The Hague Convention in [to regulate adoption]." We all knew many of these children [being adopted] had been trafficked. And I spoke out on that. I received so much hate mail. But I just thought, "No, this is the right thing. This is about children who've been trafficked."'

What is coaching?

Daniel Goleman (2000) suggested that there are at least six leadership styles: coercive, authoritative, pacesetting, democratic, affiliative and coaching. Coaching was shown to have a 'markedly positive' impact on performance, workplace climate (culture) and the bottom line.

Liberating the resources of humans

Coaching helps others discover meaningful purpose and mindful pathways of action in their lives – unleashing dreams, inspirations and potentials, assisting them to discover and unlock their *inner self-innovation*. Coaching is sometimes viewed narrowly as an element of 'managing human resources'. Coaching is not a human resources management tool – *it is a leadership mindset that liberates the resources of humans.*

Master coaches (graceful leaders) often sense and see more potential in those they coach than their coachees or clients (the people being coached) sense and see in themselves, at first. Transformation of others is achieved through the coach's use of thought-provoking questions, attentive listening, mindful reflection, observation sharing and sometimes difficult, performance-enhancing conversations. Effective coaches ask the right question at the right moment in the right way. I have included many of my favourite coaching questions throughout this book.

Coaches evoke, excite and guide; they do not propose solutions nor offer advice. They focus on the future. Although a client's past is often explored in depth, this is not to heal nor rectify but to detect signals or possibilities for future growth. Graceful leaders coach in order to help colleagues learn more about themselves and their situation, to awaken and realise their human potential, *to achieve greater personal mastery and self-actualisation.*

Individual and team coaching

Coaching can occur at the level of the individual (one-on-one coaching) and at the level of groups (team coaching). One-on-one coaching sits under the umbrella of supporting an individual's personal and/or professional development alongside other interventions such as training, consulting and mentoring. In training, consulting and mentoring interventions, however, the recipient is not considered 'the expert' nor really owns the developmental process; expertise and ownership lie with the trainer, consultant or mentor.

By contrast, in one-on-one coaching, the coachee or client is considered 'the expert' and owns and drives the self-developmental process. When a compassionate leader coaches one-on-one, through scheduled sessions or spontaneously during/after specific events, they can collaborate with a coachee 'in a thought-provoking and creative process that inspires them to maximise their personal and professional potential. The process of coaching often unlocks previously untapped sources of imagination, productivity and leadership' (ICF 2024). The goal of such coaching might include building self-awareness, self-responsibility and self-belief in colleagues.

Team coaching exists alongside team building, team training, team consulting, team mentoring and team facilitation. In team coaching (and to a lesser extent, team facilitation), the process is owned and driven by the team, not the coach, whereas in the other team development interventions, the process is controlled by the team developer. When graceful leaders coach teams, through a series of team transformation sessions or in real time (at specific *times* during task performance), they can partner in a creative, reflective process to explore team members' goal alignment (or lack thereof), unique talents and power dynamics to constructively address conflict (if needed) and, above all, to inspire the team to maximise individual abilities towards sustainable, collaborative success, ongoing team development, co-creativity and becoming a flourishing organisation: a team of teams (Woudstra 2025).

Types of coaching

There are multiple types of coaching, including life, health, nutrition, wellbeing, relationship, executive, communication and career coaching to name just a few, but from my perspective, there are two basic categories of 'workplace' coaching: for performance and for development.

Coaching for performance is typically applied to everyday, work-related issues. Professor Richard Boyatzis and colleagues at Case Western Reserve University refer to this as 'instrumental coaching' (2019). The coach offers or provides help to someone or a team to fix a performance 'problem' and thereby better fulfil an organisational need.

In contrast, coaching for development directs attention to the overall transformation of the person or team, beyond the 'problem'. Coaching for development is thus more holistic, generally more impactful and aligned with what Professor Boyatzis and his colleagues (2006) describe as 'coaching with compassion' or 'helping others in their intentional change process (ie achieving their dreams or aspirations or changing the way they think, feel and act)'.

Workplace coaching can be conducted internally (by supervisors and leaders coaching their co-workers and peers), externally (by independent coaches hired by the organisation often called 'executive coaching') or through a combination of both approaches. It is the internal approach – the leader as coach or *coaching leader* – that I emphasise in this book.

What graceful leaders say

Peter: *'I've always thought this is synonymous with good leadership. Leadership is about coaching and coaching is about leadership. I don't see a distinction. Leadership has the characteristics of coaching and, if you demonstrate leadership characteristics, that's coaching. How do you coach people to become better leaders? Leadership is about asking questions of yourself. "What do you think about this? How will you respond to this?" And so on. I'm going to ask you the questions and get you to think. It's about creating the space for the individual to say, "Hmm, who am I? What am I? And how can I build on this part and how can I perhaps take away this part?"'*

Ugochi: *'I always encourage those that I'm, let's say, mentoring or coaching to do a lot of self-reflection. So, I'm not giving them the answers, what worked for me, what didn't work for me, but I always ask them to reflect. "What are your career goals? What is it you want to do? What do you see yourself as? How do you see yourself in five years, in ten years?" So, I'm absolutely not giving direction but trying to accompany them in as helpful a way as possible on a journey that I've been on. And in the case where it's a journey that I haven't been on, obviously I have many, many years of experience. So, I would try to apply it in that context to accompany this person or persons on their own journey.'*

Gillian: *'As leaders we have that opportunity because we see how staff are going. They will often come to us for advice and if you really want to help them, you will see how they can do their work better. And it's also helping them reach their potential and to do their best work. You're able to help them with questioning, how they can move on with specific pieces of work. Because I think, as well as helping people to look at how they might do things differently and where* they might want to go, it's demonstrating that you value that person. When you have a leader who puts time and effort into your growth it can definitely help you feel emboldened.'

Hamida: 'Coaching others is really important. I believe that coaching is what brings the team together, because you have set goals, and you want to achieve those goals. You come in as a team, at different levels of being able to achieve those goals. Some team members will need coaching and tips to contribute to their fullest. So, using coaching is one of the best ways to build team confidence, to have more trust and be able to achieve what you want to achieve together. Because, as leaders, sometimes we have a tendency to work with the few who can do everything. We want to move fast with them. And we tend to forget those who need to come along with us as well, to be part of the team of those who've achieved. And if things don't go well, then blaming starts. I believe coaching is a very good ingredient to avoid all that.'

Mohamed: 'Bringing people up. You provide opportunities for your team to grow. Sometimes you have to make sacrifices. Let's say you give an opportunity for somebody to go for a two-week training [abroad] that may impact the work in the house but still, you say, "It's worth it. I will do it because I want to bring her or him to another level. And we will try to manage, as the rest of the team, what needs to be managed in the office." But I've seen many leaders who are not doing that. They block people's aspirations and potential growth in careers. They say, "No. This is not a good time to go." I mean, there's never a good time to go. You have to give people the opportunities to grow. When you do that, you get people to actually perform even better than if you don't. Everybody gets behind the opportunity. So, for me, it's about providing the necessary support to bring people up despite the risks. You have to do that willingly and you have to do that proactively to make a change.'

Graceful leadership in a nutshell

To ennoble, engage and empower individuals and teams by leading through compassion and coaching. To have deep empathy with individuals and a mindset to act with kindness to improve their personal and/or professional lives by boosting talents and addressing fears that lie within. To sincerely care for, support and coach others to become ever better human beings.

Chapter 3

Rapid response

On 4 June 2014, I received a letter from UNICEF's Department of Human Resources with details of my transition from Nepal to Iraq. I was on annual leave in Geelong, Australia. That same day, on the other side of the world, around 1,500 ISIS (Islamic State of Iraq and Greater Syria) militants began their assault on Mosul, a city that straddles the Tigris River in Nineveh Governorate, north-west Iraq.

The attack triggered an initial exodus of some 500,000 civilians. There had already been months of clashes between ISIS and Iraq's security forces throughout western Iraq, including the fall of Fallujah and Hīt, among other cities and towns. Mosul was to become the *de facto* ISIS capital and economic hub until its liberation by the Iraqi army, supported by an international coalition, on 9 July 2017. It is estimated that some six million Iraqi citizens (mostly women and children) were forced to leave their homes during the ISIS insurgency (Al Khateeb 2021).

On the eve of 29 January 2015 (my 47th birthday), thick fog descended on the northern city of Kirkuk and surrounding areas. Under this cover, an advance party of some 150 ISIS militants attacked the *Peshmerga* – elite armed forces of the autonomous Kurdistan region of Iraq – positioned along the city's outskirts.

UNICEF Iraq's emergency team and I were in Erbil, about an hour's drive north, coordinating a rapid-response mechanism (RRM) with the UN's World Food Programme (WFP), delivered by a consortium of other UN agencies and non-government organisations and designed to provide one week's worth of drinking water, high-energy biscuits and hygiene kits (which included children's toys) that could be carried by families fleeing ISIS to safer areas in north-eastern and eastern Iraq (UNICEF 2015). For many, the RRM was the only source of sustenance and comfort along the way to their final destinations.

Together with UNICEF colleagues, monitoring the humanitarian response to population displacements in and around Basrah, Iraq, 17 May 2015. Atheer is on his mobile at the back. Photo: UNICEF Iraq.

The previous week, a member of our emergency team, Atheer Al-Yaseen, an amazing professional and great human being, approached me in my capacity as UNICEF Iraq's chief of field operations. Ably supported by Atheer, the super-experienced Bastien Vigneau and the innovative Mandie Alexander, I was responsible for organising the agency's humanitarian response across the country. Atheer and I had built a level of trust that freed us to make clear decisions, frankly and quickly. For many weeks earlier, every single day, he and I would walk together to and from other people's meetings or deploy together on multiple field missions. Throughout this time, Atheer would share his snapshot analyses of the daily unfolding situation in Iraq, distilled from multiple sources. 'Spare me the details,' I would urge him, 'or I will lose the big picture.' So, he only gave me headlines. We learned how to communicate with each other.

Atheer had analysed recent advances made by ISIS towards Erbil, the capital of the Kurdistan region, the last hope and refuge for millions of displaced Iraqis, and the location of our north-eastern humanitarian operations. He pinpointed Kirkuk as a highly likely target. With large oilfields nearby, if ISIS attacked Kirkuk, Iraq's military, the *Peshmerga* and the multi-religious Popular Mobilisation Forces or PMF would combine to respond aggressively. Further population displacements were guaranteed. At the time, the city had a resident population of some 900,000, swelled further by between 200,000 and 400,000 people displaced from ISIS-occupied territories.

A few months earlier, UNICEF had secured an agreement between ISIS and the Iraqi government to allow a civilian convoy to deliver vaccines from Baghdad to ISIS-held Mosul to immunise children held captive within the city. Tragically, the agreement was not respected. The drivers were beheaded by ISIS and the trucks, together with the vaccines, vanished.

So, during that third week of January 2015, when Atheer came to inform me that Kirkuk could soon be attacked and we should pre-position trucks laden with RRM supplies in readiness to support an outflux of families, as a team we had to weigh up the pros and cons – the risks involved in such a pre-emptive move. We and UNICEF's donors were all worried that humanitarian aid intended for children could again be lost to ISIS militia.

Atheer explained that having captured Maktab Khaled, south of Kirkuk, ISIS was again on the move. Population displacements to Kirkuk had already begun. I asked him several questions as to where his sources predicted ISIS would move next: north to Hawija or maybe into the oilfields south of Kirkuk? He was convinced it would be Kirkuk itself.

We already had RRM supplies on the ground there and further supply pre-positions in Erbil and Sulimaniyah that could reach Kirkuk within 24 hours. 'Even so,' I queried Atheer, 'what if we move more supplies to just outside Kirkuk on standby? If ISIS advances to Hawija and no further movement of civilians happens into or out of Kirkuk, then we can respond to families who have already arrived inside the city. If Kirkuk is attacked and the forces opposing ISIS engage, triggering more displacements from Kirkuk, we can also activate the RRM from Erbil and Sulimaniyah. So, what if we deploy some more RRM near to Kirkuk just in case?'

Atheer agreed and rushed off to persuade our supply team to move three trucks with RRM supplies to a location east of Kirkuk on the edge of Peshmerga-controlled territory and to keep them there until the intention of ISIS became clearer.

UNICEF usually delivers supplies to partners or to warehouses and doesn't keep them on trucks out in the open. Having reached a consensus with my own senior leadership, I told the team that I would shoulder the responsibility if things went wrong.

As a child, I enjoyed playing chess, strategically moving pieces across the chequered board in anticipation of your opponent's next few moves. I remember thinking at the time that this all felt like a giant game of chess, except with far more dramatic, potentially sinister consequences.

When ISIS militants did attack Kirkuk on the night of 29 January and Iraqi, Kurdish and PMF armed units responded with force, terrified citizens fled east out of Kirkuk, as predicted by Atheer. Because of the three trucks we had already placed near their most likely escape route, UNICEF's NGO partners were able to immediately meet these families and hand out RRM supplies to ease their onward travel to safe havens in north-east Iraq. We mobilised RRM convoys from Erbil and Sulimaniyah the next day to cover the remaining families still fleeing Kirkuk.

Trust. Analysis. Consultation. Risk. Judgement. Decision. Delivery... Help given. Hope offered.

Yes, on this occasion, there was also luck involved, but to quote author and business theorist Dr Thomas Stanley in *The Millionaire Mind* (2000), 'Luck and risk-taking go hand in hand.'

By the end of 2015, when I departed Iraq for my next UNICEF posting in Iran, the RRM had reached some 4.4 million people on the move, more than half of them children (UNICEF 2016). The RRM was just one of the many humanitarian interventions – the others being in healthcare, education, psychosocial support, protection, safe water and sanitation – that, alongside other partners, UNICEF provided to the children and families of Iraq throughout the ISIS insurgency.

UNICEF had been supporting the people of Iraq well before ISIS appeared and the agency continues to assist. Sadly, Iraq still faces significant instability. In August 2023, more than one million people remained internally displaced, 4.1 million needed humanitarian assistance, and reconstruction was estimated to require at least US$88 billion (Center for Preventive Action 2024).

Graceful leadership is not about *never* giving advice but about slowing down the decision-making process (even if by a fraction in an emergency) and enticing others to offer the advice that's needed. As described above, even in times of crisis when urgent action is needed, leaders should rarely make snap decisions on their own. Instead, graceful leaders find a way to rapidly consult, attentively listen and never forget to communicate final decisions and how these are made.

Graceful leadership is not 'personalised power' (authority and decision making placed only in one heroic person's hands) but is 'distributed' or 'socialised power' characterised by a dynamic flow of inter-reliant people, each moving between leadership and followership roles, depending on the challenges in front of them and the skills required. While a form of hierarchy may still exist (in everyone's mind or on paper at least), it is downplayed in favour of utilising the available expertise pertinent to the immediate circumstance or task at hand.

Regardless of their title, rank or status, therefore, every community or team member has the opportunity to lead at many points in time, especially when their know-how is relevant to the situation. The presence of such collective leadership consistently predicts team effectiveness and can manifest when each member frequently asks questions of each other such as, 'How can I help? How can we succeed together? How can we better share responsibilities within our team?'

It is by no means easy for leaders to spread compassionate action and coaching approaches across every part of their community, team or organisation. But even by attempting to do so, levels of dignity, resilience, inclusion and creativity can be significantly raised while at the same time the overall workplace can become more sustainably 'compassion-inspired' and 'curiosity-ignited'. And it is to these and the many other benefits of graceful leadership that we turn next.

Chapter 4

Why graceful leadership matters so much

An ever-growing body of research attests that leading through compassion combined with coaching can *emphatically* improve workplace cultures and boost individual, team and organisational performance, which in turn can advance positive outcomes at individual, team or organisational and societal levels (Trzeciak & Mazzarelli 2019).

The benefits of graceful leadership at the individual level

A 2011 study of more than 5,600 participants from 77 different organisations conducted by Australian School of Business researchers discovered that compassionate leaders consistently boost employee productivity and morale (as well as bottom-line profitability); and that managers who interrelated with employees on a day-to-day basis are more impactful than the CEO (Boedker et al 2011). A 2022 survey conducted across 15 countries and nearly 15,000 employees suggested that 60 per cent of negative mental health outcomes related to work could be addressed by eliminating toxic workplace behaviours such as unfair treatment, exclusion by leaders or co-workers, derogatory and undermining actions and abusive management (McKinsey Health Institute 2022).

When coupled with coaching, compassionate leadership is an *indispensable* feature of a meaningful work environment, essential in, for example:

✦ nourishing job satisfaction and employee retention
✦ helping colleagues become more effective at accomplishing their jobs (empowerment)
✦ raising levels of energy and collaboration
✦ producing greater degrees of creativity, trust and openness to new ideas
✦ promoting individual health and better life–work balancing (lowering the incidence of sick leave and absenteeism, thereby benefiting teams and the organisation)
✦ reducing anxiety and the pressure of achieving
✦ making team members more resilient to work-related stress and burnout
✦ boosting work-related motivation, perceptions of being valued (ennoblement) and employee engagement (Kaye and Jordan-Evans 2014).

Experiencing compassion at work links co-workers psychologically and results in a stronger bond between them. Leading through compassion and coaching curbs competition, encourages egalitarianism, enhances teamwork, strengthens loyalty and positive commitment, and amplifies levels of trust, respect and inspiration (Lilius et al 2008).

Compassion breeds compassion. Those who receive compassion are subsequently better able to direct their support and caregiving to others (Zaki 2016). When supervisors perceive that their organisation is compassionate, they are more likely to show supportive behaviour towards the people they manage (Shanock & Eisenberg 2006). This is promising but *we have a long way to go.* For example, a 2018 survey in the UK of 4,626 employees (representative of gender, age, race, industry sector, region and business size) found that just 60 per cent of employees feel their line manager is genuinely concerned for their wellbeing, and a disturbing 64 per cent of managers put the interests of their organisation above staff wellbeing at some point, with 12 per cent doing so every day (Business in the Community 2018). Another survey in 2019 among 1,078 organisations across the UK (representing 3.2 million employees) found that just below 'excessive workload', 'management style' and 'relationships at work' were the second and third top causes of workplace stress (CIPD 2019).

Executive coaches Professor Richard Boyatzis and Annie McKee (2005) have identified three major benefits for leaders who coach with compassion. First, they are less focused on themselves; second, they are more connected to people and issues around them, reducing their sense of 'isolation' (which itself has been linked to many stress-related illnesses); and third, they experience regular renewal of energy (physical, emotional, mental and spiritual) that helps them to sustain their effectiveness and resilience.

Leaders who combine compassion and coaching are perceived as stronger, more competent and more effective (Hougaard & Carter 2018). By leading with grace, you can self-transform and be transformed by others to not only be a better leader but also a better human being. Graceful leaders are more likely to sustain a positive mindset, be more confident in their leadership ability and possess high levels of perceived wellbeing as well as general happiness, plus are less prone to personal distress, to being overcome by negative emotions and to succumbing to burnout (McKee & Wiens 2017).

The benefits of graceful leadership at the team or organisational level

A *Harvard Business Review* survey of the world's 20 most empathetic companies showed how compassion contributed to major successes and manifold increases in their earnings (Parmar 2016). Addressing grief and stress through compassionate leadership could save organisations hundreds of billions of dollars while generating many other benefits as described above and below (Gelles 2015). Another study revealed how, by 2030, absence from work triggered by mental health issues connected to work and family pressure will cost the UK economy £26 billion (FirstCare 2018).

Leading through compassion and coaching has a positive impact on an organisation's performance culture as a whole. Team potency and creativity can be enhanced by increasing team members' clarity of purpose, their shared confidence that they can be effective and reassurance that they will be supported (Hu & Liden 2011). Leadership that combines compassion with coaching facilitates collaborative solutions to emerge that would not have been available from hierarchical leadership structures (Maalouf 2019).

By enhancing workplace satisfaction and psychological safety, graceful leaders can motivate colleagues to exceed the requirements of their job to boost the overall functioning of their team or organisation (Walumbwa et al 2010). Compared to poor performers, top-performing teams and organisations have much greater ratios of positive statements (appreciation, support, helpfulness, approval or compliments) to negative statements (criticism, disapproval, dissatisfaction, cynicism or disagreement) within their internal communication (Diener & Biswas-Diener 2008). A ratio of around five positive statements to every negative statement has been correlated with high levels of performance (Fredrickson & Losada 2005). In short, performance is positively influenced and reinforced when a workplace is full of encouraging, kind interactions – positive energy, motivating words. This does not mean that criticism and opposing views are absent but instead they form part and parcel of daily constructive dialogues that can boost our sense of interpersonal connection (see **Practice 6**).

Graceful leadership can inspire people to go that extra mile – to become 'organisational citizens' (Organ et al 2005). When compassion is present, individuals, quiet leaders, those who lead from the shadows go above and beyond to support their team by, for example:

✦ helping a new colleague to become familiar with their role and the office; helping a co-worker who may be struggling with deadlines or facing difficulties outside of work; or volunteering to change shifts (**altruism**)
✦ checking in with co-workers about a personal problem that could affect their performance (**courtesy** – see **Practice 10**)
✦ working extra hard to ensure team targets are surpassed or developing a new procedure even when this is not part of their job description (**conscientiousness**)
✦ deciding to stay upbeat even when events do not unfold favourably (**sportspersonship**)
✦ organising or participating in agency-sponsored social gatherings (**civic virtue**).

Finally, leading through compassion and coaching establishes the enabling conditions for 'innovating' and 'collaborative success' to become the desired outcomes – sometimes called 'ecosystem' goals, driven by mutual respect and a sense of shared humanity – much more than the pursuit of individual agendas or 'ego-system' goals (see **Practice 15**). Under such conditions, abuse of power, internal competition, uncalled-for micromanagement and unjustified control of resources, incongruent with the team's or organisation's values, can be identified and addressed.

The benefits of graceful leadership at the societal level

The 14th Dalai Lama, one of the most revered Buddhist preachers, once said that individual acts of compassion have the power to promote peace on a global scale (Dalai Lama & Hougaard 2019). Leading with grace has a positive impact on society: think of Florence Nightingale, the founder of modern nursing; or the history-transforming President Nelson Mandela; or the service of Saint Mother Teresa, resulting in one million workers in more than 40 countries operating hospitals, schools and hospices for people living below the poverty line.

Then there are the likes of the late Dr Govindappa Venkataswamy – 'Dr V' as he was known – who, in 1976, together with his siblings and their families, founded Aravind, a tiny eye clinic in Madurai, in the south Indian state of Tamil Nadu. That 11-bed hospital has transformed into the Aravind Eye Care System (AECS), the world's largest provider of eye care service and surgery offered at hundreds of centres throughout India together with training programmes and research partnerships that span the globe. By March 2020, AECS had treated more than 65.5 million patients and performed 7.8 million surgeries. On a typical day, AECS performs some 14,000 patient examinations and 1,600 surgeries. With its unique high-volume, high-quality yet low-cost approach based on affordability, availability and accessibility, AECS offers cataract surgery for approximately 98 per cent less than in the USA (US$88 versus US$3,800 in 2016 figures), which is way cheaper even considering the adjusted purchasing power for both countries. Despite this low price, true to its mission to serve those in need, AECS performs close to half of its surgeries for free or highly subsidised rates, yet still operates at a profit (Srinivasan et al 2020).

In their brilliant book, *Infinite Vision* (2011), authors Pavithra Mehta and Suchitra Shenoy distil AECS rules for delivering such societal benefit: '1. We cannot turn anyone away; 2. We cannot compromise on quality; 3. We must be self-reliant. In summary, these rules meant that whatever Aravind chose to do, it would have to do it with uncompromising compassion, excellence – and its own resources.' AECS is a self-sustaining business model with its systems and procedures *saturated with grace*.

Perhaps closer to our grasp is evidence that families and close relatives of workers as well as their local communities can experience positive benefits when compassion and coaching are embedded features of organisations and businesses (Barsade & O'Neill 2016).

Graceful leaders act purposely to positively influence the world as a whole. It is not that graceful leaders change society on their own; rather they help transform their colleagues, teams and organisations to become unified agents of positive change – communities and organisations full of ever-improving human beings who diversely and collectively benefit humanity and our planet at large.

Small wonder then that leading with compassion and coaching has been embraced by an ever-expanding number of organisations – many listed in the Fortune 500 – through their leadership training or human resource support programmes as well as by embedding compassion and coaching principles into their overarching values. To name just a few: AT&T, Cisco, Costco, Greggs UK, IKEA, ING, Kroger, LinkedIn, Marriott, Natura, Proventus, Starbucks, Southwest Airlines, TechCo, The Hospital Corporation of America, The John Lewis Partnership, UnitedHealth Group, Vanguard Group, Whole Foods Market, Yodel and Zappos (Sisodia et al 2014). Organisations that want to be successful are investing in capacity-building initiatives that expand their leaders' emotional and spiritual intelligences together with skills for coaching and compassionately ennobling, engaging and empowering individuals and teams.

Graceful leadership, leading through compassion and coaching, is demonstrated daily – in what you say and do, and how you say and do – in *every single* interaction with others. And you need to commit to being the best human that you can be – bringing your best self and best energy to work and taking your best self and best energy home, whatever the challenges, and along the way, helping others likewise to live with open-heartedness and integrity.

'That's a lot of courage and areas for self-development!' you might be thinking. Yes, I know from personal experience, graceful leadership is by no means easy and I'm constantly trying to embody it. But the stakes are too high, the world's challenges too complex and the urgent need for graceful leadership too compelling.

So now comes my offer. In Part 2 of this book, I explain a set of proven practices that, if embraced, can guide you towards becoming and remaining a graceful leader.

How can one become and remain a graceful leader?

Today's most pressing leadership question is not whether leaders should be graceful, ie that they should lead through compassion and coaching – the evidence is clear on how beneficial that style of leadership is not just for individuals but also for teams, for organisations and for societies at large. No, the most powerful question we need to answer is *how* to lead with grace. And that's the purpose of Part 2.

Just as our personality can change over time, so can our ways of leading (Harris et al 2016). As a leader, you can learn to apply coaching skills (Ibarra & Scoular 2019). Being compassionate is also a trainable quality, capable of being manifested through several time-tested practices (Weng et al 2013).

There are those who might view leading with grace as a display of weakness or a whimsical concept – too touchy-feely, fluffy, sentimental, mushy, overly emotional, even cringey. By being kind and nurturing, might others take such leaders for granted, exploiting their 'human touch' or consider them pushovers?

I have come to learn that the so-called 'soft stuff' of leadership – ennobling, engaging and empowering others by means of self-caring, self-regulating, self-leading, empathising, personising, safe place-making, offering honest feedback, staying positive, healing emotions, using humour, appreciating, coaching, creating value, as well as systems thinking and collective creating – are, in fact, *the hard stuff* of leadership. These are all explored in the pages that follow.

Will showing too much compassion or providing too much coaching set a precedent that locks leaders into untenable expenditures of time and energy? Perhaps there are some leaders or potential leaders reading this book who think that they are too busy to be compassionate or to coach others because there are 'more significant matters' in the team or organisation to concentrate on. I would contend that graceful leadership is not an activity, not another item on a leader's 'to-do' list. Quite the opposite – graceful leadership is about *being* – it is an *embodied state* (Mitchell 2017). So, I agree with Alexsys Thompson (2020) when she poignantly observes, 'It doesn't require extra time… It's simply who you evolve into. So, if someone says they don't have time to be a graceful leader, what they're really saying is that they don't have time to be the best version of themselves.'

Part 2 focuses on 15 proven, *mutually reinforcing* practices that can bring or increase compassion and coaching – grace – into your leadership. Practices 1 to 4 are just for you. The remaining 11 can help to gracefully guide your daily relations with others.

Have self-compassion

Graceful leadership starts with *self-compassion*. Assisting others is one hallmark of graceful leadership, but 'wise generosity' is the key to resilient success, accomplished by carefully pacing oneself and allocating one's 'giving' time judiciously (see **Practice 12**). More fundamentally, you need to safeguard your own recharging time. You can only give what you have. As the saying, attributed to Canadian politician Norm Kelly, goes, 'You cannot pour from an empty cup.'

Richard Boyatzis and Annie McKee (2005) refer to this leadership balancing act as the 'cycle of sacrifice and renewal'. After periods of intensity, effective leaders invest in self-compassion, returning to a state of mind, body, heart and spirit that restores emotional and spiritual intelligences, positive energy and resonant relationships.

How can we practise self-compassion? Below are some suggestions – and for an excellent set of evidenced-based resources on self-compassion, go to self-compassion.org.

Keep yourself at the top of your to-do list

Please don't take yourself for granted. Keep building your *self-awareness*, *resilience* (the capacity to tolerate difficulties or bounce back quickly from hardship and to even thrive in the face of challenges), *perseverance* and *self-discipline* (Elliott 2023). Nurture self-empathy (Niezink & Train 2020). Identify, reflect on and address the challenges that you face in your professional and/or personal life. Gently and continuously recognise the *unavoidability* of being fallible, making mistakes and encountering difficulties (Brach 2003). Pause to regularly assess your mental, physical, emotional and spiritual health (Neff 2009). Self-compassion brings many benefits, helping you, for example, to:

+ recognise early signs of stress, anxiety and burnout in yourself
+ build and retain your resilience
+ be healthier
+ engage in more meaningful relationships
+ be more creative and receptive to change
+ be happier and more motivated
+ make better decisions and choices (Neff 2015).

It's impossible to help others, to participate in deeper, truly genuine and empowering interactions with those we work with and care for if you yourself are overwhelmed and off balance. Graceful leadership involves leading from a place of fullness within us, from an inner reservoir of joy, passion, wonder and positivity. But when we lead from a place of internal depletion, from an inner emptiness of sadness, tiredness and negativity, we simply bring further problems and stress to those we are trying to lead, while further risking our own burnout. What we transmit to others originates from what is within us.

Self-awareness, self-care, self-respect, self-acceptance

Self-compassion can be considered a combination of self-awareness, self-care, self-respect and self-acceptance. These are totally different from self-obsession, self-indulgence, self-promotion and self-absorption – those are narcissistic trademarks of disgraceful leadership.

Self-awareness

Self-awareness is needed in at least two dimensions:

✦ Internally, when we can fully appreciate what makes us our best selves by accurately considering our strengths and weaknesses and come to realise how our behaviours can be improved or become less conditioned by bias, emotional reactions and contexts.

✦ Externally, when we can truly comprehend the quality of our connections with others and how we impact the world around us.

Corrective actions along both dimensions, when needed, allow us to optimise our graceful leadership (more on these dimensions in **Practices 2** and **3**).

Self-care

There are those who believe that the harder situations become, the harder they should push themselves – captured by the idiom 'When the going gets tough, the tough get going!' – and thus pausing to take care of oneself is perceived as a display of weakness or softness. But an ever-growing body of research proves the profound health and social benefits of self-compassion (and showing compassion for others). Enough evidence to perhaps modify the idiom to 'When the going gets tough, the tough pause for self-care before they get going again!' Furthermore, recent research has shown a link between leader self-care and employee health. Self-caring leaders seem to focus on staff care much more than leaders who do not care for themselves, with employees of self-caring leaders perceiving higher levels of staff care investment and reporting lower stress and better health (Klug et al 2022).

Self-respect

Self-respect can emerge by cultivating positive self-talk – recognising our own value and celebrating our own successes – which can help us break out of the cycles of self-sabotaging thoughts most of us get trapped in (Germer 2009). In his impactful book *Focus on the Good Stuff* (2007), Mike Robbins (former baseball pitcher with the Kansas City Royals and now executive coach) warns, 'Self-criticism… kills off the possibility of loving ourselves, appreciating others, and creating the kind of relationships, success and happiness that we want.' Self-respect is not the same as bragging or being arrogant; it is about internally lifting our self-worth and self-confidence. It's about self-acknowledgement – too few of us practise this but it's so important because appreciating others (see **Practice 12**) becomes almost impossible if we are constantly criticising ourselves.

Professor of psychology at the University of California and the world's leading scientific expert on gratitude, Dr Robert Emmons (2016) gives us this simple advice just before going to sleep each night: 'Try to focus on pleasant thoughts – good things happening to your family or friends; the soothing sounds in your bedroom; how fortunate you are to be in good health; future plans, such as holidays or an upcoming trip; enjoyable things you did during the past few days; how relaxed you are feeling; good things that other people have done for you in the past few days.'

Self-acceptance

Finally, reframing your mistakes as learning experiences to draw out what you will do differently next time is fundamentally an act of self-compassion. *It can be powerfully cathartic to simply accept that a mistake happened but does not define who you are.* As Sonia Ricotti, CEO of Lead Out Loud Inc, bestselling author and expert in personal transformation, once said, 'Accept what is, let go of what was and have faith in what will be.' We will reflect a little more on mistakes and failures in **Practice 6**.

Mindfulness

Classic self-care habits are well known but not universally practised. Start today! Get quality sleep (seven to eight hours is recommended). Maintain a healthy diet. Drink plenty of water. Isolate time for regular physical exercise. But there are perhaps some less familiar self-care habits that are proven to enhance leadership skills and generate compassion. Adopting a daily mindfulness practice through meditation, tai chi, qigong or yoga, for example, especially deep, rhythmic breathing, allows you to focus powerfully, not on the past nor the future, but on what you sense and feel in the moment without judgement.

But for many of us, resting into mindfulness is difficult. We carry around so much 'interference' or 'clutter' in our minds, for instance from anxieties about work, family, health or finance, alongside constant notifications, whether emails, calls, texts or social media alerts, to regrets about past conversations, mistakes and misfortunes. It's not easy to shut this 'noise' off so that we can be quietly 'present' in the present. When I started practising mindfulness, to overcome the chatter inside my head, I would doggedly remind myself of the many advantages it offers. Thinking about these benefits helped to block out my gaggle of otherwise perniciously incessant voices urging me to be preoccupied, distracted and worried.

When we engage in, for example, yoga or meditation, we gain greater calmness, self-awareness, energy recovery, mental acuity, connection with others, greater authenticity and leadership competence in the form of improved resilience, capacity to collaborate and the ability to lead in complex conditions (Gelles 2015). People who are highly resilient are not particularly unique but, to continually refresh themselves, they do actively practise a variety of skills such as mindfulness and cultivating compassion as well as hope (Reivich & Shatte 2002). Mindfulness can supercharge your ability to:

✦ think clearly even when in the midst of a crisis or confronted with multiple deadlines

- ✦ emotionally self-regulate (see **Practice 2**)
- ✦ engage in more cerebral responses instead of snap reactions (see **Practice 3**)
- ✦ remember more, and more accurately
- ✦ be less distracted in meetings and conversations (see **Practice 6**)
- ✦ synthesise seemingly unrelated information (see **Practice 15**).

Mindfulness practice can also reduce aggression, anxiety, self-criticism, irritability and anger (Gillions et al 2019). Sitting quietly and visualising how you will successfully perform, for example in a future task or an upcoming meeting, can help to rewire your brain's neural circuitry, resulting in better performance (Robertson 2000). But be mindful (excuse the pun) – to gain all these benefits requires dedicated mindfulness practice.

Mindfulness costs nothing and can be practised anywhere, anytime. Nowadays there are courses and several apps that can help us practise meditative breathing (see the links in the References). I practise mindful breathing in short bursts, for example, when at my desk (to refocus), in a car heading to a meeting (to generate empathy), riding my motorbike, washing the dishes or walking our dogs (to re-energise). When I introduce mindfulness as part of my mentoring and coaching, I begin by encouraging a simple focus on deep, measured breathing (officially called 'focused attention'). Your breath becomes an intentional anchor to the present moment. When your mind wanders, as it always will, you can bring it back to the anchor, to your breathing. Nothing else matters, just the sensation of air moving in and out of your lungs. I silently count to six for every breath I inhale, and again count to six as I exhale. A minute or two of this works wonders. You can also place one hand flat on your chest and the other flat on your abdomen. Your lower hand should move in and out further than the hand on your chest.

When I know I have a difficult conversation coming up, an important speech to make, a worried colleague to support or I'm just feeling tired, I calm and re-centre myself by simply focusing on deep, rhythmic breathing.

Galleries and sanctuaries

For some, self-compassion might include or even be as simple as going regularly to your personal 'art gallery' (to re-energise) or to your 'sanctuary' (to find peace). My 'galleries' are walking our huskies, Boopy and Tokyo, along a beach or through forests, taking a smooth ride on my motorbike, playing archery with friends, swimming underwater (these are forms of ecotherapy), cooking a new Indian recipe, coaching someone, publicly singing karaoke or (and this is the best) performing with a live band.

My sanctuaries, places of reprieve and reverence, are a quiet morning coffee alongside Ranjana, my soulmate, together with our cats, Gypsy and Whiskey (when the dogs are snoozing), chilling with our children, curling up with a great book, watching an inspirational movie, writing (eg this book), listening to my favourite vocalists and bands, drawing by hand, adding another intricate scene to my model railway or just enjoying a sip or two of smooth Australian merlot or dark Irish stout.

Former Harvard Medical School professor and founder of the Circadian Light Research Centre Dr Martin Moore-Ede likens these intermittent periods of soul restoration to 'time cocoons' (Moore-Ede 1993).

Energy management
Circadian rhythms

Are you 'an early morning person' – bright and chirpy in the first part of the day? Or are you 'a late afternoon/evening person' – in your most active flow in the latter part of the day? Or do you have a few bursts of action across the day?

From the field of chronobiology (the study of how processes within living organisms relate to time), these are the three broad patterns of our 24-hour energy distribution – our *circadian rhythms* – linked to how we each adapt to our environment as well as to solar- and lunar-related cycles.

I'm an early bird or lark and therefore find mornings the best time for tackling my major tasks. That's when my 24-hour distribution of energy is at its peak. As the day progresses, my general energy level depletes and I'm usually in bed by 8 pm. I try to schedule lower priorities for the afternoons. Then there are night owls, those whose optimum energy periods are afternoons and evenings. Their best work is achieved later in the day. The third, and largest, group of people are known as 'hummingbirds', who experience at least two peaks of energy, one in each half of the day (Kreitzman 2009).

Noticing your unique circadian rhythm can help you better schedule your daily tasks to match your optimum energy flow, achieving what biologists refer to as *allostasis* – balancing your internal environment to meet perceived and anticipated external demands (see 'Task prioritisation' below). Within a team, appreciating each other's circadian rhythm can assist in ensuring such tasks as meetings and urgent collaborative work are aligned as much as they can be with when the majority have their highest levels of drive or at least are distributed proportionately over time across the variations in circadian rhythm.

Ultradian rhythms

World-renowned performance psychologist Dr Jim Loehr and Tony Schwartz, CEO of The Energy Project, in their ground-breaking book *The Power of Full Engagement* (2003), note how the world's best athletes all build highly structured routines of performance (energy sacrifice) followed by recovery (energy renewal) into their lives. They argue that top-performing corporate or organisational 'athletes' need the same type of renewal routines.

The physical, emotional, mental and spiritual dimensions of energy are interrelated and require competent management to function at our best. We and our teams are compromised in whatever we do if we don't have the proper amount, type, focus and force of energy. Inclusive work cultures foster higher levels of commitment and productivity by promoting *periodic energy recharging.*

The good news, of course, is that our energy can be replenished. Nature has ingeniously developed a second energy pattern within each 24-hour cycle known as our *ultradian rhythms,* found in behavioural activities such as feeding habits and in physiological functions, including cellular processes, respiration, circulation, hormone release and sleep stages. Our brain has its own ultradian rhythm known as the '90/20 cycle' – roughly 90 minutes of high-frequency neural activity interspersed by 20 minutes of lower-frequency brain activity, possibly controlled by a delicate balance between potassium and sodium. Consider this as our *internal productivity timer.* At least in terms of work-related tasks, for 90-minute bursts or sprints our brain is hyperfocused and then disengages or 'takes a break', if you will.

There's a huge body of neuroscientific research on the brain's ultradian rhythm but for most of us it's enough to know that 'periodising' or stepping away from an intense task or taking a break between a series of tasks every 90 minutes and doing something different for 20 minutes is highly beneficial (Davidovich 2023). Whether the 20 minutes is spent daydreaming, taking a stroll, listening to music, chatting with colleagues (if they're also taking a break), mindful breathing, playing a game (**Practice 11**) and so on, this 'downtime' allows us to shift from our brain's analytical mode of thinking (its task-positive network) to its social mode of thinking (its default-mode network), reorganise our thoughts and recharge so that we can return to our work-related tasks with a fresh perspective and motivation (Lieberman 2013). To fully benefit from these 20 minutes of respite means to *fully* disengage and seek renewal. Turning to another work-related task for 20 minutes isn't the solution (just in case you were about to ask). It's about cultivating the self-discipline to oscillate or flow between periods when you expend and then renew the four dimensions of your energy.

The Pomodoro technique

One final way to manage energy at work is to consider using the famous Pomodoro technique, which can also be applied within any 90-minute task-focused sprint of our brain's ultradian rhythm. Developed in the late 1980s to help him get through his studies while at Sapienza University in Rome, Francesco Cirillo employed a kitchen timer that happened to be shaped like a tomato or 'pomodoro' in Italian. He would set the timer and work in 25-minute intervals and then take a five-minute break. Adopted by individuals and teams worldwide, this technique has helped users tackle projects of any length, greatly boosting their output, improving their focus and assisting them in reaching their goals (Cirillo 2018).

So, the first of two invitations here is to monitor your energy flows to identify your own circadian, ultradian (90/20) and pomodoro (25/5) rhythms – and then, if it makes sense and is practical for you, honour your natural chronobiology by organising your workday priorities to match these cycles as much as possible.

Task prioritisation

Most people maintain a to-do list of tasks in some form, whether handwritten on a sheet of paper or typed into a mobile, tablet, laptop and so forth. Though sadly hardly any of us put our wellbeing at the top, such lists offer some sense of order to the multiple demands on our energy and time. Some of us are comfortable just progressing through our list in the order we construct it. There is something immensely pleasurable about either drawing a line through each completed task or deleting it from the screen.

Others prioritise their duties or responsibilities using criteria such as a task's importance, urgency, value and effort relative to other tasks. Probably everything on our list is important, but is it urgent? Is this event or activity time critical or day specific? If it's not completed before the end of the day or in the next several hours, will there be serious consequences? What's the worst that could happen if this doesn't get done today? Are there any high-priority dependencies that rely on me finishing up this piece of work now (eg a task that needs to be completed today to prepare for a workshop in two weeks' time)? Which of the urgent tasks has the highest value for my team? Which task will require the most effort? And then the next, etc? What is the payoff of completing this task compared to the time I'll invest in it?

Prioritising our to-do lists can help bring an even deeper sense of order. But in my coaching and mentoring of colleagues, I've noticed many do not take what I believe are two further important steps. One is to match their priorities against their circadian rhythm – placing the most critical tasks, those that are important, urgent, of high value to others and need lots of effort (or a combination of such criteria) in the periods of the day when their natural energy flow is at its highest. I noted that I'm a lark, so I always place my top priorities in the morning knowing that my daily energy reserves will start to deplete during the afternoon and further into evening. Night owls prefer to place their top priorities in the second half of the day when their energy rises. Several hummingbirds I know tend to plan their day around a mid-morning priority and a mid-afternoon priority.

Time allocation

The second important step missed by many of my colleagues is to organise their day in terms of how much time needs to be allocated to each task. You might be using a paper-based calendar or an electronic tool such as Microsoft's Outlook calendar to map out all the meetings that you must attend during each day, week or month. But the times in between meetings are often left blank on these calendars and it's during these blanks that many of us try to plough into our to-do lists, often getting frustrated and stressed when we have to interrupt our desk work or personal tasks and go to 'yet another meeting' (which may not be well organised, as we shall see in **Practice 6**). We might even be tempted to take our tablet or laptop with us and try to continue working on our to-do list *in the meeting,* believing that we can multitask. I'll come to the myth of multitasking in a moment. But first let me quickly share how I go about organising my work calendar.

While my weekly calendar usually contains several 'meetings' (whether they be events, workshops and group discussions), I also plan my time *in between* meetings to complete work-related tasks using three time-allocation techniques: timeboxing, timeblocking and something I call 'wriggle room'.

Timeboxing is the allocation of my time for *single,* top-priority tasks – those that are important, urgent, of high value to others and need lots of effort. From experience, I've learned to estimate how much time a proposal, report or policy document, for example, will need to be worked on. These are my timeboxed single tasks and in tune with my circadian rhythm are usually scheduled in the mornings. Sometimes a particular timeboxed task requires more than one scheduled time slot or there's simply not enough time on that given day so I split the task over two or three timeboxes.

Timeblocking is an allocation of time in my calendar for a set of small, often similar tasks such as responding to several emails or letters or completing electronic surveys. My timeblocked tasks usually get placed in the afternoons. During these timeblocks, I work through my sets of smaller tasks in sequence, one task after the other.

Within both timeboxes and timeblocks, I try to maintain the ultradian energy flow of 90 minutes of focus on the task or tasks followed by 20 minutes of brain recharging. And within each overall 90-minute burst, I try to use the Pomodoro technique of 25-minute bursts of intense focus interspersed by five-minute breaks. I say 'try', because breaking my focus can sometimes prove tricky if I'm experiencing a creative flow of writing or reviewing. For more on timeboxing and timeblocking, see asana.com/resources/multitasking.

Wriggle room is my own term, taken from my potholing experiences (exploring underground caves, sometimes when there was only just enough room in a rock tunnel to wriggle through). In my weekly calendar, I purposively leave around 90 minutes of unallocated time every day for any urgent tasks that come at me unexpectedly, such as a new priority emailed overnight from UN headquarters or a colleague needing to see me urgently. I therefore always reserve some extra space for tasks or meetings I cannot anticipate.

MONDAY	TUESDAY	WEDNESDAY	THURSDAY	FRIDAY
Timebox 📎	Timeblock 📎	Timebox	Meeting 📎	Timebox 📎
	Meeting 📎			Meeting
Meeting	Timebox 📎	Meeting 📎	Meeting	Timebox
Meeting 📎	Meeting		Timebox 📎	
Timeblock 📎		Timeblock	Meeting	Meeting 📎
Meeting	Timeblock 📎	Meeting	Timeblock 📎	Timeblock

A typical week in my calendar might look like this. It does not include evening and weekend invitations to attend events, launches, virtual calls and workshops. The blank spaces are my wriggle room. And you will see paperclips in several of the timeslots, which is when I've copied and pasted the documents, emails, speeches, talking points or meeting agendas (that I need to work through) in my laptop's Outlook calendar so I that save time not having to search back through my email inbox.

My second invitation is to consider using your calendar as a form of one-stop shop – where you maintain your to-do list, prioritise tasks and allocate time in timeboxes (single, big tasks), timeblocks (multiple, small tasks) and wriggle room (for unexpected tasks) – *alongside scheduling meetings*. I use a quiet hour on Monday morning to organise my weekly calendar and then 15 minutes every morning to organise/reorganise each day. It may feel a little odd when you start trying this but by allocating desk time to tasks (and if you can, paste critical emails or documents that you need to act on within the relevant time slot so that they are easy to locate), it could make you more task effective *and* time efficient, additionally reducing stress and improving your life–work balancing all at the same time. This also requires self-discipline or willpower to not get distracted or disrupted from the orderly schedule you've created.

Some further tactics to allow you to focus on tasks with no interruptions include removing email functionality from your phone (I don't receive emails on my phone and haven't done so since 2015); switching off emails when working on key tasks; and sticking to your timetable of scheduled tasks and not being tempted to disrupt your focus by answering emails or joining *ad hoc* meetings. By doing so, you may feel an even stronger sense of control, energy and positivity permeating your time at work and time outside of work. So aside from meetings, how will you divide your time to maximise job priorities? Are you prepared to take charge of your schedule and your life as a result?

On multitasking

I'm often asked if I 'multitask' at work – perform multiple tasks at the same time, for example answering emails while participating in a meeting. My answer is that I used to try to, but over the years I've learned to unlearn this habit, for several reasons. First, it's largely a myth. What we think of as multitasking is just our ability to rapidly switch between single tasks, known as 'task-switching' or 'context-shifting' (Madore

& Wagner 2019). Simple processes such as brushing your teeth while tuning into the radio or cooking while listening to music are forms of multitasking, but for complex processes such as writing emails while attending a team meeting, most of us are task-switching, consuming time and expending energy as we move back and forth between each task, and not really paying attention to the task we are not primarily focused on. To use my example, it's either the email or the team discussion. There's a reason we admire the expression 'undivided attention'.

Only about 2.5 per cent of us, known as 'supertaskers', possess the amazing capacity to *simultaneously* complete two tasks that require a great deal of focus, which more than 97 per cent of us are unable to do without suffering significant performance consequences (Watson & Strayer 2010). For most of us, multitasking is ineffective, despite how reassuring it may feel because we seem to be leaping through our to-do lists! In most cases, we're not. By hopping from one task to another, we're losing energy and time while our brain re-engages with each task. Such milliseconds add up. According to research, multitasking *wastes* 28 per cent of a typical workday. Multitaskers also make more mistakes than singletaskers – those who work on tasks in a linear fashion, one task at a time. In short, if you try to do too much at once, you can actually end up working more slowly and not doing anything well (Rock 2020).

Second, research has also demonstrated that the brain is not inherently designed for multitasking, as it can only store so much data and use so much processing power at once. Multitasking diminishes our creativity, our 'out-of-the-box' thinking. To be creative, we need time for our minds to analyse and mull over new ideas (**Practice 15**). Multitasking also prevents us from entering that amazing mental state known as 'flow' when we're so laser focused on a task that our output soars. According to Kotler (2014), CEOs who were in a state of flow reported being 500 per cent more productive!

And third, for us non-supertaskers, our efforts to multitask are not only unproductive but can also be harmful – from reducing grey matter density in our brain's cortex to increasing stress and anxiety; from diminishing our short-term memory to increasing the time we take to complete simple tasks; from reducing IQ to losing sleep; from distorting our beliefs about how long tasks really take (chronic multitaskers overestimate how long tasks actually take) to diminishing trust and respect – and thus psychological safety – when others sense we're not giving them attention (see **Practice 6**) (Davidovich 2023).

Hyperfocus

I later learned that productivity expert and author Chris Bailey labels this method of prioritisation coupled with allocating time to priority tasks as 'hyperfocusing' one's energy and attention (Bailey 2018). Entrepreneur Gary Keller and business executive Jay Papasan, in their fascinating book *The One Thing* (2012), also debunk some of the myths that can prevent us from achieving hyperfocus. For example:

✦ 'Every task carries equal importance' – not true and only results in us attempting too much and accomplishing little. The truth: not everything matters equally. So, when prioritising tasks, it is vital to identify *what matters the most* using the 80/20 principle (realising that 80 per cent of our impact usually comes from 20 per cent of our efforts). This can turn a humdrum 'to-do' list into a 'daily success' list. For me, this has always been a combination of working through the relative urgency × importance × value (for the team) × estimated effort of each task to distil my to-do list of tasks to the essential few. In sum, internally deciding between what I *could* do today versus what I *must* do today.

✦ 'Extraordinary success can be achieved by working simultaneously on several tasks' (multitasking) which, as explained above, is also not true – once we have the essential to-do list of tasks it is much better to complete work one task at a time because success is sequential not simultaneous.

So, over the past decade, I've unlearned multitasking and embraced the liberating power of singletasking, coupled with careful energy and time management – hyperfocusing. Through first investing energy and time in prioritising the tasks that then feature on my to-do list and by precisely organising my weekly calendar (meetings *plus* tasks), I've got closer and closer to optimal life–work balancing.

Life–work balancing

There is a growing body of research including meta-analytic reviews on the concept of work–life balance as it correlates to productivity, engagement, wellbeing and so on (Wood et al 2020). But while the analyses point in favour of making sure our workplaces offer better work–life balance, I still prefer to use the expression 'life–work balancing' for two reasons.

First, as the late Dr Louis 'Studs' Terkel, a Pulitzer Prize-winning writer, historian, actor and broadcaster, once famously quipped, 'Too many people are searching for a life that is not a Monday-through-Friday kind of dying' (Mcfadden 1997). Most of us work to live. A lucky few, those whose life purpose perfectly aligns with their profession, find the sweet spot of living to work, in fact they may not even call it 'work'. They follow this sage advice: 'Choose a job you love, and you will never have to work a day in your life.' Discovering one's life purpose (**Tool A**) can bring several benefits. One might be to clarify that your current job is not allowing your highest self to flourish, so it could be time to seek greener pastures. Or as O C Tanner Institute researchers David Sturt and Todd Nordstrom (2015) observe, another benefit might be to realise that you can infuse your current job with elements of what you love to do.

And second, in my experience a perfect balance can rarely be achieved. The challenge is to *keep balancing* priorities in our personal lives with those required by our profession or employer. The Covid-19 pandemic allowed individuals and organisations to experience what virtual teams already knew – that quality performance is still possible regardless of people's physical and temporal locations. The widespread use of flexi-working arrangements gave many of us (not all, mind) the chance to achieve better balance between personal and professional commitments.

But as Gary Keller and Jay Papasan have noted, prioritisation is the key to balancing. Sometimes personal life must take precedence, and we can compensate at work with extra effort later. At other times work requires our hyperfocus but we must subsequently counterbalance by investing in ourselves, family and friends. By prioritising and mindfully managing energy and time in both our personal and professional domains, I believe it's possible to become better at balancing life and work.

Compassionate networks

As a leader, you certainly need know-how (clear strategy) but you also need 'know who' (social capital). Leadership can be distressing and lonely, so try to build a support community who will fortify your resilience and empower and celebrate you. When you have a place to go for questions and help, a place where you can show up authentically and connect with others to recharge, you'll find the strength to help you through the most challenging times. Being a part of a network and feeling appreciated and supported reduces stress, strengthens our immune systems and helps us to avoid burnout (Gilbert 2009).

Some call such social capital a developmental network, a tribe of like-minded people, a reciprocity ring, a spiritual support system or professional/personal learning network – people with whom you have networked and with whom you have trusting, caring relationships. They can also be accountability partners who hold you accountable for the personal and professional changes you want or commit to make.

Different types of networks that you might have already and can enhance might be labelled as follows:

✦ The comfort network, a place of safety and reassurance made up of family and friends.

✦ The community network, for which you volunteer your time and in return, receive gratitude and more contacts.

✦ The board of personal advisors network, a small group of professionals you respect to whom you can reach out for regular advice such as when you want to change jobs or have major personal decisions to make. This board might consist of peers, colleagues, mentors, coaches, counsellors, therapists, family and friends.

✦ The cheerleaders network, people within organisations who know your talent and can put in a good word on your behalf to hiring managers (members of your board of personal advisors might also be cheerleaders).

✦ The thought leaders network – experts who inspire you intellectually and may be people you have met or heard in conferences or podcasts, or read their books, articles or blogs. LinkedIn is a place where you can connect to many such experts.

Rain for our brain

Psychologist and author Tara Brach (2019) has encapsulated a very useful stepwise approach to practising self-compassion through the acronym RAIN:

✦ **R**ecognise what is happening to me in this moment (eg negative thoughts, sensations or emotions).

✦ **A**llow or accept whatever is happening to me just as it is.

✦ **I**nvestigate or be curious about what is happening to me, what it truly represents.

✦ **N**urture or care for myself in the context of this difficult experience.

In the words of Professor Paul Gilbert (2009), the take-home message from all this is that through self-compassion, 'We can stimulate patterns in our brains that are self-nourishing, supportive, encouraging and soothing, so that in whatever we do to help ourselves... we practise creating in our heads an experience (brain pattern) of warmth, kindness and support as our primary starting position.'

And it is to the further exploration of our brains that I turn next.

Train your brain

Have you ever considered what's going on inside the brain of individuals you're leading or in your own brain as you lead? If you haven't yet, I invite you to plunge deep into the refreshing and uplifting world of neuroscience (the study of our nervous system).

Neuroscience

Neuroscience is transforming our knowledge of the human brain and thus the hows and whys of our emotions and behaviours. If wisely applied, these new insights could radically change the way leaders engage with, coach and motivate others (Dimitriadis & Psychogios 2021; Brann 2022). Exploring outer space is enticing, but perhaps exploring our *inner* space and then utilising this understanding for good could be the much more important game-changer that humanity, and ultimately our planet, urgently needs. And the bonus here is that by searching inward, we might possibly learn more about what lies outward, beyond Earth. You see, while it is both humbling and at the same time awe inspiring (well, to me at least), there are scientists who argue that, at an atomic level, our inner space, our brain, is itself 'the billions of years in the making' manifestation of outer-space activity. Our evolutionary foundations were forged from elemental particles emitted by exploding stars or supernovas (LeDoux 2019).

Neuroscience is fascinating but deliciously complicated and rapidly advancing. There are just too many intriguing features within this second practice to do it justice here, so let's just reflect on some headlines.

First the bad news

Our brains are virtually the same in basic function as those of Stone Age humans. The head-brain's structures (I say 'head-brain' because we possess other 'brains', as we'll see) that were once highly essential for our survival when we hunted *but were also hunted by predators* some two million years ago up to the Bronze Age (around 3,300 BC), are not very appropriate for the 'threats' we now encounter in today's world.

Though not all agree with his theory, physician and neuro-scientist Dr Paul MacLean hypothesised that our head-brain evolved in three main sections. First, the reptilian (the brainstem and basal ganglia). Second, the limbic (wrapped around the reptilian brain and consisting of the hippocampus, amygdala and hypothalamus), which controls most of our emotions, helps us to judge situations and often unconsciously determines many behaviours. And last, the neocortex (wrapped around and on top of the limbic brain), home to our reasoning, imagination, creativity and problem solving – the seat of compassion – but which needs to be consciously activated (MacLean 1990).

The catch here is that while elegantly designed to help us survive during the Stone Age, in today's modern workplace our brain still perceives a confrontational manager, aggressive co-worker, competitive colleague, harsh email (called 'flame-mail' in some circles), verbal criticism or a flippant supervisee as a life-or-death 'threat'. Evolved for and honed by survival, our primitive brain's default setting is hypersen-sitive to threats – left untamed, it just keeps overreacting. And once we have auto-switched into self-defence mode, we can misperceive even neutral comments from colleagues as disparagement. This presents *trying to remain graceful* with at least two hurdles.

First, once triggered by 'threats', our more ancient neural structures make us want to be in control, focus on the negative, get ready for trauma, become overly emotional and repeat earlier actions (even if they were not useful). We react stubbornly, devoid of compassion (empathy plus kind action). In this defensive, autopilot mode, emotional balance and moral reasoning slip away – we become hostile and inflexible. Not pleasant. Certainly *not graceful*.

The second obstacle is that our ancient fight–flight–freeze reaction can shut down higher brain centres such as the neocortex. Our threatened state impairs our ability to perceive and think clearly. Executive coach Dr Laura Delizonna (2017) writes, 'Quite literally, just when we need it most, we lose our mind. While that fight-or-flight reaction may save us in life-or-death situations, it handicaps the strategic thinking needed in today's workplace.' Overemotional reactivity is the opposite of mindfulness (**Practice 3**). So, this ancient, once vital design feature is now perhaps a modern-era design fault which, if left unrealised and unaddressed, can severely affect workplace cultures.

Now some good news

Our brains have incredible, lifelong... yes lifelong neuroplasticity. Neuroplasticity is the capacity to grow new neurons (nerve cells) and to create new connections between neurons in response to internal and external stimuli. Through learning new information or practising a new skill or repeating an experience, for example, our brain can reorganise its functions and structural connections allowing for positive mental states that we can cultivate to become more heightened and ever more resilient (Fuchs and Flügge 2014). We can alter our neural default settings.

This neural reconfigurability is remarkable. It means, for example, that while the basic function and structure of our brain are still the same as our Stone Age ancestors', the more fine-tuned neural pathways of modern-day humans can be quite different. This is due, in part, to the many external, ecosystem changes that have occurred over time to which our internal epigenetics (gene expression) have responded and transformed. But is also because, in part, we've had an increasingly intrinsic role to play, for good and (agonisingly) for bad, in these ecosystemic changes. Climate change, biodiversity loss and pollution – our very real triple planetary crisis – are tragic manifestations of humans' (or their leaders') incapability to tap into our higher selves, our inner space.

In order to improve our emotional and spiritual intelligences, neural reconfiguration only occurs if we consciously and *proactively* enable it. In short, to unleash our neuroplastic potential *we must keep working at it.*

And now some further good news: *there are at least two other 'brains' that can help us* – both of which communicate with and can modulate our head-brain's responses.

The heart-brain (or intrinsic cardiac nervous system) is a complex network within and around the heart that constantly communicates with the head-brain and other parts of the body. In his spellbinding journey to comprehend compassion, *Into the Magic Shop* (2016), Stanford University neurosurgeon Professor James Doty powerfully describes the heart-brain's influence, 'the heart sends far more signals to the brain than the brain sends to the heart... The brain knows a lot, but the simple truth is it knows a lot more when it joins with the heart.'

The gut-brain (or intrinsic enteric nervous system) consists of more than 500 million neurons within our gastrointestinal tract. Sending signals back and forth to the head-brain, our gut-brain contributes to vital functions such as appetite, digestion, metabolism, mood, behaviour, stress management, pain sensitivity, cognition and immunity (Brierley & Costa 2016).

Accessing all three brains – by, for example, trusting that 'gut instinct' (your intuition, thought to be manifested via the bidirectional vagus nerve that links our head-brain and gut-brain) or through mindful breathing, slowing your heartbeat and thus generating calmness – can make you a more effective leader (Cooper 2000).

The magic of the pause

The more primitive parts of our brain can be tamed over time to become less selfish and more selfless through engaging in habits described in **Practice 1**, especially mindful breathing and meditation, and by investing in spiritual intelligence (see **Practice 3**). We can learn to recognise what causes us stress and become far more self-aware of our instantaneous emotional reactions and then mindfully intervene. But we only have microseconds every time our ancient neural structures are triggered – and remember, evolution has honed them to be super-ready! That's when the magic of the pause comes in.

One way to describe what happens and how our brain can be trained is as follows. The whole reactive process starts when a sensory stimulus – be it auditory, tactile, taste based or visual – reaches our hypothalamus. This, in a fraction of a second, sends the information to the amygdala via three channels:

✦ Directly, to create an immediate impression of the situation and generate an emotional response. *We need to learn to bypass this pathway by building agile self-awareness.*

✦ Concurrently, the same information is transmitted to the prefrontal cortex, where it's analysed to provide a more comprehensive understanding of the appropriate reaction before reaching the amygdala. *We need to enhance this pathway through self-regulation practice.*

✦ Instantly, the prefrontal cortex sends information to the hippocampus to check whether anything in our memory bank can add more detail to help the amygdala better determine the emotional response. *We need to slow this pathway down, again through self-regulation practice.*

Nobel Prize-winner Daniel Kahneman, the late professor emeritus of psychology and public affairs at Princeton University, in his classic book *Thinking, Fast and Slow* (2011), distinguishes between two cognitive systems that our brains appear to possess. System 1 is fast, instinctive and automatic; System 2 is slower, deliberative and logical. The hard work of self-regulation, of pausing before responding, is to strengthen the neurological bridge or 'cortical overpass' as it were, which connects System 1's reactions more consistently to System 2's more measured responses.

Name it to tame it

Emotional self-control or self-regulation begins by identifying common stress triggers (certain actions or words from others, threatening circumstances) and becoming familiar with your own stress signals – physical and/or emotional cues such as body tension, a racing heart, tightness in your chest, a 'knot' or 'butterflies' in your stomach, anxiety, the volume of your voice rising, anger and so on. Then, in that split second before impulsively reacting to any menacing remark or situation... pause, breathe mindfully (**Practice 1**), appraise, clarify or remind yourself of your higher purpose (**Practice 3**), and put yourself in the shoes of those in front of you (**Practice 4**). This is not about avoiding or removing emotionality; this is about learning to consistently channel the energy of our emotions (which are just electrical impulses in our brain) in more constructive ways (DiGangi 2023).

Neuroscience has shown that by simply labelling a triggered emotion, we can lessen the intensity of our amygdala's reaction (Lieberman et al 2007). In other words, 'name it to tame it'. Recognising, examining and naming an emotion momentarily moves our neural energy from the primitive, emotionally reactive brain structures to the more sophisticated, analytically responsive prefrontal cortex. Even a split-second transfer of focus to the more evolved parts of the brain where language is created can be enough to short-circuit this ancient neural pathway, allowing us to slow down or reframe our response.

This is about developing *emotional literacy – the ability to express our emotions and feelings using speech and other forms of communication* – which underpins attainment of higher forms of intelligence (emotional and spiritual). I find it useful to ask myself, 'What feeling/s am I detecting in myself right now? Where am I feeling it in my body? How helpful is this feeling? If the feeling continues, will it be unhelpful or harmful to myself or others?'

Labelling and probing the emotion elevates thoughts to the neocortex. Allowing ego (the creator of emotions) to 'speak up' is also helpful, though we must recognise that ego is only telling us its self-defensive version of the story, not the whole truth. I might further ask myself 'What's really going on here?' and then 'What worries me about that?' and then 'How might I view this differently? Is there anything I can be grateful for?'

Six seconds

So, when confronted by a stressful situation or challenge such as a harsh word, an insult, an angry colleague or stranger, a curt email or offensive behaviour, we can learn to be more aware of the emotions that are being aroused and at the same time pause or slow down before responding. But how long should our mindful pauses be?

Inspired by the incredible research of the neuroscientist and pharmacologist, the late Professor Candace Pert, studies are emerging that suggest it takes around six seconds to recognise an emotion and somewhere between 90 seconds and several days – sometimes weeks, due to rumination or repetitively thinking or dwelling on negative feelings and distress and their causes and consequences – for various emotions to dissipate (Pert 1997). So, one school of thought seems to be that even just six seconds might be sufficient to interrupt or at least slow down the rapid amygdala-hypothalamus-neocortex-hippocampus exchanges I described above (Freedman nd; Tan 2015).

Harvard-trained neuroanatomist Dr Jill Bolte Taylor, author of the transformative book *My Stroke of Insight* (2006), describes our ability to self-regulate emotional reactions through what she calls the '90-second rule' – a 90-second time frame from the initial trigger to when neurochemicals that cause emotional responses dissipate from our bloodstream. When emotions linger beyond 90 seconds, it's usually because we're choosing to remain in the 'emotional loop' or for other reasons, including pharmacological factors (Verduyn & Lavrijsen 2015). Longer-term feelings such as grief need to be considered differently (see **Practice 10**).

Detection and measurement methods, including electro-chemical, optical, magnetic and neuroimaging techniques, continue to advance, generating greater clarity on the timespan of neurohormones and neurotransmitters once they are released in our bodies. But while the research continues, I like to think of this possibility to self-regulate our emotions within the first six seconds of Dr Taylor's 90-second rule as equivalent to the 'golden hour' in emergency medicine – in which an injured or sick person must have effective treatment within the first hour following the trauma or the onset of symptoms. Thus, to me, the six-second rule is a form of self-regulatory first aid in which I've learned how to focus inwards on my breath – slow counts of six as I breathe deeply in and out (**Practice 1**). Some say a mantra such as 'I can deal with this' – first said with your eyes closed and then eyes open – which also gets you to six seconds.

Hot letters

Another, though somewhat longer way to learn the magic of the pause is to follow a method described by President Abraham Lincoln as writing 'hot letters' – these were letters that he handwrote to those who had outraged him but which he never dispatched because he sensed they would do more harm than good. For him, however, these letters were a form of healthy catharsis.

In our hyperconnected cyberworld, hitting our internal pause button or writing a social media response but leaving it to 'cool' for 24 hours and then rewording it (if you still decide to post it) is becoming a vital peacekeeping skill. I've typed a few emails that were the equivalent of Lincoln's hot letters but they remained in my draft email folder until I eventually deleted them. By the way, should you be tempted to type such 'hot emails', always remove the email address of the person you're writing to – one slip of the fingers on your keyboard can unleash untold repercussions into the ether!

Mindsighting

To do all the above requires us to work hard at developing metacognition – *the act of thinking about our thinking*. Daniel Siegel, professor of clinical psychiatry at the UCLA School of Medicine and executive director of the Mindsight Institute, calls this *mindsighting*. 'It helps us to be aware of our mental processes without being swept away by them, enables us to get ourselves off the autopilot of ingrained behaviours and habitual responses, and moves us beyond the reactive emotional loops we all have a tendency to get trapped in' (Siegel 2011). Mindsighting is the brain's 'overhead construction work' that elevates our *response flexibility* – combining self-awareness, emotional appraisal and perspective taking, deliberately setting aside the negative interpretation that set off our triggered responses and looking for alternative, neutral or even positive interpretations.

I'm also intrigued by the invitation of neuroscientist Dr Dan Radecki and his colleagues at the Academy of Brain-based Leadership. When you find yourself in an inflammatory situation with another person, try to depersonalise and defuse the moment by internally reminding yourself that 'it's not them, it's their brain' (Radecki et al 2021). While somewhat dispassionate, this is another way to adopt a different perspective – to try to interpret their emotional turmoil as simply an electrical discharge that is beginning to get out of control and for which their soul, their better self, is no longer in charge.

One final piece of good news is that there's an ever-growing body of science that demonstrates how consistent emotional self-regulation can dampen the amygdala's reaction to stressful stimuli (Denny et al 2015; Weng et al 2018). We can literally train our brain.

It is rain that grows flowers

The deliberate pause, during which we use unhurried breathing and reflective questioning, can help to *short-circuit our instinctive reaction* and transform it into mindful intention, metaphorically (perhaps even literally) lifting our response to the uppermost part of our brain – doing so can also generate oxytocin, which underpins trust and bonding behaviour (Quinn et al 2021). The words that then leave your mouth, *if required at all*, will likely be wiser and more compassionate, as well as spoken more gently, more slowly, more positively.

As you respond in your mind or through speaking, ask yourself, 'What emotion would my ideal self be feeling right now? Is it my ego or my soul talking? Am I being threat provoking or thought provoking to the other person/s? Am I being mean or measured in my response? What can I learn from this? How can I be kinder and wiser in this situation?' If you are rigorously disciplined in applying this self-regulating practice when threats appear (pause, breathe, reflect), through neuroplasticity, calmer responses can become almost automatic. By gaining a better neuroscientific understanding of how our brains function and by training them accordingly, we can indeed self-engineer a compassionate mind and coaching mindset (the cortical overpass).

But neuroscience is not our only source of guidance here. Rumi, the famous Persian poet (and my all-time favourite), Islamic scholar and Sufi mystic, wrote 700 years ago…

> Raise your words, not voice. It is rain that grows flowers, not thunder.

Practice 3

Lift your spiritual intelligence

Sunday 19 May 2002. The Rockefeller Foundation had gathered the leading scholars of communication to its Bellagio Centre on the shores of the mesmeric Lake Como, Italy. Then part of the social mobilisation team within the World Health Organization's communicable diseases programme located in Geneva, I was thrilled to be in the company of these global experts. But to be honest, I was puzzled as to why Alfonso Gumucio Dragon, filmmaker and development communication specialist, who'd met me in Papua New Guinea a few years earlier, had invited me. He later explained that my writings at that time were very much aligned with the principle of 'community participation', one vital axis of the emerging discipline that would later become known as communication for social change (CfSC). This gathering was to distil the essential competencies that should be possessed by CfSC practitioners.

I watched in awe as diametrically contrasting opinions and diverse ideas were debated by these intellectual giants, with exquisite grace. Never was a harsh word uttered, nor any voice raised, no matter how opposed they were to each other's views and suggestions (see **Practice 4**).

During the afternoon break on the first day, I plucked up the courage to join one of the small groups huddled around the coffee dispenser. I looked around at these wise, caring faces. 'If I may ask,' I began nervously, 'how is it that you can each hold such divergent views and yet argue with such calmness and even reach a final consensus with no heated exchanges?'

They looked across at each other. It was the late Professor Juan Díaz Bordenave, always with a sparkle in his eyes, who answered my question on behalf of the group. 'Well, Will, you're from Australia, right?' I nodded. 'OK. So, picture yourself standing on one of those beautiful Australian beaches. Out in the blue water is an orange buoy, anchored to the seabed, bobbing up and down on the surface about 100 metres from where you're standing. Now visualise the swim to and from that buoy represents one's career, one's life. At the beginning, on the way out, you want to get ahead of everyone; you want to be the first to reach that buoy. So, you thrash and thrash through the water; you swim as fast as you can, not paying any attention to the other swimmers who have joined you in the race. In fact, you push past them should they get in your way. That's the first half of your career, when you believe that you must outdo others, compete against everybody, win every argument. But once you turn around that buoy and start swimming back to shore, you realise that everyone needs to reach land safely. That's the second half of your life. Having already made it to the buoy, having argued your point, having made your mark, you have nothing left to prove. So, on the way back, instead of racing and contesting, you start to care for others; you make sure everyone gets back to the beach unharmed. So, what you see here,' as he gestured around the huddle, 'all of us, we are heading back to the shore. There's still a need to debate, but we have no more need to argue.'

I remember this conversation as if it were yesterday. At that point in my life, I was indeed still on my way out to the orange buoy. A technician, a self-labelled 'expert', in sum, an *ego*. In early 2007, when I started to live my boyhood dream of working for UNICEF, I sensed that I had finally reached the buoy, that I could begin to let go of my ego. I started to unlearn self-serving habits that were preventing me from doing what mattered most – serving others. It did not happen overnight! But ever since, I've been swimming back to the beach, trying my best to look out for colleagues as they embark upon their own professional and sometimes personal journeys of trans-formation.

Deep intelligence

Do you admire people with high integrity who are brave, caring, calm, open-minded, inspirational yet humble, unselfish, forgiving, nonviolent, resilient, centred and determined to have positive impacts on humanity and our planet, who seem to be leading a distinctly noble life? They have high levels of multiple 'intelligences'.

Graceful, genuine leadership involves *leading ourselves first* (Janosky 2017). To do so, we require several intelligences, including not just cognitive or mental intelligence (IQ) and relevant technical know-how or rational intelligence (RQ), but also:

✦ positive intelligence (PQ) – fostering an optimistic, resilient outlook to overcome our own, frequently self-sabotaging, self-berating thoughts (usually triggered by us succumbing to 'imposter syndrome')
✦ body intelligence (BQ) – carefully managing our health
✦ emotional intelligence (EQ) – intense self-awareness and good interpersonal skills
✦ cultural intelligence (CQ) – the ability to understand and master interactions with people from different cultures or when working in cross-cultural settings
✦ and, above all, in my view, spiritual intelligence (SQ).

When combined, we find leaders who possess what might be called *deep intelligence* (Wigglesworth 2014).

What is spiritual intelligence?

Spiritual intelligence was first coined in 1997 in the writings of two unconnected authors – Ken O'Donnell, an international consultant in organisational development, and Professor Danah Zohar, a management thought leader (O'Donnell 1997; Zohar 1997). SQ has been defined as 'the ability to behave with wisdom and compassion while maintaining inner and outer peace, regardless of the situation' (Wigglesworth 2012). Dr Altazar Rossiter, a modern mystic and gifted facilitator, defines spiritual intelligence as 'an organic wisdom that we all carry, one that is constantly trying to inform us and support us. [SQ is] an innate quality of knowing' (Rossiter 2006).

SQ can be closely associated with *calmness* (**Practices 1** and **2**) and with *creativity* – our ability to make sense of complexity, to uncover root causes, to discover subtle patterns, to see possibilities, to innovate, and thereby focus on the big picture (see **Practice 15**).

For Stephen Covey, 'Spiritual intelligence is the central and most fundamental of all the intelligences, because it becomes the source of guidance for the others' (Covey 2004). SQ could be thus described as the ultimate pathfinder, enhancer, stabiliser and integrator for all the other types of intelligence. In short, SQ is the ability to consistently *move above and beyond one's ego* – to strive to always be all we can be in all situations. This is not easy because our egos can be highly influential and disruptive to our relative state of mindfulness. But even becoming aware of when our ego is trying to take over is a positive start!

So, if **Practice 2** was about taming our primitive brain structures, then **Practice 3** builds on that, allowing us to move and be consistently above and beyond our ego. In some respects, this practice is about transitioning away from being a manager to becoming a leader. I know because I was for some time an ego-driven manager (see the beginning of this section).

Is the calmer, wiser 'higher self' in charge of your life, your day-to-day interactions, or are you dictated by an immature, short-sighted, self-interested ego and/or the beliefs and ideals imposed on you by others? SQ ultimately determines the type of relationship we have with *ourselves*. And this relationship dictates how we relate to others and the world at large. This is why SQ is so important. SQ runs through all the practices in this book, from cultivating inner peace (see **Practices 1** and **2**) to generating outer peace (**Practices 4** through **15**). SQ is the DNA or the golden binding thread of graceful leadership.

Brainwaves

Referencing the work of Austrian neurologist Wolf Singer in the 1990s, Professor Danah Zohar offers us a fascinating neuro-scientific explanation as to what SQ might look like. Prior to Singer's research, neurologists and cognitive scientists identified only two types of neural organisation in the brain. Danah continues: 'One of these forms, serial neural connections, is the basis of our IQ... In the second form, neural network organisation, bundles of up to a hundred thousand neurons are connected in a haphazard fashion to other massive bundles. These neural networks are the basis of EQ, our emotion-driven, pattern-recognising, habit-building intelligence' (Zohar and Marshall 2012).

But Professor Singer discovered there were also unifying synchronous 40 Hz (cycles per second) neural oscillations that travel across the whole brain. Are these brainwaves the first indication of a third type of unitive thinking – a third mode of intelligence (SQ)? Professor Danah believes so and continues, 'Just as linear or serial neural tracts enable rational, logical data processing (IQ) to take place and parallel neural networks allow preconscious and unconscious associative data processing (EQ), the 40 Hz across-the-brain oscillations provide a means by which our experience can be bound together and placed in a frame of wider meaning (SQ).'

Spiritual intelligence can be developed

While these exciting neurological investigations continue, some good news again. In whatever form it manifests, like all intelligences, SQ can be developed and tapped into. Yes, most of us have the capacity to keep lifting our SQ, and this capacity increases with our age and levels of experience, but developing SQ is not predetermined or automatic. We need to *work at developing it and practise using* SQ (some also engage a mentor or coach to help) – but develop it we can.

In her pioneering book, SQ21 (2012), Cindy Wigglesworth offers 21 skills designed to help us to become more fully who we are, to keep transforming, and to live with more wisdom and compassion – to become fully human. There are at least two reasons I really like Cindy's writing. First, she does not claim this SQ skill set will lead us along a predetermined path, but rather we can use these skills on whichever unique path we have chosen or choose to take to make our self-transformation more effective and thoughtful. Second, unlike many who have written about spiritual intelligence, Cindy has created an extensively validated tool (the SQ21 assessment) that can be used to inform and monitor our own efforts to raise our levels of spiritual intelligence.

The SQ21 assessment is an online instrument that asks approximately 170 questions to measure the 21 skills, with a report produced for anyone undertaking the assessment. This contains a skill development score from 0 (not yet begun development) to 5 (highest level measured) based on the answers given across the 21 skills together with suggested steps to take to improve or sustain skills. Go to: deepchange. com/assessments

SQ is not about becoming more religious or gaining spirituality

One thing to clarify before we delve more deeply into how to lift our spiritual intelligence: developing SQ is not about religion or spirituality (though faith in the divine may be an important foundation for many). Most anthropologists I've met down the years are agnostic (non-religious). So, as one of these anthropologists, allow me to reassure you, if you had concerns before beginning this section, lifting your spiritual intelligence is *not about becoming more religious or gaining spirituality.*

Religion has been defined multiple times across the centuries but a simple description might be that a religion constitutes a particular system of faith in or worship of a divine power or powers that decree a set of beliefs, commandments, behaviours and identities to which followers adhere. There are many definitions of spirituality but this one by episcopal priest and Jungian analyst Dr Pittman McGehee (2016) struck a chord in me: 'Spirituality is the deep human longing to experience the transcendent in our ordinary life – it's the expectation to experience the extraordinary in the ordinary, the miraculous in the mundane, and the sacred camouflaged in the profane.' Spirituality is to *know* who you are in relation to sensing that there is something greater than just existence.

Spiritual intelligence, on the other hand, is to *manifest* who you are, to have a passionate vocation and to live your life at peace, with calmness, through this heightened self-awareness and purpose. SQ is about tapping into your soul – your spirit, moral essence, inner vitality – or connecting to your honourable, most gracious, purest self. SQ is the soul's intelligence. SQ makes religious expression possible but is not dependent upon religion.

So, yes, SQ is faith friendly but it is faith neutral.

Skills and steps to lift spiritual intelligence

Here's more good news. SQ can be broken down into specific, measurable 'skills' that can each be practised and then, once reunified, can help us to lead with greater wisdom and compassion. For example, Cindy Wigglesworth's 21 measurable skills for SQ growth are organised into interlinked quadrants with the ultimate being 'social mastery and spiritual presence' – the outcome of developing skills in the other three quadrants (**Tool B**).

I personally find even *trying* to master these skills extremely beneficial. While the framework may seem complex, the self-transformation required can be expressed simply – your actions become less ego driven and more guided by your wiser soul. *It is the subtle yet crucial difference between impulsively reacting and thoughtfully responding.* As we will see in **Practice 13**, this transition is akin to moving from a manager who quickly succumbs to the urge to give advice towards a leader who frequently pauses and asks questions to nurture the innate talent in others.

SQ is raised gradually by practising, observing and then learning, followed by practice, in a constant cycle of action and reflection. Developing SQ is not about dwelling in a secluded place to achieve full 'enlightenment' to become perfectly developed on the inside before we re-enter the world in a higher state of consciousness and grace (though, of course, some among us embrace and succeed through that isolated metamorphosis). In my experience, how we learn to show up with increasing levels of SQ is accomplished through daily, honest interaction with others, following which we carefully reflect and learn. For most of us, spiritual intelligence is gained not via a miraculous self-awakening but from an incremental dedication that sees us first try out SQ skills and then learn from our answers to the types of reflective questions posed in **Tool B**.

That's why I talk about *lifting* one's spiritual intelligence. Indeed, Cindy refers to this transformational process as a form of 'spiritual weightlifting'. It takes regular and painstaking effort to try to move above and beyond our ego towards our higher, better self. This process of lifting links directly back to **Practice 2** where we can, if committed, train our brain to raise our impulses and thoughts to the neocortex. This shift allows us to tap into our SQ, thereby accessing more measured and caring responses while at the same time contagiously transmitting calmness and perhaps some reassurance to others (whose egos might have been triggered and taken over their behaviour).

In her highly recommended book, Cindy provides nine SQ 'weightlifting' steps to follow, shortened into a memorable and meaningful acronym – SOUL – which is super handy for tapping into your SQ, especially when faced with stressful moments, difficult conversations or broader turmoil such as a crisis:

S = Stop and disrupt the reactive ego's desire to hijack the situation. Mindfully breathe. Slow down. Ask your higher self (or faith) for some advice.

O = Observe what is going on inside you (name the emotion and take responsibility for handling it) as well as in front of you (noting the emotional state of others).

U = Understand more is likely happening than meets the eye. Say to yourself, 'I don't fully know what's going on here.' Ask questions. Try to see through others' eyes.

L = Lean into a loving (compassionate/wise) response: 'Thanks for the update. How can we solve this together?' or even if it's just 'Hmm. I hear you. Allow me a little time to think about this.'

Leaders with high SQ deal with complexity or adversity using patience, agility, holistic wisdom and a deep concern for the welfare of others. By using their SQ skills, they can go from ego-driven, immature behaviours to more mature, higher soul-driven behaviours. Spiritual intelligence is also about embracing the world view of others, which requires deep empathy, the subject of our next practice.

Practice 4

Step into others' shoes

Early in my career, I started to notice how, as soon as I thought of people I'd met before and was about to meet again, or when I'd meet people for the first time, I would attach subjective thoughts to them. I wasn't meeting people from a 'pure' perspective in which I held no preconceptions. Instead, I would prejudge people, for better or for worse.

Judging others tells us more about ourselves than about them. Back then, my interactions with others would always be 'contaminated' by my own mental projections. It has taken me *a lot of difficult self-awareness work since* (see **Practices 1** to **3**) to consistently meet people with my biases suspended.

Empathy

At the heart of this graceful leadership practice is *empathy* – one of life's most essential skills (McLaren 2013). Empathy is about making an emotional connection that leads to *attunement* – the state of resonating with and validating another person's emotions (Forlè 2024). Think of a room in which there are two violins that are tuned to the same frequency; when the strings of one are plucked, the strings of the other also vibrate. I love to sing, so when I consider relationships or partnerships, I think about these questions: 'How can we reach a state of harmony? How can we move onto the same song sheet?'

Attunement in this sense is *emotional resonance*. It's not 'groupthink' or when people reach a collective decision without using critical thinking skills – not taking the alternatives or implications into account. Attunement permits calm disagreement in the quest for mutually agreeable solutions. The opposite of attunement is an unsettled or disordered connection (Fosha et al 2009). Or, in singing terms, a state of discord or disharmony.

Empathy requires neurological effort to actively engage the neocortex. The late Chris Argyris, professor of business theory at both the Yale School of Management and Harvard Business School, explained this brainwork as learning how to journey across two cognitive models – from Model 1 to Model 2 (Argyris 1982). The implicit goals of Model 1 thinking are to appear logical, gain the upper hand and control the situation. When we're in a Model 1 frame of reference we tend to think negatively about other people and their intentions. Even worse, we don't consider what else we could be overlooking or discovering. On the other shore, Model 2 is *full of curiosity* and aware of the gaps in our own knowledge – but requires a lot of effort to engage and sustain. We'll look at some ways to reach Model 2 thinking in a moment.

Empathic attunement is a foundational state for healthy relationships. Project Oxygen was an extensive study conducted within Google which revealed that besides skills in coaching, empowering and communicating, when leaders have the capacity for attunement their team members perceive them as better performers (Garvin 2013). Likewise, attuned co-workers have more seamless, higher quality collaborations (Worline & Dutton 2017).

Our innately human capacity to connect *on a cognitive level* has been called mentalising, theory of mind or cognitive perspective taking. Professor Tania Singer, psychologist, social neuroscientist and scientific director of the Max Planck Society's Social Neuroscience Lab, together with cognitive scientist and clinical psychologist Professor Olga Klimecki at

Dresden's Technical University, observes that this capacity 'makes it possible, for instance, *to understand that people may have views that differ from our own*' (Singer & Klimecki 2014).

The emphasis in this quote is mine and underscores a simple yet profound truth that is immensely uplifting because there's another important dimension to this graceful leadership practice, one that I learned more about when I moved to the Islamic Republic of Iran to take up my first UNICEF represent-ative role at the end of 2015. That other dimension is *diplomatic negotiation.*

On the high sea of diplomacy

I spent more than three and a half years living and learning in Iran, one of the world's oldest continuous major civilisations. I came to admire many dimensions of Iranian culture – the architecture, art, literature, music, poetry, cuisine, resilience and, above all, her people's gracious hospitality. To truly get to know down-to-earth Iranian individuals and families – who are so genuinely warm-hearted despite the difficulties they experience, whether from internal or external pressures – dispelled the less than complimentary preconceptions that non-Iranian media had tried to instil in me before I arrived there. My time in Iran was truly one of the most eye-opening while also most introspective periods of my life.

Advocacy on behalf of children in Iran exposed me to the diplomacy of the country's top ministerial officials as well as its more progressive religious authorities. One such leader was Dr Mohammad Javad Zarif, former Iranian ambassador and permanent representative to the United Nations in New York (2002–2007) as well as former foreign minister (2013–2021). A career diplomat and scholar in international policy, foreign relations and law, Dr Zarif has built a global reputation for his gracious, affable if occasionally gritty conduct – for instance, his intelligent eloquence (**Practice 3**), his personability (**Practices 4 and 5**), his pragmatism and his sense of humour (**Practice 11**), among other qualities.

During his time in government, Dr Zarif handled some of Iran's most complex challenges, which are too numerous to mention here, but as examples, he was a member of the multiple delegations that negotiated a ceasefire ending eight years of war with Iraq in 1988 and secured the release of American hostages in Lebanon in 1991. Notably, he was crucial in negotiations for a new Afghanistan government following the 11 September 2001 terrorist attacks on the United States, and, perhaps most visibly, the 2015 Joint Comprehensive Plan of Action, better known as 'the Iranian nuclear deal', an accord reached in July 2015 between Iran and several world powers, including the United States (in the deal, Iran agreed to disassemble much of its nuclear programme and expose its facilities to more extensive international inspections in return for billions of US dollars' worth of sanctions relief). The foreign minister's connection with his American counterpart at that time, Secretary of State John Kerry, represented a seismic shift in bilateral relations – the first such official high-level American–Iranian contact since the US Embassy in Tehran was overtaken by Iranian students on 4 November 1979.

Without my meaning to cause any offence, and like *every* nation, Iran presented and continues to present challenges for anyone concerned – Iranian and non-Iranian alike – with children's, particularly girls' wellbeing. Negotiating in favour of children on complex issues with such finessed diplomats from within Iran's authorities was a steep learning curve for me. In the days ahead of moving from Iraq to Iran, I reminded myself, 'Will, if you can't sharpen your diplomatic skills while in Iran, you never will.' How to engage in *diplomatic negotiation* for children thus became another self-transformational voyage.

Once an anthropologist

I had trained as an anthropologist so understood the basics and merits of building my cultural intelligence. But I'd also learned the value of using intent observation skills to notice small details such as facial, eye, jaw, head, hand and body movements as well as the frequency, duration and quality of eye contact between a speaker and myself. We all know that body language can either complement (to emphasise the speaker's point) or be misaligned with verbal communication, which in the case of the latter, sends telltale cues of inauthenticity or even untruths.

Anthropology also taught me the need to listen to not only *what* was being said but *how* it was being said – quite tricky through a translator, hence the value of carefully observing the original speaker – and above all, to pay attention to what was *not being said* or 'reading between the lines' as well as to what I expected to be hearing but was not.

The tattered book

Over the years, I've been lucky enough to read up on 'diplomacy' for which there is an ever-enlarging collection of excellent texts (eg Cooper et al 2015; Berridge 2022). But the book that stands out and the one that I return to time and again is academic, anthropologist and negotiation expert Dr William Ury's *Getting Past No* (1991), which now sits 'nicely' tattered in my bookcase. This was a sequel to his equally insightful *Getting to Yes* (1981), co-authored with Roger Fisher (Fisher & Ury 1981). If in a rush I was forced to choose two books on leadership out of the immense selection that now exists, my fingers would hover over William's (jump to **Practice 15** to see which two I would finally choose). But for now, I want to share what I gained from Dr Ury's brilliant exposition on negotiation in *Getting Past No* and provide an example of how I deployed his time-tested tips. What I describe below in relation to empathetic diplomacy applies equally well should one want to collaborate better with team members when tasks or situations or conversations get tough.

Breakthrough negotiation

For Dr Ury, negotiation is 'the process of back-and-forth communication aimed at reaching agreement with others when some of your interests are shared and some are opposed.' He warns that, on the one hand, if we are worried about harming the relationship, we might be 'soft' and give up our own position. On the other hand, if we are 'hard' in defence of our own position, we might move further and further away from the other's position – a process known as 'attitude polarisation' – and can end up damaging, perhaps even losing the relationship altogether. I've come to understand that this is indeed the dilemma faced by *all* diplomats and negotiators in *all* settings (from families to international relations). But Dr Ury points out that there is an alternative: joint problem solving that is *soft* on people, *hard* on the problem. He enthuses, 'Instead of attacking each other, you jointly attack the problem.'

Point fingers or offer an open hand?

You see, on many occasions I've witnessed so-called 'diplomacy' take its more classical Argyris Model 1 form of *finger pointing*, often across a bureaucrat's table. Rigid, hard-nosed, immovable and opposing positions. No willingness on either side to understand the other's viewpoint (to engage in cognitive perspective taking, Argyris Model 2 or Kahneman System 2 thinking), nor to journey even some of the way toward the other shore. In short, no attempt at *joint* problem solving.

In Iran, perhaps naïvely, I took a different tack to learn whether offering an open hand might make a difference. It was an open hand not to capitulate but to *share perspectives* and to ask in relation to upholding children's rights, 'What could we all do differently?' I adopted the perspective that government counterparts were not adversaries but respected allies trying to resolve tricky issues together (and helping me to learn and grow).

Fierce compassion

Unless we can embrace a sense of common humanity, it's all too easy to demonise others. And what makes us all human is precisely *our differences*. Let me be clear. Deep within, I never lost and never will lose this grounded sense of what Dr Chris Germer later came to powerfully describe as *fierce compassion* (Germer 2020).

Not that I am one, but fierce compassion is like being a martial artist who has *equanimity* (balanced awareness) on the inside and is a *warrior* on the outside. In diplomacy, fierce compassion is not about combat but the courage to have tough conversations *about our differences*. 'Should we get angry at *injustice* or feel hostile toward a *person?*' asks Chris. Like Dr Ury's breakthrough negotiation, for Chris fierce compassion always *spares the person and focuses on the problem.*

Preparation is key

Diplomatic negotiation begins with *thorough preparation*. Like readying for a long sea voyage, you must ensure that you have everything you need in the boat before you leave shore. You cannot afford not to prepare because often the stakes are just too high. As a leader you are often speaking – and have been bestowed with the honour to do so – *on behalf of the voiceless.* The more difficult the negotiation, the more intensive the preparation must be. Dr Ury's book has offered me a great template by which to prepare each time I needed to engage in diplomacy.

First figure out your interests. Ask yourself, 'Why do I want this? What problem am I trying to solve?' And then rank your answers so that you know what your real priorities are. Next, think through what the interests on the other side of the negotiating table might be. What do they seem to care most about? One way that's worked for me has been to try to understand the other person's or counterpart's reality *and* their view of me – a move from 'me' to 'we'. Before meetings, for example, I ask myself preparatory questions such as:

+ How do they see things?
+ What are their hopes and fears?
+ What interests them?

✦ What disappoints them?
✦ What might they be experiencing daily?
✦ How do they like to be communicated with?
✦ How do they absorb information and make decisions?
✦ How do they like to be acknowledged?
✦ What do they want to happen here and why?
✦ What is in it for them? Their colleagues?
✦ Who else has an influence on them and how does this influence help or hinder?
✦ What is another way a person could view this situation?
✦ What are their experiences with me?
✦ How do I want them to experience me?

Just like thinking through and then ranking our own interests, it is equally important to imagine how the other side might prioritise their interests. 'What would be their top priority, and why? Their second?' And so on.

Tony Schwartz, CEO of the Energy Project, together with its former COO Dr Catherine McCarthy, likened this form of perspective taking to viewing the situation through three different camera lenses. Through the *reverse lens* we ask, 'What would the other person say and in what ways might that be true?' Through the *wide lens*, 'Regardless of the outcome of this issue, how can I grow and learn from it?' And through the *long lens*, 'How will I most likely view this situation in six months or a year from now or five years or even 30 years from now? What advice would a more mature, future version of myself give the current me?' (Schwartz & McCarthy 2007).

This last question links to the SQ self-mastery question, 'During challenges, how willing am I to trust that, in the long run, life is purposeful?' (see **Tool B**). Quietly asking such questions to prepare myself provides me with at least three perspectives – opposite, wide and deep – as well as diminishes my temptation to prejudge others.

In their extensively researched book, *Difficult Conversations* (2010), Doug Stone and Harvard Law School colleagues Sheila

Heen and Bruce Patton offer one further tip before embarking on a negotiation journey. Be prepared to let go of trying to control the other party's reaction and accept in advance that it's OK for them to react in their own way, even negatively.

I've come to appreciate that these types of questions asked within your mind *during* actual meetings also help to maintain strong empathy in the moment. I'm still learning how to combat my unconscious bias by deploying empathy and curiosity, making such questions a mantra driving my intents, moment by moment, meeting by meeting. Regular use of these questions can hone both one's cognitive and active understandings of counterparts and co-workers alike, two of the three core pillars of compassionate leadership according to Professor Thupten Jinpa, a well-respected Buddhist philosophy scholar and the Dalai Lama's long-time English translator (Jinpa 2015).

Different lamps, same light

The lamps are different, but the Light is the same. – Rumi

At the beginning of 2016, the UNICEF team in the Islamic Republic of Iran began discussions with the government to co-create a new programme of cooperation for 2017–2021 – written up in a short paper known as a country programme document or CPD. UNICEF's CPDs are based on extensive analyses, consultations and reviews. Once agreed with the respective national authority, each CPD is presented for final approval at UNICEF's executive board, an intergovernmental body consisting of 36 UN member state representatives (UNICEF 2023). While it's only 6,000 words, a CPD signifies a crucial multi-year agreement between the government and UNICEF for the children of that country. *Every single word in a CPD carries weight and thus must be carefully negotiated.*

My Iranian government counterpart at that time was the graceful Rashid Bayat Mokhtari, then director of the Office of International Specialised Agencies at the Ministry of Foreign Affairs (MFA). Rashid is another of Iran's impressive diplomats, an eloquent scholar and author as well as a tough yet empathetic negotiator. He was appointed as the Iranian ambassador to the Republic of Cuba just before my mid-2019 departure from Iran. Rashid and I debated numerous issues, including some of the toughest that I've had to deal with such as adolescents held in adult detention centres – sadly, a problem in numerous countries. But I don't recall any occasion when, despite approaching the issue from different perspectives (Rumi's two lamps), we did not find a solution (Rumi's one Light).

An illustration using a relatively open example was when we created the 2017–2021 CPD. In March 2016, we received the Iranian MFA's feedback on the zero draft we had sent them a few weeks earlier. The MFA team requested multiple edits and rephrasing of the text. All these were negotiable. But I was perplexed when I saw that every reference to children's 'rights' and to the Convention on the Rights of the Child or CRC – the most widely ratified human rights treaty in history (including by Iran) and which also guides UNICEF's work – had been cut (UNOHCHR 2024). It was the first CPD I'd been involved in drafting that did not refer to the CRC. For UNICEF was this a non-negotiable? How could we find a win–win workaround for the children of Iran?

Overcoming negotiation barriers

In *Getting Past No*, Dr Ury identifies several barriers to negotiation as well as ways of breaking through each, which I've condensed into four steps and labelled with a maritime-inspired acronym: SAIL. Let's take a quick look...

1. Seek perspective on your reaction

If you react defensively to the other party's 'No!' (or to criticism) you'll likely trigger their emotions and needlessly heighten the tension. At the other extreme, to avoid damaging the relationship you might give in but thereby expose yourself to future exploitation – you become a 'pushover'. One middle-road, breakthrough move is to first 'step to the balcony' or to use my sailing analogy, climb to the bridge or crow's nest of your ship. Imagine yourself looking down from there onto the negotiation. In other words, leaning into the magic of the pause (**Practice 2**) and tapping into your spiritual intelligence (**Practice 3**) to gain reverse, wider, deeper and longer-term perspectives.

Ask yourself, 'Am I in Model 1 (controlling) or Model 2 (curious) thinking right now?' Recall your life purpose, should you have one. Focus on the problem, not the person. Instead of an immediate reaction, it can be as simple as asking for some time to think further about what you've heard or read. 'Your response makes me curious. I'd like some time to reflect on it. Shall we take a break?' you might communicate. Despite the best of preparations, perspective is easy to lose in the heat of a negotiation. Such is Rashid's grace, I never had to do this when in face-to-face discussion with him. But in several other countries and situations, I've needed to occasionally pause before returning to the discussion.

2. Appreciate the opposing side's emotion and position

Behind their upfront 'No!' may lie misunderstanding, fear, distrust or even other pressures that you may not be aware of nor fully understand. A breakthrough negotiation manoeuvre here is to 'step to their side' by mentally repeating some of the preparatory questions I referred to earlier but during the negotiation itself. 'How might they be viewing this right now? What does this situation signify for them? What do they see that we are unable to see or are unaware of? What previous experiences are shaping their view? Who, perhaps not even present, might be influencing their position? What do they hope to achieve? What would their ideal outcome be from this conversation? What impact does it have on who they are? What's their stake in this?'

This is about suspending your judgement, seeing through their eyes, showing respect and giving them trust *even if you don't agree* with their current stance. It's not necessary to give up your own story in order to comprehend someone else's. Ask yourself, 'What if both of us are partially right?' It's about reframing your understanding of their position: 'Tell me more. Help me understand *why* you want that?' (eg to remove all reference to the CRC). After listening to their explanation, you might say, 'Allow me to explain my viewpoint...' And add, 'What else could I share that might help you reconsider your view?' (and ask yourself what you would have to learn and unlearn to change your view). Followed by, 'Now that we understand each other a bit better, what's a good way to work through this problem? Maybe we can try to come up with some creative solutions here to satisfy both of our interests. What do you think? Are you up for the challenge?'

3. Ignite co-creativity

Start this third step from where the other person or party is. You're inviting them to help figure things out initially from their vantage point. 'From your perspective, what would success look like if our discussion results in a win–win? And what might be our options for getting there?' A hazard to avoid is announcing that you already have a solution to the impasse. It's plausible that the other party doesn't find a mutually beneficial arrangement appealing or advantageous, especially if it's 100 per cent your proposal. They might reject it entirely because of hidden, unmet interests that you didn't discover in the previous step (eg 'My agency demands that I push this through as it is'), or for fear of losing face (eg 'High-level authorities expect me to land this the way they want it').

If you're too pushy, they may remove themselves from the negotiating table entirely or you might need to turn to third-party arbitration (of course, only if that's relevant and feasible). So, one breakthrough move is simply to invite *their* wisdom and build on *their* thinking, not immediately tell them how you would reach a win–win – you need to tame your 'advice monster' as will be explained further in **Practice 13**.

For Dr Ury, the best breakthrough negotiators co-create

multiple possibilities for mutual gain. Don't stick to and then try to work through one solution but co-generate and move on as many possibilities as the situation allows. Sometimes you might need to jump back to the two previous steps to further advance the co-creative process. In our case, over a few weeks, Rashid and I debated several words to include in the CPD (recalling every word matters) that could represent situations when children's rights were not being met. 'Child poverty', 'vulnerabilities' and 'disadvantaged children' became possibilities.

There are times when the other side doesn't come up with options or refuses to do so. Only then should you offer some suggestions: 'I'm curious if doing it this way might work for both sides?', allowing others the room to disagree with you. 'How about we consider this... or this... or this...? Which alternative would work for you?' If the situation permits, you might even propose pilot-testing some of the proposals either in parallel or in sequence before reaching a final agreement: 'How about we try this for a while before we decide?' – not possible in finalising a CPD.

4. Land the agreement

If all has gone well through the first three steps, you reach the last negotiation stage: finalising the agreement. Hopefully with multiple options on the table, you and the other party can hone down which is the optimum for both of you. Seeking mutual satisfaction not 'victory' for one or other side. And then validate: 'Let's recap what we've agreed to here.'

In this final step, any lingering power games – Model 1 thinking through which one party desires ultimate control – can torpedo the deal or 'capsize the boat' so to speak. Here, Dr Ury's expert advice is to look together at the consequences of failing to reach agreement. I never needed to do this with Rashid because we both empathised with each other's viewpoint. But let's suppose we had not. One option then might have been to explore a *reality test* question: 'What would be the consequences of not having UNICEF as a development partner in Iran?' Reality testing is not about threatening but about co-creating and examining future scenarios should the negotiation fail. If reality testing doesn't resolve the power play, further processes for both sides might involve mediation, dispute resolution, third-party observers, building coalitions of supporters for the opposing positions, offering escape routes for either side and so on.

Both of us were fiercely compassionate but through this four-step process I also came to understand the internal pressures Rashid was under, and he mine. The topic of 'international human rights' is not part of the Islamic model of socioeconomic development. We agreed that 'Islamic rights' and 'citizen rights' (as featured in Article 24 of Iran's Sixth National Development Plan 2016–2021) should be referenced in the CPD. But Rashid argued that the Iranian government used other channels such as the Universal Periodic Review and CRC State Party Reporting to deal with international human rights (including the CRC) and thus, he explained, these channels sat outside of the CPD (UN Human Rights Council 2024). I argued that the executive board would be expecting recognition of the CRC. So, if the word 'rights' could not be used or the CRC referenced, what was our compromise to ensure the board's approval and preserve UNICEF's partnership with Iran?

It sounds simple now but together we settled on the word 'disadvantaged', which appears 16 times in the final CPD 2017–2021. I gave up insisting that the CRC had to be mentioned in the CPD as the Iranian government was already committed to reporting through other international channels. UNICEF's executive board approved our CPD in September 2016 (UNICEF 2016).

This is not a magic four-step recipe since every negotiation is unique, but over the years it's helped me to navigate troubled seas. And while the steps are sequential, you may need to return to the crow's nest to seek perspective on several occasions during a negotiation. But with grace, you and the other party can find and share the common light between you.

Tack with tact

Dr Ury uses another sailing analogy to explain that negotiation seldom goes in an orderly straight line. Sailors use 'tacking' to manoeuvre around reefs and shoals, and to zigzag through tides, winds, storms and squalls. Likewise, diplomatic negotiation is a deep flow and mix of some gains, some compromises and some losses during which opposing sides move towards consensus.

To conclude this practice, in addition to the suggestions, questions and steps outlined above, here are three other items that I've found useful during empathetic conversations (and negotiations) and would pack in my boat before leaving shore. All three relate to the art of using *tact* or how to deal with difficult issues in a way that considers other people's feelings and reactions.

Tact through using 'powerless communication'

It might seem a paradox to use the term 'powerless communication' in reference to negotiation. But here I'm reflecting on the many occasions I have approached colleagues and counterparts with statements such as 'I'd like to seek your guidance on...' or 'I'd welcome your advice on...' or 'I'm curious to learn what you think might be a way forward on this...' As Adam Grant, professor in organisational psychology at the University of Pennsylvania, explains, 'Advice seeking is a form of powerless communication that combines expressing vulnerability, asking questions and talking tentatively. When we ask others for advice, we're posing a question that conveys uncertainty and makes us vulnerable. Instead of confidently projecting that we have all the answers, we're admitting that others might have superior knowledge' (Grant 2013).

Advice seeking must be done with humility and sincerity. Deceitfully asking for help and then conceitedly trumping their recommendations with your own ideas is not tactful or graceful. But if there is authenticity, I've found that requesting advice can in and of itself be persuasive. Not only are you raising an important issue just by seeking guidance on it, but to offer their advice, those you're asking must start to consider the problem from your point of view. Asking for advice not only demonstrates our appreciation for their knowledge and wisdom but is also a humble way to invite them to sail towards our shore, even if just for that conversation.

Tact by listening with fascination

In her enduring classic, *Time to Think* (1999), Nancy Kline, founder and president of Time to Think and visiting lecturer at the UK's Henley Business School, sets out ten components – from appreciation to encouragement and from asking incisive questions to giving attention – that together cultivate what she terms 'A Thinking Environment'. This is a compelling combination of asking powerful questions and listening attentively in ways that *ignite the minds of others*. Curiosity must be your keen companion on the journey to another's shore. We shall explore more of what this feels and looks like in **Practice 6**. Suffice to say for now that, like coaching, this is the art of asking the right question at the right moment in the right way, and then listening with genuine fascination as others offer up their thoughts.

Tact when presenting 'evidence'

Many leaders and diplomats place enormous value upon 'their evidence' and I can understand this conviction. But what constitutes evidence is notoriously subjective and is often a matter of perspective (Rumi's lamps again). Whose version of 'truth' should we accept? Rather than descend into an underground warren of arguing about who is right or wrong – often an ugly debate that leads to a dead end creating only heat and no light (**Practice 6**) – I've found it more productive to explore the respective *reasoning behind* differing interpretations of the 'facts', 'data' or 'story'. This can move us from trying to prove that only one side can be 'right' to sharing and weaving together how we each make sense of the world.

While we all have our inner, fiercely compassionate warriors guiding us – our core values, uncrossable red lines and zero-tolerance principles – in our crisis-riddled, volatile, ever more complex world, we increasingly need as many diverse perspectives as we can muster to have any chance of solving the wicked issues that confront all of us. All parties need to have the courage and curiosity to leave their familiar shores to venture into the unknown. Tacking with tact permits sustainable problem solving and diplomatic negotiation to become judgement-free flows of co-creative energy. More on this in **Practice 15**.

Always keep the moon in mind

> Load the ship and set out. No one knows for certain whether the vessel will sink or reach the harbour. Cautious people say, 'I'll do nothing until I can be sure.' Merchants know better. If you do nothing, you lose. Don't be one of those merchants who won't risk the ocean. – Rumi

Alongside charts, landmarks, coastlines, tides, lead-line depth soundings and other means such as the movement of fish and birds, ancient maritime navigators also relied on the moon, stars, constellations and the sun to find their way. As Rumi points out, our ancestral sea merchants risked it all. And like them, are we not all travelling through life trading our goods, plying our wares, whether they're individual talents, corporate products, organisational mandates, national policies, international treaties and so on?

As with navigation, *empathy is an ancient perspective-taking skill* that has allowed our species to not only survive but also thrive. I'm no scholar on warfare but I've witnessed first hand the tragedies that armed conflicts cause. So, as we say in Australia, it's a no-brainer – wars are the most disgraceful outcome of miserably inept, failed negotiation. With due accord to meerkats, rabbits and other precious burrow-dwellers, absence of global concord on climate change is likewise forcing us rapidly down an adjacent warren of lose–lose negotiation.

There's so much accumulated collective wisdom among us, yet humiliatingly at some of our most critical moments that later become chapters in a shameful chronology, we don't even have the humility to follow the basics of listening to the best versions of ourselves, nor seek the wise counsel of others, nor dare venture to the opposite 'shore' to understand our fellow humans. Our individual egos and even nationalistic tendencies storm the citadel of grace. In the absence of reverse, wider, deeper and longer-term perspective taking, the 'other' becomes our so-called 'adversary' *through our own negotiation shortcomings.* There is no artistry in a non-deal.

All the while the moon, a gentle, less confronting light than the sun, softly beams down from her position far above us. She's played a crucial if unimposing part across civilisations past and present as well as those yet to come. You name it – time, tides, biological rhythms, nutrition cycles, mythology, religion, art, poetry, songs, theatre, gender debates, geophysics and space flight, to name just a few of her many influences – our gracious moon's 29.5-day cycle around Earth inspires and animates each of us, whether we acknowledge her or not. As an energy nexus, what must she be thinking through all this? I like to imagine that our moon is consistently entreating us to be a positive, creative part of each other's stories. *She's gracefully inviting us to combat the problem, not the person nor the people involved.*

Practice 5

Personise

We all have a need to belong, to make connections outside and inside our places of work. Relationships are intrinsic to humanity. Indeed, some might propose that our *greatest* strength is... *other* humans (Berscheid 2003). Our social connections are dynamic, altering in accordance with emotions, thoughts and actions, and can vary in quality depending on how healthy our interactions are at particular points in time (Stephens et al 2012).

Organisations depend on our ability to connect with others to accomplish work (Edmondson 2012). As with all practices in this book, investing in workplace relations brings multiple benefits:

✦ creating vitality, trust, care and resiliency
✦ building commitment, engagement, learning and job satisfaction
✦ fostering psychosocial support
✦ providing inspiration and supporting divergent thinking
✦ turning conflict into a space for personal growth
✦ establishing a climate of fairness
✦ promoting creativity and self-discovery
✦ enhancing self-image and organisational citizenship
✦ improving physiological responses to stress and anxiety
✦ lowering the risks of death and increasing lifespans

✦ strengthening immunity
✦ generating more energy
✦ enhancing adaptability
✦ transforming productivity and performance (Rosales 2016).

What is personisation?

Developing effective and energised workplace relations requires us to humanise or 'personise' relationships through understanding colleagues' backgrounds, dreams, job/career objectives and obstacles. In their meticulously researched book, *Humble Leadership* (2018), Edgar and Peter Schein define *personisation* as 'the process of mutually building a working relationship with a fellow employee, teammate, boss, subordinate or colleague based on trying to see that person as a whole, not just in the role that they may occupy at the moment.'

Personisation is a socioemotional and interpersonal competence. This is not about favouritism; it's about appreciating individualism. The interpersonally competent leader can individualise their relationships so that every connection they have with team members is uniquely motivational for each member (Yammarino & Dansereau 2002). Understanding others enables leaders to guide individuals, groups, teams and organisational cultures more effectively. Besides the many benefits listed above, personising also helps teams to become more cohesive, builds team spirit and increases talent retention (Pentland 2012).

Personising is important for leaders at all levels. Psychologist Susan Fiske and others have shown that those who occupy more powerful positions or higher-status roles tend to rely more on stereotypes about co-workers than on obtaining distinctive information (Fiske 2013). This suggests that graceful leaders, particularly those in more senior positions, must not only elevate their levels of attunement to others (see **Practice 4**), but also pay much more attention to the character nuances of people around them. Getting to know colleagues' patterns of energy and engagement also builds your ability to discern deviations from those patterns, offering insights into when things might be affecting them so that you can offer emotional healing (see **Practice 10**) (Bazerman 2014).

Check in with people, not on them

Personising means being passionately curious about others' aspirations, fears, interests, challenges and so on, as well as sharing something more personal about ourselves while always respecting the boundaries of privacy and decency. The premise is simple: if we know more about one another's beliefs, hopes, concerns, character, experiences and behaviours as these show up at work, we can collaborate more effectively.

When I first meet new colleagues, I like to ask them, 'What inspires you to get out of bed each morning? What gives you the energy to go about your day? What was one of your best days at work? What are you passionate about?' These questions get to the heart of *why* they do what they do. But I also ask, 'What frustrates you? What takes up most of your time? What holds you back?'

In a sequence of further conversations, I like to pose more entertaining questions such as, 'Outside work, what are your current interests or hobbies? What's your favourite food? Favourite form of art? What's the best gift you've ever received? If expenses were not a hurdle, what place on Earth would you like to visit and why? Which three adjectives would you choose to describe yourself? If you chose to be an animal that most closely resembles your character, which animal would you be and why? Which three things would you like to change about yourself? If I remove all the barriers that might be in your way, what would be your dream job? Where do you want to be three years from now? Where do you think you should be? How can I help you get there?'

Employees are more likely to be engaged if they believe that their leader or manager cares about them personally. Engaging in regular check-in conversations and, most importantly, paying close attention to what colleagues have to say builds trust. You'll be able to view each team member as a unique individual if you pay attention to the things that matter in both their personal and professional life.

As I move around the workplace or meet colleagues elsewhere, I'll ask questions such as, 'How are you feeling? What's happening for you today? What's on your mind today? What's a word that describes you right now?' As much as I can, I'll learn about their family members: 'How's your family doing? How's your daughter doing at her new college? I hope your dad's feeling better,' and so on. And sometimes I'll enquire about any pets they might have (given I have two cats and two dogs). Checking in also helps me know more about their preferred style of communication and how they like to show up at work (and detect when things might not be going so well).

The more information we have about each other's cultures, customs, interests, families and aspirations as a whole, the easier it will be for us to relate to and empathise with each other. Not only is this one of the most interesting aspects of any job, but in diverse work settings especially, culturally appropriate personising can help to build our cross-cultural intelligence (Earley & Mosakowski 2004).

The chances of getting along rise with our level of familiarity with one another. There's a neuroscientific reason for this. As neuromanagement expert Dr Carlos Davidovich (2023) explains, 'What really happens in our brains is that the more information I have about those around me, the less likely they are to activate my amygdala's negative responses, thereby decreasing the chances of triggering my survival reaction. Basically, as we get familiar with each other, we actually start to sidestep biased reactions at the neural level!'

Two-way conversations

Regular check-ins and personising conversations in general should be two way. Of course, striking a balance between selective sharing versus oversharing is part of the art of graceful leadership. But when they share information about themselves, leaders definitely add to levels of trust. So, with grace, talk about your life purpose, your priorities, your passions and the things that challenge you.

Colleagues are often intrigued when they discover that I love to cook (especially Indian savoury dishes), ride a motorbike, draw and paint dogs and landscapes, create model cities that include miniature electric trains that actually move along tracks, was an archer in Bhutan, once sang in a choir and a band, acted in a movie (OK, I only said three lines), learned to hand-produce Shiraz wine in Iran, used to be a 100-metre sprinter and thoroughly enjoy playing rugby, hockey and cricket.

Inviting colleagues and teams to get to know each other as people (their hopes, hobbies, life experiences, etc) through regular social events outside of work is also a great way of fostering creativity, collaboration and cooperation back at work. Finally, and perhaps crucially, personising builds and feeds psychological safety which, as the next practice reveals, is vital for optimum individual and team performance.

Practice 6

Strive for psychological safety

Known as Project Aristotle, Google's famous study across 180 of its teams, all of which, at face value, seemed to possess equal expertise, revealed five core factors that set super high-functioning, high-performing teams among the sample apart from the rest:

+ **Psychological safety:** team members feel safe to take risks, to be vulnerable in front of each other.
+ **Dependability:** team members get things done on time and meet Google's high bar of excellence.
+ **Structure and clarity:** team members have clear roles, plans and goals.
+ **Meaning:** work is personally important to team members.
+ **Impact:** team members think their work matters and produces change (Duhigg 2016).

Google's data indicated that psychological safety *above all* is critical if teams are to function and perform at their best levels. It is not who is on the team nor how brilliant they are but *how well* all team members interact, determine their tasks, collaborate, help each other and appreciate everyone's efforts.

In short, factors 2 to 5 above are redundant unless psychological safety is present and permanent.

So, what exactly is psychological safety?

The concept of psychological safety was introduced in the 1960s by Professors Edgar Schein and Warren Bennis (Schein & Bennis 1965). Their research examined psychological safety from an individual's perspective. The concept was later linked to studies by Professor Carol Dweck to suggest that those with a disposition for learning (a 'growth mindset') and possessing emotional stability (connecting to Professor Daniel Goleman's theory of 'emotional intelligence') are more likely to perceive their workplace as being 'psychologically safe'. Why is that? Such individuals tend to be calmer, more relaxed and self-secure when compared to those with more 'fixed mindsets' and less emotional intelligence, who tend to be anxious, hostile and vulnerable to stress (Dweck 1986).

Building on these earlier works as well as those of Professors William Edwards Deming and William Kahn, Amy Edmondson – Novartis professor of leadership and management at the Harvard Business School and Massachusetts Institute of Technology (MIT) – has extensively studied psychological safety at the team or group level. Her superb book *The Fearless Organisation* defined the concept as 'a shared belief that the team is safe for taking interpersonal risks'. Psychological safety is not about feeling good or being in a 'cosy' workplace, nor does it imply that there'll not be pressures and problems – it's about high performance among teams *despite* the challenges they regularly face (Edmondson 2018).

Psychological safety is present when you can be your genuine self, take risks, make errors, request and offer help, raise problems, ask questions, speak up and disagree with *anyone in the team, regardless of your or their position, and without fear of ridicule or retribution.*

Early in my UNICEF career, I attended a regional meeting on emergency preparedness. At one point, we listened to a presentation about a new online portal into which UNICEF country teams were expected to upload our disaster contingency plans (what we needed to prepare for and how we would respond to natural or human-made emergencies as relevant to our country context). In the question and answer session that followed, I asked, 'I'm curious. If this is the solution, what's the problem?' (It's still one of my favourite questions.)

Seated on the stage, the panel of experts who had presented the new e-platform looked at each other and, somewhat irritated, declined to answer my question. At the afternoon drinks break a colleague walked up beside me and quietly cautioned, 'If you ask that type of question, you won't last very long.' That was many years ago and UNICEF has genuinely intensified its efforts to boost psychological safety, particularly in recent years. But back then, I could perceive the lack of it in certain *patches* of the agency. By 'patches' I mean that it's possible to have psychologically unsafe teams coexisting alongside psychologically safe teams within an overall organisation, even within the same office. Google's Project Aristotle revealed exactly that.

Psychological safety is a workplace (and community) *climate* – a cooperative pattern and tone co-created and maintained *by teams or groups of people*. This collaborative atmosphere cannot be built and sustained by only some individuals on a team but needs every team member committing to interactions and behaviours that co-create mutual respect and trust, allowing everyone to be authentic and to take interpersonal risks. And of note, though senior leadership in organisations must act as role models in promoting psychological safety, research proves that it's the mindset and behaviours of our *nearest supervisor* that can make the most difference (Frazier et al 2017). Thus *every employee and every line manager* needs to contribute to creating and preserving psychological safety, not just top leadership. I like to think of psychological safety as a collective trust fund into which everyone invests so that everyone reaps the rewards – and the benefits are huge so it's well worth striving for.

Why is psychological safety so important?

Besides Google's finding that psychological safety is the *number one ingredient* needed for super high-functioning, high-performing teams, there are other compelling explanations as to why psychological safety is so important. First, when we're low on psychological safety and we're low in our 'motivation and accountability' (Project Aristotle's factors 2–5), then *apathy* usually sets in. Second, if we're super psychologically safe but not motivated and have little accountability, there's a chance we might ease off and enter (even remain) in our *comfort zones*. Third, if we have no psychological safety but many responsibilities, we'll likely be highly anxious, under constant stress and *drained of all energy* despite efforts to recharge (**Practice 1**).

Some may believe that creating psychological safety – sparking too much 'freedom of expression' – could lead to a less productive and less accountable workplace. More than two decades of research, however, shows that the more psychologically safe we feel, the more willing we are to work and be more accountable and thrive as an innovative organisation. There's a neuroscientific reason for this. When we feel psychologically *unsafe*, our lower, more primitive brain structures are triggered for survival – to protect us from any perceived threat, shutting down our self-control, creativity and prosocial behaviours (**Practice 2**). When we feel psychologically *safe*, our higher, more advanced brain structures are in charge, permitting more productive team discussions that can lead to innovation, early detection and prevention of problems (such as letting others know about a problem as soon as you discover it), and ultimately more efficient and consistent accomplishment of shared goals (Radecki et al 2021).

The upside is that although psychological safety can take a while to engender, once protected and sustained, it can *supercharge* an employee's ability to contribute, grow and learn, as well as to collaborate with others, and in doing so, boost a team's creativity and effectiveness. The presence of a leader's compassion and coaching play three key roles also. First, by helping to create and sustain psychological safety in the first place; second, by motivating team members to step forward with new ideas; and third, by helping people open-mindedly and open-heartedly embrace errors and failures. All of which also leads to enhanced learning, insight and innovation = performance results + wellbeing.

In sum, when we're high in psychological safety *and* accountability (*self*-accountability such as driving our own performance and *mutual* accountability such as driving each other's performance), we'll be learning, taking risks and innovating – on our way to becoming super high-functioning, high-performing teams and, ultimately, organisations.

Hungry lions

Inspired by Aesop's fable of four oxen who stand together, facing outward, tails touching, to defend each other from a hungry lion, in his classic *Leaders Eat Last* (2014) Simon Sinek underscores the need for teams and organisations to build their own *circle of safety*. Simon elaborates, 'By creating a circle of safety around the people in the organisation, leadership reduces the threats people feel inside the group, which frees them up to focus more time and energy to protect the organisation from the constant dangers outside and seize the big opportunities.'

In such complex, turbulent times as we are experiencing now (and will do so long into the future), psychological safety not only unleashes the highest levels of performance *from within* but it can also build our resilience to external threats as well as liberate our best energies to tackle problems that lie *outside* our organisation. For almost every team and organisation, it's not on the *inside* but in the *external* world that our struggle for positive change and impact should be taking place. That's where 'hungry lions' hide and prowl – be they, in humanitarian terms, poverty, inequality, stigma, discrimination, epidemics, famine, disaster, climate change, war and so forth. Sadly, we are often thwarted, even paralysed by our own *internal* struggles.

Besides the current global vacuum in graceful leadership, I contend that the potential of organisations (public or private) to positively change the world is often shackled by their absence of or limited psychological safety. The consequence... hungry lions continue to pounce and devour.

Psychological safety is vital but fragile

> Trust comes on foot but leaves on horseback.
> – Dr Johan Rudolph Thorbecke, 19th-century prime minister of the Netherlands.

The term 'social architecture' can be defined as the composite of at least the following: social network structures (such as affiliation webs, patterns of interactions and energy flows); workplace culture (founded on humanistic values, social norms and basic assumptions held by workers about 'acceptable' interactions); the definitions of work roles (internalised expectations and scripts); the ways that routine work is accomplished, and non-routine work is absorbed; and the meaning and modelling of behaviours that leaders must provide (Madden et al 2012).

Together with formal structures, processes and systems, social architectures help to shape an organisation's workplace culture. But psychological safety is a product of the *attitudinal and behavioural* sides of culture, built and sustained person by person, team by team, interaction by interaction, moment by moment, day by day.

Building psychological safety takes collective time and energy but once it starts to emerge, *sustaining* psychological safety requires even greater communal effort. Similar to happiness, there is no end state or final destination. Instead, we need to keep 'striving for' psychological safety as a worthwhile but non-stop pursuit. You see, like trust, which is a key foundation, psychological safety is undeniably vital but is also *highly fragile* – 'coming slowly on foot and leaving swiftly on horseback'. Its emergence can *make* an employee's ability to contribute, to grow, learn and collaborate – and a team's creativity and happiness. Its disappearance can *break* all this and more. Unsuitable remarks or inappropriate behaviours – for example, a harsh email, a hostile conversation or public humiliation – can easily damage ingenuity, personal growth, willingness to speak up and cooperation. Psychological safety is akin to a collective heartbeat. Once that pulse weakens or ceases, individual engagement and team performance both deteriorate alongside co-creativity, joy and wellbeing.

How can we strive for psychological safety?

There are several actions that we can take when striving for psychological safety. My top six are below.

1. Assess psychological safety levels

Assess and brainstorm (and regularly reassess and re-brainstorm) whether your workplace or team is psychologically safe (and how to make it so). Here are some typical signs and symptoms that your office or team might *not* be psychologically safe:

✦ Staff don't ask many questions during meetings.
✦ Staff don't feel comfortable owning up to mistakes or blame others when mistakes are made.
✦ The team avoids difficult conversations and hot-button topics.
✦ Senior and team leaders tend to dominate meeting discussions.
✦ Feedback is not frequently given or requested.
✦ Staff don't often venture outside of their job descriptions to support other teammates.
✦ Staff don't ask one another for help when they need it.
✦ There are hardly any disagreements or differing points of view.
✦ Staff don't know one another personally, just professionally.

A more precise assessment (that can also be used to re-measure the effect of efforts to build/maintain psychological safety) can be done in at least two ways – through a survey and through team discussions; one can be followed by the other. A simple survey can be conducted using a tool like SurveyMonkey. For example, the Fearless Organisation Scan (fearlessorgani-zation.com/engage/free-personal-scan) includes statements such as:

✦ If you make a mistake in this office, it is often held against you.
✦ People in this office sometimes reject others for being different.
✦ It is difficult to ask other people in this office for help.

Those taking the survey are asked to rate the statements on a scale of 1–5 (1 being strongly disagree, 2 being disagree, 3 being neutral, 4 being agree and 5 being strongly agree). You might first conduct the survey with a focus on the organisation or office as a whole, then follow up with additional surveys that are team or unit specific. If you do, just update the questions to reflect a team focus (eg I feel safe to take a risk on this team). The office-wide results will provide insight into cultural issues that may impact psychological safety. The team-specific results can be compared to the organisation's benchmark to see if certain teams are better or worse at creating/sustaining psychological safety. Then you could hold office-wide or team-specific discussions. It is wise to first create a safe space for such discussions. Team coach Geraldine Anathan calls this 'creating the container' – a container that allows people to speak freely, has no other distractions, is safe to have emotion of any kind and encourages people to trust the discussion process (Anathan 2021).

One way to begin the discussion would be to present the survey findings and ask the office or team to reflect upon what the results mean to them. 'Anything jump out? What else?' Later, you could split into smaller groups to explore what options there might be to improve poor results or preserve good results (group discussions might adapt or use questions provided in **Tool C**).

Once you understand which aspects of your office or team are contributing to low or high levels of psychological safety, you can co-create a plan of action to address/sustain them. It is best to adopt a holistic approach to creating and maintaining psychological safety – it's usually not about addressing one aspect, but rather *all of them*.

2. Pay attention to paying attention

We're talking about the importance of *being present*. Trust, a vital ingredient for psychological safety, is not built through gallant or highly noticeable actions but through a stream of small moments, such as simply listening with genuine attention and acts of authentic connection. As Simone Weil, the French philosopher and mystic, once said, 'Attention is the rarest and purest form of generosity.'

Giving others your undivided attention can be accomplished through *active, empathic listening*. This is listening intently, without judgement and without distraction. Active, empathic listening requires a listening *heart* – being mindfully present in front of others with a genuine interest in understanding them (Nichols & Straus 2021).

Being present also involves asking open-ended questions ('Who?... When?... How?... What?... Why?... Tell me more... What else?') as well as acknowledging and recapping or paraphrasing what colleagues say ('What I hear you say is... It sounds like... If I understand you correctly...') in every conversation and meeting. Cultivating mindful listening in such ways can significantly increase the quality of our interactions with others.

It was Stephen Covey, in his famous book *The 7 Habits of Highly Effective People* (1989), who wrote, 'When you listen with empathy to another person, you give that person psychological air' – later describing this type of listening as equivalent to offering 'emotional oxygen'. I can't think of a better way to describe this powerful leadership skill. In short, active, empathic listening (a vital element of holding a learning conversation) is a deep coaching skill that can help others settle matters for themselves (**Practice 8**).

But when we ask others an empathetic or coaching question, what is most important (and for most of us, very difficult) is *allowing for the silence that might follow*. Many of us find it hard to cope with even three to four seconds of quietness. But these moments of silence, as Michael Bungay Stanier (2016) observes, are 'often a measure of success' because it means our colleague is contemplating, seeking an answer, developing new neural pathways 'and in doing so literally increasing [their] potential and capacity.'

Another challenge is to listen without thinking 'How shall I respond?' or 'How about you try this?' or 'Here's what I think...' while the speaker is *still* talking! Too many of us start to make judgements or formulate our responses, when all our colleague might really need is for us to, well... just listen. But often we end up interrupting them.

In 2017, Focus Features, Perfect World Pictures and Working Title Films released *Darkest Hour*, a biographical film about Winston Churchill's leadership at the start of the Second World War. The actor Gary Oldman, who plays the British prime minister (winning an Oscar in the process), delivers a classic line during a heated war cabinet meeting, 'Would you stop interrupting *me* while I am interrupting *you*!' I now always remember this quote when my ego grows restless to speak in conversations when I should just be listening.

On par with the problem of thinking that we have all the answers is the ease with which we can become distracted: 'What time is my next meeting?' or 'What must I prepare for this evening's engagement?' This is our wandering mind speaking. If colleagues feel that you don't pay attention when they speak or that you don't value their thoughts and opinions, they'll shut down and won't speak up. Humans are tuned into recognising disingenuous behaviour, so inauthentic listening is quite easily picked up (Bowden & Thomson 2018).

I just wish someone had told me years ago that if you want to become a better leader, become a better listener… and breathe deeply, more often.

3. Treat meetings as 'sacred time'

Ohh… This is another basic I wished I'd learned at the start of my leadership journey!

Planned and facilitated in the right way, meetings provide leaders the opportunity to communicate their vision, be authentic and inspire and engage their teams. Well-run meetings also function as democratic, inclusive spaces in which employees exchange ideas and engage creatively, ensuring all voices are heard and can flourish. But over the years, either as a participant or, more embarrassingly, as the chair, I have experienced many meetings that are *ineffective* (they end with no clear actions to carry forward), *bloated* (in terms of both the time consumed and the number of people attending), and *non-inclusive* (just a few voices dominate the airtime). Research has shown that this is not just a widespread workplace frustration but also has enormous financial implications when you tally up the average salaries of meeting attendees. A conservative estimate is that more than US$250 billion is lost every year *in the USA alone* due to poorly organised and badly facilitated meetings (without adding indirect costs such as staff frustration and meeting-related stress) (Rogelberg 2019).

No matter the purpose, size, duration or modality, all meetings should be considered sacred time. But how well are most meetings organised and run? And are all meetings really needed? Elsewhere, I have considered the preparation for and flow of meetings involving just two participants, such as performance conversations (**Practice 8**). Then there are 'group meetings' – gatherings of between roughly three and 25 attendees – used for information-sharing, coordination, and/or decision making. This particular type of meeting can sometimes define, even dominate (perhaps sadly contaminate) our working hours. Of course, there are meetings that have many more participants, such as stakeholder consultations, community meetings, team retreats and 'town halls'. Meetings might be just five minutes (if we are lucky) or can last a day or so. Meetings might be face to face, virtual or 'hybrid' (in person and virtual).

There are several excellent resources on how to prepare for and facilitate stellar meetings (Smutny 2021; Shannon 2023). For example, in his practical, science-based book, *The Surprising Science of Meetings* (2019), Professor Steven Rogelberg provides numerous tips on meeting facilitation skills, meeting length, agenda setting, attendee numbers, seating arrangements, walking and standing meetings, meeting mindsets, fostering positive moods, brainstorming (including brainwriting or the silent creation of ideas) and meeting virtually. I won't dive into these topics. Here I want to focus on how well-run group meetings (as defined above) can enhance psychological safety, and therefore highlight just a few key suggestions that do exactly that.

Meeting facilitation capacity. As a first step towards psychologically safe meetings, leaders need to receive meaningful facilitation training. Such training should ensure leaders can, at the very least, design and lead meetings with purpose so that *the time and talent of those participating are honoured* and participants have a quality experience *every time*. Basic questions to pose before each meeting might be as follows:

- ✦ What is the meeting for?
- ✦ Who must attend?
- ✦ What kind of energy will I bring?
- ✦ How do I want to show up?
- ✦ During the meeting, what do we want to have accomplished by the end of it?
- ✦ What might we be missing here?
- ✦ Are all voices being heard?

✦ And at the end of the meeting, what do we take away from it?
✦ What crisp decisions and time-bound follow-up actions have we made?

To spread leadership skills for psychological safety, one idea is to regularly rotate the chair of group meetings, especially if you have frequent meetings with a group that has stable membership.

Meeting ground rules. Many teams and organisations co-create a 'charter' or an 'alliance' detailing expected, acceptable behaviours for meetings, workshops and sometimes general daily interactions. Such mutual agreements or social contracts are useful to pinpoint ground rules for how everyone would like to 'show up' in front of each other – what's behaviourally acceptable and unacceptable to all team members. In effective teams, everyone takes responsibility to help each other adhere to the rules and call out anyone who does not. Such charters should be co-created and remain living documents that can be adapted to any changing circumstances and to the evolving nature of the team.

In their timeless blueprint, *The Psychological Safety Playbook* (2023), Dr Karolin Helbig and Minette Norman offer three more useful suggestions that, if appropriate, can be combined (and woven into a team's charter):

✦ *Appoint an inclusion booster* with the role of listening and observing intensely to make sure all voices and dissenting ideas are being heard. The inclusion booster is not an active meeting participant but helps the meeting chair to ensure that no one dominates or disrupts the meeting and that everyone gets an opportunity to contribute. Like the meeting chair, the role of the inclusion booster can be rotated among group members.
✦ *Establish a rule of 'no interruptions'* where the group accept that the chair will step in if a group member is being

interrupted. This rule can also be used to urge meeting attendees to speak concisely so that others have more chances to speak.

✦ *Set a rule that nobody talks twice until everyone has spoken once,* which can help to share 'airtime' more equally as well as foster diversity of opinions. This rule can also be used in a series of intervention 'rounds' during a meeting where everyone is invited in turn to speak on relevant agenda items.

Meeting presence. And how attentive are we in meetings? During meetings, everyone should demonstrate engagement by being *truly present*. This includes culturally appropriate eye contact, shutting laptops and resisting the mobile phone (Washington et al 2014). Distractions come easily but even small acts of disengagement can be perceived as uncivil and negatively impact psychological safety (Roberts & David 2017).

Meeting expectations. American businessman and former US ambassador Matthew Barzun, in his perceptive analysis of political leadership *The Power of Giving Away Power* (2021), pinpoints three expectations that we should have for every meeting, 'Expect to need others. Enter with the intention to make differences and diversity fruitful in order to make something together. Expect to be needed. Bring your whole self to the meeting... Expect to be changed... You should expect to leave a meeting not quite the same person as when you entered.' I think these are concise and highly constructive expectations if we are to treat the time and energy we expend in every meeting as *sacred*.

4. Avoid blaming by assessing contributions

The problem we face in most workplaces with low or zero psychological safety is that when something goes wrong or there is a failure of some sort, people tend to blame others in order to shield and defend themselves. When work is highly pressurised and stress abundant, this tendency can turn into a viciously recycling habit:

stress ➜ mistake ➜ blame ➜ stress ➜ mistake ➜ blame ➜ stress…

Under these circumstances, most of us engage in disagreements about what happened or should have happened. We focus on who's 'right', who's 'at fault', and therefore who's to blame. 'It could have been either of us, but it was definitely not me. It can't possibly be both of us at fault here!' But like negotiation, engaging in conversations from such fixed positions does not lead to learning, it only leads to incrimination, self-defence and denial (**Practice 4**). In these situations, the large amount of energy often expended by the antagonists does not create any needed light, *only needless heat.*

Doug Stone and colleagues (2010) offer us a solution to disrupt this 'blame frame' of reference and move towards higher levels of psychological safety. Instead of spreading blame, focus on what else could have contributed to the problem and what contributory role did everyone involved play? All relationships and their products and most problems are co-creations. This is about embracing 'both/and' instead of 'either/or' thinking (see **Practice 3**).

When things go wrong, instead of asking condemnatory questions such as 'Who's responsible for this error? Why did you let this happen?', you can ask coaching questions to create a learning conversation (see **Tool D**). These questions use collaborative language whereby 'we' reveals the contribution system, identifies solution-oriented intersections between colleagues as opposed to stagnated insinuations of who's right and who's wrong, and turns the responsibility for improvement into a group or team effort rather than singling out an individual for blame and sole accountability 'to do better next time'. This isn't to suggest that there are never mistakes made because of one individual's action or lack of it. But it is how the team then *rallies around* rather than *reacts against* the individual that will determine if psychological safety is going to emerge or be maintained. *Problem solving should be a team sport.*

And as a graceful leader, keep reflecting upon these questions:

✦ How can we explore mistakes, errors or missed deadlines in ways that do not create blame?
✦ When we experience a failure, are there ways to engage each other so that we regard it as a learning opportunity?
✦ How can I ensure that I keep seeing things from the other's perspective, especially during a disagreement or when my expectations are not met?
✦ How can I facilitate team reflections about errors and mistakes that foster learning and compassion?

5. Demonstrate situational humility

Architect, systems theorist, author and futurist Buckminster Fuller once said, 'Dare to be naïve.' Asking others 'What am I missing here?' is one of the most effective things a leader can do. Through just these five words you're indicating your willingness to respect opposing viewpoints and even accept criticism. This is *courageous communication,* which is not just about what we say but also about allowing people to participate in the conversation, being open and honest about our emotions, and letting go of the urge to be correct, flawless and all knowing. It signals a *secure leader.*

Accept and openly acknowledge that you don't have all the solutions to tough problems; in short, be vulnerable about your challenges, but not for sympathy's sake – vulnerability is not about revealing weakness but about having the *courage to show up when you cannot control the outcome* (Brown 2018). Detecting those situations or moments when displaying vulnerability and humility (putting one's ego aside) will ennoble, engage and empower others. Invite colleagues to be your sounding board. Co-create and discover something new by continually encouraging others to bring their luminosity to conversations, to the edges of the unknown. And by inviting others to help you, not only might you uncover amazing ideas that you may never have thought of, but you also build their thinking and leadership wisdom.

Finding oneself monopolising conversations and meetings is a definite red flag. Create space for others to express themselves, remembering that some colleagues may require more time to do this than others. My leadership experience has been that there is no shame in being the quietest, least-spoken voice in the room. Often, I will only speak at the end of team meetings and even then, very briefly to summarise the key points or bright ideas that I have heard. Sometimes, in *ego-tantalising* inter-UN, regional or global meetings, I don't speak at all. Achingly and too slowly, I've come to understand the saying, sometimes attributed to Plato, the Greek philosopher, 'Wise men speak because they have something to say; fools because they have to say something.'

6. Celebrate failure

Nobody likes to fail. Even if they are informative, our mistakes can feel humiliating and undesired. Ironically, most of us *erroneously* assume that our achievements stem solely from our own efforts and prefer to believe that any blunder we make was not our fault. Accordingly, we defend our actions as 'right', refuse to accept criticism and look to blame anybody or anything other than ourselves. Fear of failure can even prevent us from making any decision at all.

Why is admitting to and learning from failure so hard? Why do we fear failure so much? Why can we not embrace failures and celebrate them instead? There might be several reasons. For example, many leaders have devoted significant time and effort to becoming experts in one or more intellectual fields and then using this expertise to address issues in the real world. It's tricky to accept and learn from failure if you think you already know all there is to know. Second, because many leaders are often successful at what they do, they seldom fail. And because they haven't failed very much, they haven't really learned how to learn from failure. Last, many leaders get to positions where they are increasingly cut off from candid criticism, so they rarely receive (nor ask for) feedback that would help them to reflect and learn (Argyris & Conant 1991).

How can we begin to change our approach to failure? Dan Bongino, author of *The Gift of Failure* (2023), urges us to reframe failure, not as the opposite of success but as 'a necessary part of the journey towards success'. Failures are simply ways that didn't succeed this time around. Don't be cast down or held back by them. Mary Pickford, an American film industry pioneer, once said, 'If you have made mistakes, even serious ones, there is always another chance for you. You may have a fresh start any moment you choose, for this thing we call "failure" is not the falling down but the staying down.' I love this positive mindset from inventor Thomas Edison who tried thousands of different materials before finding the perfect light bulb filament, 'I have gotten a lot of results! I know several thousand things that won't work.'

Failures are not woeful attempts; failures are wisdoms acquired. For me, embracing and 'celebrating' failure is not about rejoicing in the failure itself – it's about *honouring that we had the courage to risk failing in the first place.*

Are we prepared to accept failure if it happens? Are we ready to allow failure to serve as the foundation for whatever comes next? Are we willing to frame failure as a learning opportunity? What's the worst thing that can happen? If everything that could go wrong did go wrong, can we live with the consequences? These are some of the questions I have used with teams to start our journeys into reframing and celebrating failure. And I've also noticed that if failures go uncelebrated, or if we blame ourselves for them, it can justify not taking any more chances in the future. To avoid such withdrawal, *celebrate failure.*

In her enlightening research on various forms of failure, Professor Amy Edmondson provides an inspiring summary of companies that have embraced *failure celebration*: CEO of European fashion retailer C&A Giny Boer's 'Failure Fridays', Melanie Stefan's advocacy for more of us to produce a 'CV of Failures', Jon Harper's 'My Bad' podcasts, The Failure Institute's '****up Nights', Eli Lilly's 'Failure Parties', Grey Advertising's

'Heroic Failure Award', Tata Group's 'Dare to Try Award' and NASA's 'Lean Forward, Fail Smart', among others (Edmondson 2023).

Professor Edmondson also provides a useful categorisation of failures, allowing us to distinguish and learn from the differences between a careless error (basic), a catastrophe (complex) and a praiseworthy failure (intelligent).

✦ **Basic failures:** These are unintended mistakes, normally with a single cause, that occur in familiar surroundings, often due to overconfidence, distraction or negligence. Basic failures take place in everyday situations, and while few have deep impacts, some can be highly disruptive. Generally preventable, they tend to waste resources, time and energy, and can harm relationships. Learning from basic failures can increase our levels of acceptance that mistakes are just a part of life; help us overcome our fear of failure; reduce our negative tendency to ruminate; cause us to question our usual way of doing or thinking; and, of course, assist in preventing repetition of the same mistake. I will share one of my basic failures shortly.

✦ **Complex failures:** Like basic failures, complex failures occur in familiar circumstances or terrain, but despite the familiarity there is much more complexity. Usually heralded by subtle warnings, complex failures have multiple causes – lots of factors, both minor and major, coming together in unexpected ways with at least one external, ostensibly unpredictable factor. To illustrate complex failures, Amy Edmonson analyses examples such as the Torrey Canyon oil tanker catastrophe that occurred on 18 March 1967 (which remains Britain's biggest oil spill to date); the Columbia space shuttle's tragic disintegration upon re-entry that occurred on 1 February 2003 (the second shuttle mission to end in disaster after the loss of the Challenger in 1986); and the terrible Boeing 737 MAX air crashes on 20 October 2018 (Lion Air Flight 610) and

10 March 2019 (Ethiopian Airlines Flight 302, which included 22 souls affiliated with the United Nations). All these sobering analyses are well worth reading.

✦ **Intelligent failures:** These are intended and occur in unfamiliar settings to advance a valued goal. An intelligent failure occurs with intention (to learn more), knowledge of risk and acceptance that you might not succeed. If you already know how to avoid a mistake and yet still make it, then it's a basic failure. Of course, both basic and complex failures can occur in unknown territory. The key difference here is that intelligent failures are carefully planned and prepared for with high levels of situational awareness – for example, anticipating what might happen, expecting the unexpected, predicting the risks and how to manage them, and staying aware of what's at stake (see **Practice 15**).

Some other tips to encourage intelligent failures include adopting a mindset that expects and accepts mistakes and errors; taking time to map out the implications if your idea does not work; working out how to limit your exposure; rehearsing; amplifying early warnings; failing small, failing incrementally and failing fast – do not fail slowly. Amy's book is replete with numerous examples of what can be learned from intelligent failures across multiple sectors and industries.

Off the record

When the Covid-19 pandemic erupted at the beginning of 2020, I had been working with UNICEF in the Royal Kingdom of Bhutan for several months. The country's response to the pandemic became a shining example of excellent planning, coordination, mass mobilisation and graceful leadership (more about that in **Practice 7**).

Among many negative impacts, Covid-19 harmed the psychological and emotional wellbeing of children and adults around the world, Bhutan included (Parks 2021; Tsheten et al 2023). Starting in June 2021, UNICEF and sister UN agencies supported the government in a series of participatory dialogues with various stakeholders (eg young people, academia, media, religious bodies and civil society) to listen to their ideas as well as share global good practices to promote and invest further in mental health.

On 3 September 2021, I was invited to an audience with the Queen of Bhutan, the *Gyaltsuen* (Dragon Queen) Jetsun Pema Wangchuck – an extremely rare event for any foreigner. She had recently become the nation's figurehead for mental health promotion. Ranjana, my wife, was granted permission to accompany me. We were joined by His Majesty the *Druk Gyalpo* (Dragon King), Jigme Khesar Namgyel Wangchuck. For almost three hours that autumnal afternoon, the four of us sat discussing mental health and what could be done about it in Bhutan. I confess, Ranjana and I were awestruck in the presence of such royal grace.

Five days later, on 8 September, the UN held a briefing with a group of media representatives. I used the opportunity to continue my mental health advocacy but neglected to check if the meeting was 'off the record'. Overconfident, negligent and simply not pausing to consider what the implications might be, my opening line was, 'Bhutan is heading down the wrong path on mental health and suicide...'

What was I thinking?

I wasn't thinking. This was known territory for me. My mistake was a basic failure.

The 11 September headlines in *The Bhutanese*, a national newspaper, quoted me directly That evening as I read the article my heart sank and my stomach reeled. I felt embarrassed and afraid of the repercussions in this tightly knit society.

Her Excellency Dasho Dechen Wangmo was the intelligent and super-energetic minister for health at the time. Over the next few days, I heard through several back channels that she was incredibly disappointed with what I had said. I could appreciate why. But together we had built a trusting relationship, strong enough for forgiveness and, a few weeks later, she graciously thanked me for all the efforts I had made. But upon seeing that headline, I felt guilty. What I did was bad. Yet, strangely, I did not feel ashamed. This was an unintended error. I did not let it define me. It's not helpful to beat yourself up. So, I brushed myself down and over the next few weeks continued to compassionately advocate.

On 8 October, at an event in Thimphu alongside Dr Tandi Dorji, Bhutan's then foreign minister – yet another wonderfully graceful leader – we launched UNICEF's annual flagship report, 'The State of the World's Children', which that year focused on mental health (UNICEF 2021).

On 3 November, Her Majesty the *Gyaltsuen* graced the *Salhang Tendrel* (ground-breaking) ceremony for the Pema Centre – a new, 60-bed hospital for mental health and wellbeing. During her speech, she said, 'We must put in every effort and all possible means to provide timely intervention and services to support the wellbeing of our people. It is crucial now that as a nation, we embody that spirit of community and nurture a society that works to ensure that no person suffers in silence, and that we support each other with compassion and kindness through any struggle or adversity. Mental health will have the national priority it deserves.'

Psychological safety stages

Convinced by the evidence that, as a concept, psychological safety is fundamental if individuals, teams and organisations are to thrive, I've been constantly grappling with the concept's 'how to'. Fortunately, the likes of Dr Timothy Clark, CEO of LeaderFactor, neuroscientist Dr Dan Radecki and colleagues from the Academy of Brain-based Leadership, alongside mindset coach Dr Karolin Helbig and leadership consultant Minette Norman, have recently shone practical light on the subject (Clark 2020; Radecki et al 2021; Helbig & Norman 2023). I highly recommend their respective books.

For example, in *The 4 Stages of Psychological Safety* (2020), Dr Clark identifies and illustrates progressive phases of psychological safety – a pathway to inclusion and innovation that graceful leaders and co-workers, at all levels of an organisation, can help themselves and others move securely along. This framework can also be used as a diagnostic tool to assess the stage of psychological safety that any social unit, team or organisation has reached at a given point in time. Each stage must be reached before the next can begin and sometimes, because of changing dynamics or context, there's a need to return to a previous stage in order to advance any further. With each progressive stage comes the need to collectively amp up the levels of two-way mutual trust, respect and empowerment to mitigate the increasingly constrictive risks of personal exposure to harm or retribution.

Alongside suggestions already provided in this section, I indicate below when other graceful leadership practices will be of particular use in each growth stage of psychological safety. **Practice 1** ('Have self-compassion') permeates every stage.

Over the course of my career, I've found many teams can get to Stage 3, producing results by contributing, yes, but only occasionally by challenging (Stage 4). Leaders need to lean into team dynamics and tackle whatever barriers are limiting a team's shift from Stage 3 to Stage 4. Among other graceful leadership practices, team coaching can be a key bridge between these two stages (**Practice 13**). I've also seen many individuals oscillate between Stages 2 and 3, but none can move to Stage 4 unless their team or wider community also moves. Again, coaching both individuals and teams can be the elixir for positive and safe transition as well as in helping everyone to keep investing in and striving for psychological safety.

Stage 1. Inclusion safety (BELONG): First, recognise that we all want to be included. The need to create workplaces of belonging is paramount. For example, people who have recently joined a team or community (including new leaders) or become a member/leader of a newly formed team, can be assisted through this stage by using **Practice 4** ('Step into others' shoes'), **Practice 5** ('Personise') and **Practice 10** ('Be an emotional healer').

↓

Stage 2. Learner safety (LEARN): Once we feel included, we generally want to learn more about the community or team to which we now belong. By using **Practice 7** ('Apply compassion every time') and **Practice 13** ('Help people transform'), you can help people move from safe spectators to curious participators, encouraging them to ask more questions, seek help, try things out and learn from mistakes without fear of criticism or ridicule.

↓

Stage 3. Contributor safety (CONTRIBUTE): Now that we belong and have begun to engage in tasks at hand, we want to contribute more, to display our ability to deliver results. This signals the end of apprenticeship and the start of more self-determined performance. This stage is the bedrock for individual and team performance. *Signs of innovation begin to emerge.* **Practice 8** ('Be ethical and candid'), **Practice 9** ('Assume the best in others'), **Practice 11** ('Use humour and play'), and **Practice 13** ('Help people transform') are especially relevant here.

↓

Stage 4. Challenger safety (INNOVATE): And finally, we reach a stage when we all feel comfortable enough (ie there are no personal threats) to challenge the *status quo* or to ideate and invite disruption if we believe things need to change or could be done better. *This is when innovation truly kicks in.* This should be every leader's end goal for workplace culture. Alongside all other graceful leadership practices, **Practice 2** ('Train your brain'), **Practice 3** ('Lift your spiritual intelligence'), **Practice 8** ('Be ethical and candid'), **Practice 12** ('Embody generosity and gratitude'), **Practice 13** ('Help people transform'), **Practice 14** ('Create value for the community') and **Practice 15** ('Focus on the big picture') will greatly assist leaders and team members to advance to and keep everyone in this ultimate state of psychological safety.

Building and sustaining psychological safety offers a surefire return on your investment, including improvements in individual and team performance and collective wellbeing. Try just one – or all – of these various ways to strive for psychological safety and track how *your* team, organisation or community is impacted.

Apply compassion every time

A Chinese proverb says, 'There is no way to compassion; compassion is the way.' I've noted already that compassion is grace expressed – it is to have empathy and then act with kindness. Whether you're a leader by title or not, seeking daily chances to be compassionate can be transformative for not only yourself but especially for your colleagues, your team and ultimately your organisation.

Land of the Thunder Dragon

In August 2019, following almost four years in Iran, I took up my second UNICEF representative post, this time in Bhutan – *Druk Yul* or Land of the Thunder Dragon.

A Buddhist kingdom on the eastern ridges of the Himalayas, Bhutan is renowned for its rich traditions, tranquil monasteries, pristine forests, crystal-clear rivers, diverse wildlife and striking topography, stretching from mountains to subtropical plains. I will also never forget the clouds drifting across sapphire skies that, to me, perhaps unsurprisingly, always resembled dragons.

Bhutan is also known for the concept of gross national happiness or GNH. GNH implies that non-economic factors of wellbeing should be given equal weight to other sustainable development factors such as economic growth. The GNH Index is a single number index derived from 33 indicators measured across nine domains: psychological wellbeing, health, education, time use, cultural diversity and resilience, good governance, community vitality, ecological diversity and resilience and living standards: gnhcentrebhutan.org/gnh-happiness-index

The population of some 780,000 people is led by Jigme Khesar Namgyel Wangchuck, the fifth sovereign of Bhutan. Cherished and respected throughout the country, he is known affectionately as the 'People's King' (Kuensel 2017). I had the privilege to meet him on several occasions. I also witnessed first hand his extraordinarily graceful leadership during the Covid-19 pandemic.

Madeline Drexler, journalist and a visiting scientist at the Harvard T H Chan School of Public Health, has written a brilliant synopsis of how Bhutan staged a world-class response to Covid-19 that was largely guided by His Majesty (Ministry of Health & WHO 2022). Organising and funding social protection schemes (cash support and scholarships) to the country's most vulnerable, travelling tirelessly to all corners of the country, attending all-night meetings to help decide on next steps and reading voraciously to better understand the pandemic's epidemiology as well as the latest science behind promising public health interventions were just some of the king's countless acts of compassion and dedication.

I'm humbled to note that with the great support of our supply division team located in Copenhagen, together with our regional team based in Kathmandu, the UNICEF Bhutan team played a key role in supporting the kingdom's Covid-19 response. For example, after many late-night calls in June 2021 with His Excellency Tshering Gyaltshen Penjor, Bhutan's ambassador to several European countries based in Brussels, we managed to deliver thousands of Covid-19 vaccines collected from Bulgaria, Croatia, Denmark and the US, as well as cold chain equipment (certain Covid-19 vaccines needed to be stored at extremely low temperatures) from across Europe and Asia at a crucial point in Bhutan's response to the pandemic, all against overwhelming odds. This included organising a fearless Indonesian cargo crew who flew with vaccines from Kentucky (in the US) and had to be navigated by a brave Bhutanese pilot to Paro (the location of Bhutan's only international airport) through one of the world's most dangerous runway approaches. Despite ruffling some government feathers, we remained adamant that, after they were shut in early 2020, schools needed to be safely reopened and must remain open, and we were successful in our persuasion. And again in 2021, we boldly led the UN in encouraging the country to make mental health a new national priority, contributing to a whole-of-government, whole-of-society initiative spearheaded by Her Majesty, Queen Jetsun Pema Wangchuck.

In her book, Madeline cites a UNICEF statement we issued on 27 July 2021 that Bhutan organised 'arguably the fastest vaccination campaign to be executed during a pandemic.' Voice of America's Asia correspondent Anjana Pasricha interviewed me for a VOA *News* bulletin, 'If Bhutan can succeed in a monsoon with so few health workers to get almost the entire population vaccinated and then move to the children,' I said, 'maybe Bhutan can be a beacon of hope in a region that is on fire' (Pasricha 2021). Anjana had asked me whether there were any lessons for other countries. I replied, 'If there are lessons to be learned from Bhutan, it is about compassionate leadership that has to come from the top. By compassionate leadership I mean having deep empathy, really walking in the shoes of others, and then actively making efforts to support people throughout this terrible, terrible pandemic.'

It didn't surprise me that the 'People's King' was also named the 'Compassionate King' (Kuensel 2021). If ever there was a complete example of what graceful leadership looks and feels like, then *Druk Gyalpo* Jigme Khesar Namgyel Wangchuck and *Druk Gyaltsuen* Jetsun Pema Wangchuck are it. The world would do well to learn from their examples.

Communication graces

Frequently seeking moments to give and receive compassion is deeply rooted in the evolution of our brains. Jessica Cabeen (2019) eloquently labels these everyday actions as our *communication graces*. Mindful listening skills (**Practice 6**) can be heightened enormously by your disposition to always communicate with others more kindly. To ignite compassionate interactions, one simple question that you can ask frequently is, 'How can I help you to have a better day?' Check in with colleagues if you learn that they have challenges inside or outside of work – a supportive phone call, a text message or a house visit can lift spirits, theirs and yours (**Practice 10**).

Compassion architects

John Chambers, former CEO of Cisco, recognised how compassion was not just the right thing to embody but also to advance his company. He created an alert system to make sure that if any member of his staff, anywhere on Earth, was going through severe loss or sickness, John would be notified within 48 hours (Kanov et al 2004). He would then write a personal letter offering help to that employee. The importance of care and compassion spread throughout the company.

Jeff Weiner, executive chairman of LinkedIn, has oriented the entire company around compassionate leadership as well as developed an online training course (Weiner 2017). Some of LinkedIn's compassionate workplace interventions include: each employee is given an annual budget to invest in self-compassion (**Practice 1**); employees have regular 'in days' when they focus not on tasks but only on spending time with their teams to help build better trust and connection (**Practice 5**); and a Compassion Award has been launched to encourage leaders around the world to scale up initiatives that promote more compassion in communities and workplaces (Simas 2020).

So, try to bring compassion into any interaction that you have. And keep reminding yourself that practising continual compassion is good for your health and the health of those you lead. A calendar reminder or sticky note on your desk – 'Remember compassion!' – is a simple but powerful aid. Ask yourself at the beginning of every working week, 'How do I make the beginning of this week feel different for everyone, including myself, from the end of last week? What positive changes can I make through my leadership this week? How can I use my leadership to help others today and each day of this week?' This is the daily investment in others made by those Dr Monica Worline and Professor Jane Dutton (2017) describe as 'compassion architects' – individuals who continuously strive to enhance specific features of their organisation, such as networks, culture, roles, routines and leadership actions so that compassion awakens and propagates.

What graceful leaders say

Mohamed: *'Keep in mind every second, every minute, every hour, every day, every week, every month, every year that you, as a leader, are nothing without your colleagues, your team. And therefore, as I like to say to my colleagues all the time, I am there to serve them. I do have oversight, I get informed about how things are going, but I let people be themselves and do things by themselves. So, yes, be compassionate all the time and that's for sure the only way. But unfortunately, we are also in a world that more and more I think is being transformed, where being compassionate can actually take you to sometimes be exploited. Not everybody's genuine, not everybody is a good person. The second challenge is, and I also hear this very often, not everybody sees compassion as a quality. Some people see it as a weakness. But I think again you have to use your emotional and spiritual intelligences and put yourself way above that, otherwise you may even change the way you are. Because at the end of the day it's about your feelings, your values and how you see this humanity, how you want your role to be in this world.'*

Gillian: *'You can have small acts of kindness throughout the day, throughout the week. It's how you make your team members feel valued. So, if you have something tough to say to them, you can put it* in a kind way. Being courteous, always treating everyone with respect, I think is very important.'

Hamida: 'If you are taking care of others most of the time, they will also take care of you because as a leader, you also need people to take care of you. And I have this strong belief that as you take care of people, you try to lift them up, you try to care for them, you try to show all your support and guidance rather than just pushing, directing and instructing, then in turn, I find that it's reciprocal.'

Ugochi: 'It is very, very important for me to be able to demonstrate my kindness very early on in the relationship. So, I try to find situations very early to show who I am, what my values are and what's important to me. And to me, kindness goes with empathy, goes with respect, goes with being humane. I don't think you would meet anybody who would say, "Having a kind leader is not important to me." Because I'm also known for pushing my team, for setting high standards and for having high expectations. And so, kindness is the way to temper that so that you can still push people, but people recognise that you are also a kind person. Otherwise, I would've been labelled as a slave driver, taskmaster, demanding. Listening is a form of kindness and making time for a colleague's priorities or something that's important to a colleague. Or a colleague knowing that they mean more to you than just the work.'

Peter: 'That's what makes us graceful leaders. That's what makes us kind leaders. But compassion is not just kindness and grace. It can be hard. It can be difficult. You start with compassion and then you move from there. I mean, your entry point is compassion. Your exit point might have to be slightly different. Let's not forget, you need a return on your kindness. You need a return on your compassion. You could be compassionate about everything and achieve nothing. You can be heartless and achieve a lot, but it goes back to the way you do it. Compassion will sustain your achievement if the entry point is there.'

Acceptance

However, this is also perhaps the hardest of all graceful leadership practices since everyday hurdles and complexities constantly threaten to unsettle our mindfulness. One tactic I use is *acceptance* (**Practice 1**): accepting that I'm trying to be compassionate and to coach but I might not always succeed. This is the meaning behind the final line of my life purpose (see page 1).

When I sense the rising threats, I also remind myself of the multiple benefits of remaining calm – compassionate *intention* creates inner *contentment* for those you interact with and for yourself (**Practices 2** and **3**). My 'go-to' mantra of calm is Mother Teresa's 'Let no one ever come to you without leaving happier.' And I remember what the poet Maya Angelou once observed, 'I've learned that people will forget what you said, people will forget what you did, but people will never forget how you made them feel.'

There is another important benefit to remember. In times of stress and tragedy, if we are not mindful, our brain and emotions can easily be hijacked by more primitive reactions (**Practice 2**), so there is tremendous value in applying compassion in everyday work interactions in *times of peace* as a form of preparation or resilience training ready for *times of crisis*. So, each time you meet colleagues, family, friends or stakeholders who might be struggling with a problem, try to ask, 'What's on your mind? And what else? How can I help? What do you need from me? In this instance, what would my support look like? Who else can help?' Consider lending a helping hand to colleagues when they have tight deadlines; this can lead to higher engagement and more productivity among the team. Ask team members, 'What can I do today to be a better leader? What barriers can I help you dismantle so that you can do your job? What does a great day at work look like for you, and how can I contribute to that?'

Practice 8

Be ethical and candid

Graceful leaders do not compromise on ethics or standards. Behaving ethically is doing the right thing in the right way – being open, honest and fair. For example, I noted earlier that allowing poor performance or bad behaviour is the opposite of compassion – it is unethical and misleading. If you conceal or withhold concerns to appear 'kind' (or play the 'popularity game'), people will neither know your expectations nor benefit from your wisdom. Being kind is being honest, direct and transparent (Avolio 2016). You must accept that not everybody will like you. Indeed, it is not necessary to be universally liked.

Let's be clear. Graceful leaders are not there to make friends (though friendships may arise), and while they do invest in fostering positive interpersonal relationships, they carefully balance collegiality with accountability to advance organisational efficiency and effectiveness towards results. Liane Davey, a team effectiveness advisor, author and professional speaker, notes that there is a delicate balance between ensuring accountability for results and demonstrating kindness to individuals, 'The secret is to over-index on clear expectations and then provide frequent, low-impact coaching and feedback to give your team members assistance without ever transferring ownership. It's a winning formula for a happy, healthy, and productive team' (Davey 2023).

Co-create clear expectations and frequently reassess them

To effectively lead others, you must first co-create and then regularly review firm, crisply defined expectations. For example, agreeing on unambiguous behavioural standards – the three to five things 'we should always do' and the three to five things 'we should never do' in the form of a psychological contract, social pledge or team charter (best if documented for future reference) – and then frequently reconvening to discuss and refine these expectations, are steps that I believe supervisors and supervisees as well as whole teams should take together way more (**Practice 6**).

In my many engagements as both a one-on-one and team coach, I don't know how many times absence of clarity combined with lack of flexibility regarding roles, boundaries and responsibilities is *the underlying reason* for workplace anxiety, tension and friction. Among the prerequisites for strong interpersonal trust and high performance are:

✦ gaining clarity about work-related goals, the roles involved and the tasks required
✦ agreeing on accountabilities while embedding fluidity and renegotiation as needed, in simple as well as in more complex tasks requiring teamwork (and here I always emphasise the importance of colleagues discussing *beyond* or digging *beneath* what is laid out in policies and regulations since interpersonal friction due to role ambiguity often arises at the uncertain edges of or due to the haziness within many organisational procedures)
✦ getting to know each team member's preferred communication and work style
✦ learning what resources people need in order to flourish
✦ identifying how everyone's contributions will be appraised.

These also represent great areas in which graceful leaders can coach individuals and teams for even higher performance.

Beware the micromanager!

Graceful leaders empower those they lead by first agreeing on clear individual, team and organisational expectations of performance and then, crucially, assisting with these various performances.

Early in my UNICEF career, I learned how important it is to match expectations with support mechanisms such as regular performance coaching. I recall a time when I was supervising a leader whose team could not meet deadlines, even those we had jointly pre-agreed. According to this team leader's perspective, I had an unwarranted focus on controlling subordinates, an unhealthy drive for perfection and a fixation with details (the deadlines). In short, I appeared to be a 'micromanager'. My ego will forever gleefully dispute the accusation, but despite noticing that deadlines kept being missed, I didn't bother to find out *why* nor provide any *assistance* (something which micromanagers indeed tend not to do). Instead, I just indifferently wrote a critical end-of-year performance review. Not once did I offer compassionately tough coaching feedback when it was obvious that I had regularly needed to. I also became aware of the need to acknowledge differing perspectives ('both/and') – there's *never* just one side to a performance story.

Compassionate toughness

There is nothing kind or earnest about failing to give timely, constructive criticism or not relaying bad news – this is the opposite of compassion. Avoiding tough interactions or always saying what people want to hear simply allows bad behaviour and poor performance to continue, no matter how well cared for and supported you have made that colleague feel. In her superb book, *Radical Candor* (2017), founder of Candor Inc and well-known Silicon Valley CEO coach, Kim Scott, calls this avoidance behaviour 'ruinous empathy'. And by not dealing with low performers, you also send demotivating signals to high performers.

Leading with grace means respectfully, authentically and firmly offering criticism or breaking bad news by being candid, fact based and respectful. Not doing and being so all but guarantees that team members will not learn or grow. By consistently listening, understanding, empathising and helping, you can forge the very conditions that allow for difficult performance management conversations if needed. When colleagues feel cared for and supported, you build trust and earn respect. These in turn create the safe spaces for honest, tenacious hard talk – *compassionate toughness.*

One reason *compassionate toughness* can emerge is because graceful leaders purposively forge high-quality connections with their team members. These connections possess great tensile strength, able to withstand high emotional loads or tensions, whether positive or negative. For example, an inadequate piece of work can be discussed in terms of both a leader's disappointment but also their concern about the team member's personal circumstances without harming the work relationship (Dutton & Heaphy 2003).

Graceful leaders can be assertive and compassionately tough when the situation demands it but never aggressive, reckless or mean spirited. Graceful leaders communicate difficult messages and get hard things done in a *human* way – with genuine concern for people's souls and welfare. In **Practice 4** I introduced 'fierce compassion' (an inner steeliness when engaging in diplomacy), and it possesses another dimension when giving performance feedback. My experience has been that people can generally handle 'tough' once you've won their trust and respect through your kindheartedness; when they repeatedly witness from all you say and do that you *absolutely* have their best interests at heart. Graceful leadership makes crucial performance conversations not only possible but more meaningful and impactful. As leadership scholar Ken

Blanchard once observed, 'People don't mind being challenged to do better if they know the request is coming from a caring heart.'

Certainly, it takes courage to give (and receive) feedback. For example, a leader may dread the impact her feedback could have on the person about to receive it but she courageously cares enough to give it anyway. Additional ingredients for having kind yet assertive performance conversations include *consistent proportionality* (giving tough feedback always to the same level as you did previously for similar instances of unacceptable behaviour or poor performance) and *dependable fairness* (never turning a blind eye to some while calling out others) – this is *ethics in action*.

Calling out disgrace

Through their acute empathy, graceful leaders are attuned to workplace undercurrents, identifying and tackling any hidden rules and tactics (such as gossiping) that are being used by those who have power (or falsely believe they have the power) to shut down ideas, stymie risk taking, belittle others, preserve their own internal faction or to rationalise their own ruthlessness (Chapman 2009; Sutton 2017). Allowing incivility can devastate any organisation in a number of ways, including financially and culturally (Pearson & Porath 2009).

Similarly, graceful leaders use their comprehension of team dynamics to call out toxic employees who deliberately harm co-workers or pollute others with their poisonous attitude (Frost 2003). Workplace conflict due to toxic relationships, caustic politics, chronic underperformance and other forms of disruption can produce significant misery. For example, if toxic employees are not attended to, they can cause others to suffer poor mental and physical health; have low levels of confidence and dignity; decrease their quality of work, along with work effort and time at work; lower their organisational commitment; and experience exhaustion, even burnout – as well as increase overall rates of staff turnover and absenteeism

(Lewis 2021). Indeed, beyond the adverse impacts on other team members' performance and wellbeing, the broader financial losses can add up to millions if workplace incivility is tolerated or the negative influence of toxic employees is ignored. This is true *even if* such individuals deliver results (see below) – and in organisations where only 'the results' matter and not the people, this is one reason why toxic workers tend to survive (Purushothaman & Stromberg 2022).

Dealing with workplace toxicity requires graceful leaders to, in the words of University of British Columbia professors Peter Frost and Sandra Robinson, accept and handle being a *toxic handler* – someone who 'voluntarily shoulders the sadness, frustration, bitterness and anger that are endemic to organ- isational life' (Frost & Robinson 1999). People suffering from toxic co-workers often turn to such toxic handling colleagues or leaders because they are perceived to be trustworthy, calm, kind and non-judgemental.

Peter and Sandra have identified several ways by which toxic handlers alleviate organisational pain: they listen empa- thetically (**Practices 4** and **6**); they reframe difficult messages (**Practice 6**); they work behind the scenes to prevent pain (**Practices 7** and **10**); and they carry the confidences of others and help them to find solutions (**Practice 13**).

Organisations can recover from or at least keep handling toxicity at work thanks to these difficult and frequently selfless acts of compassion. But toxic handlers also need to ensure that their own physical, emotional, mental and spiritual health is not damaged. Thus, self-compassion becomes essential if they are to maintain the integrity of their own anti-toxin armour (**Practice 1**).

Other ways to reduce toxicity at work should be obvious – how an organisation goes about hiring and firing. Comprehensive recruitment processes that screen out those with a history of disruption or overt aggression are vital. As are the firm and consistent use of strong workplace regulations such as zero-tolerance policies. But are these too costly? Interestingly, a 2015 Harvard Business School study of almost 58,542 workers across 11 different firms found that not hiring a toxic worker or quickly releasing them if already employed delivers twice the cost savings compared to recruiting a stellar employee with desired values and consistent performance. In other words, *not hiring or dismissing a toxic worker is more profitable than recruiting a superstar*. Thus, the Harvard researchers recommend that it's better to avoid or let toxic workers go than to hire outstanding, non-toxic performers. They even found that replacing the toxic worker with a non-toxic but mediocre performer is still a more profitable option, with the added benefits of improved workplace wellbeing (Housman & Minor 2015).

Of course, some workers can *become* toxic because of the environment in which they are placed – and this might be due to the pre-existence of other toxic workers who have not been held to account. Graceful leaders deploy a systemic approach to foster and coach improved team dynamics and workplace culture. An initial question to ask might be, 'How could we keep improving and enjoying things around here?' (see **Practice 6** for more coaching questions). Thus, graceful leaders can help to *transform* polluting environments while, if resources allow, counselling and coaching may help to *reform* toxic workers (**Practices 10** and **13**).

Tough performance conversations
Mindful preparation

Just as with any diplomatic negotiation (**Practice 4**), holding a difficult performance conversation cannot be *ad hoc* nor done on the fly but requires thorough preparation and dedicated time. A graceful leader always uses compassion as the conversation's lens (Rimm 2013). In doing so, it is useful to again heed Doug Scott and his Harvard colleagues' caution that every difficult conversation is actually three dialogues subsumed within one – in which perceptions of being blamed, risks of having feelings hurt and fears of losing a sense of self-worth bubble just beneath the surface and, if not mindfully handled, can instantly terminate the conversation (**Practices 4** and **6**). So, preparing one's mindset or steadying one's mind's eye to observe through the lens of compassion matters enormously for tough performance conversations in at least five ways.

First, I always begin with the assumption that the individual or team wants to do a good job (**Practice 9**). Underperformance or bad behaviour is not their *purpose* but perhaps there are factors holding them back, running interference or unsettling them. My task is to better understand the situation, to work out what, if anything, might have triggered this low standard or discourtesy – what is their perspective, are they suffering in some way, what challenges are they experiencing?

Any tough performance conversation has at least two basic aims: to jointly identify the problem and then co-create some actionable solutions. The key challenge is to identify the 'right' problem but, many leaders, myself included, frequently leap too early to what we think the performance problem is and then set about 'fixing' what turns out either to be the wrong problem or not the most important one. To use a swimming analogy, we end up just snorkelling in the shallows. So, this is the second mindful preparation step that I take: to *remember to dive as deep as I can* as to why there is underperformance or bad behaviour. When a colleague's performance falls short, ask yourself whether they might be grappling with issues beyond their control.

In his motivational book, *Compassionate Leadership: Creating Places of Belonging* (2019), Chris Whitehead, CEO of Damflask Consulting, offers a handy question: *have they been equipped to succeed?* Do they have the right training, resources and experience? Do they have adequate help from colleagues? Do they fully understand their role and contribution to the organisation's broader mission and strategy? In addition, they might be feeling swamped with too many tasks or too many competing deadlines, have rarely received feedback on or guidance about their job, be dealing with interpersonal conflicts, coping with a health issue, struggling with personal challenges outside of work or any combination of these and other underlying problems. While I might end up not needing to dive too deep to identify the problem, I still prepare my intent to do so.

Third, my mindful attention remains on the *problem*, not the person/s. I remind myself that a person's or team's under-achievement or wrongdoing is much more likely due to their situation rather than their personality. For instance, and as I noted earlier, poor team performance or even toxicity within a team more often occurs because they don't share the same understanding of their goals, haven't clarified each other's roles, fail to regularly review collective performance and face constantly excessive workloads. These are not 'personality problems'.

Fourth, I approach the conversation as a *positive opportunity* to help my colleague/s while also improving individual and team performance. This positivity must be carried into and through to the conversation's end. This is not easy, because my colleague or team may react with anxiety or anger. It requires that I stay calm, present and grounded. Thus, I prepare myself to respond constructively to negative emotions should they arise (**Practices 1** to **4**).

Finally, I ready my mind to engage in a *partnering journey*, unfurling compassion and coaching as the twin sails to help get us through the rough waters that might lie ahead. This conversation is about *learning*. It's not going to be about my instructive advice, though of course I might be asked to provide or sense that I need to give it. But that will only happen once I have asked open-ended questions and then listened with fascination to deeply understand the other person's or team's perspectives and their own corrective solutions. It will mean that I must remain comfortable in any silence and purposively leave space for my colleague/s to think and respond (**Practice 6**).

The last part of preparing for a tough performance conversation is less about mindset and more about margins.

How wide should the conversation's focus be? What do I wish to accomplish through this conversation? Even if there is a long track record or office memory of substandard performance or incivility and you happen to be the first one to openly confront the individual or team about this (and you could be – **Practice 10**), it's just not possible to resolve years of transgression. So, I set narrow margins for each performance conversation and focus on dealing with one, up to a maximum of three 'fresh' (so they are more easily remembered) and 'clear' lapses in performance or judgement ('clear' as in obviously something has happened, and we need to find out why).

The performance conversation flow: SHINE

For me, providing kind, direct feedback in both tough and not-so-tough performance conversations follows this straight-forward acronym: SHINE.

It begins with a *Signal*, an *Honest* acknowledgement and an *Invitation* (not imposition). So, the start of a tough performance conversation might flow like this:

'What I'm about to share may be tough for you to hear but all I want is for you to perform well. Honestly, it's not been easy to prepare for what I now need to explain to you. However, I'm going to try to be as clear and as brief as possible, so I invite you to let me know if I'm not and you'd like me to go back over any part... All right?'

And after pausing to check in with my colleague/s, I might continue my invitation like this: 'As I hope you know by now, I strive for everyone to be at their best, so when it seems they're not, I always wonder what might be going on, and if needed, how they can be supported. And that's what I'd like to explore with you today. So, I know I don't have the full picture [remember SOUL in **Practice 3**] but the facts as I understand them are... And based on these facts, here's what I'm seeing... This is how I'm reading the situation... This is the story I'm telling myself... [And after I've shared my perspective] I want to check whether or not any of that makes sense to you... [or you can invite them to paraphrase back to you] Would you mind just summarising what you've heard me say so far?… Is there anything you'd like to ask me at this point?… Now, I am keen to learn your perspective so that I can better understand, and we might be able to move forward together. What do you think I need to know?… What do you know that I don't?… How are you reading the situation?… In what ways might you be seeing this differently?… What do you think was going on?' and so on.

If my invitation is accepted, then the performance conversation can proceed, during which I listen intently and might ask at an appropriate juncture: 'Sounds like you're quite/really… [adjective to acknowledge how you sense they are feeling] about all this. Is there anything you're curious, unsure or worried about? What are you proud of? Where are you struggling? What's really at stake for you here?'

If they deny the underperformance or wrongdoing, I might say, 'OK, for now, let's not debate whether or not this happened, but what would it imply for you if it actually had?' And later follow up with: 'What solutions or options might you suggest? What's the best way forward? What support might you need?… I have some observations and some ideas. Would you like to hear them?'

And eventually, the performance conversation moves to a *Negotiated* agreement about what needs to happen next (the commitments to take subsequent corrective action from both the colleague/team as well as from myself). And concludes with an *Expression* of my thanks for being open to the feedback.

Graceful leadership is about helping others to shine, so using SHINE as a flow for performance conversations, tough or otherwise, has always felt apt. And easy for me to remember! If my invitation is not accepted, I accept my colleague's decision not to continue and suggest that it's best if we circle back on another occasion, just like diplomatic negotiations sometimes need us to pause and 'go to the balcony' (**Practice 4**).

Finally, after every performance conversation, documentation is always necessary for at least a couple of reasons. First, any subsequent follow-ups can be informed by and build upon what was previously discussed and committed to. And second, these records will be needed if more formal performance management proceedings must be conducted in accordance with your organisation's human resource policies and procedures (Gallo 2016).

This may all seem overly sanguine but my experience in many contexts has been that when others see that you both care for them and you want them to *shine* by solving the performance problem together – that you believe in them – feedback in positive *and* negative forms is readily embraced, even sought.

Receiving feedback

It's not easy to listen intently to sometimes tough feedback from those you lead. But honesty is a two-way process. If you offer it, you must be equally curious and willing to receive hard, constructive feedback. This includes having the courage to graciously accept that your own understanding can be questioned, even rejected.

Receiving feedback always challenges self-identity and we need to be mindful of not succumbing to what Doug Stone and colleagues describe as the '*all-or-nothing* syndrome' (Stone et al 2010). None of us are supremely competent nor are any of us abysmally incompetent. We are magical mixtures of both good and not so good, wise and not so wise, graceful and not so graceful. We are never *permanently* anything: always polite; always punctual; always perfect. If we cannot shake these all-or-nothing self-delusions either we slip into a state of denial and dismiss the feedback (and thereby learn nothing from the advice) or we exaggerate the feedback to imply that we must be hopeless, forgetting all the competency we do have (and thus also learn nothing). Our ego takes over either in defensive or in self-sabotaging mode and cuts off our more discerning, reasonable, curious soul (see **Practices 1** to **3**).

Proactively and regularly asking others these kinds of questions to encourage feedback can help to prepare and tame the ego, 'How am I doing? If you chose one word to label how I lead, what would it be? In what way do you think I should change? What should I do more of? Less of? Start doing? Stop doing? What can I do to make your job more enjoyable and to help you better meet your goals? What two or three things could I do differently to better lead you? In that last project/meeting/workshop/report, what could I have done better? What little mistakes should I watch out for next time? What (if any) concerns do you have when it comes to giving me feedback? How can I alleviate those concerns?'

And for the times when you feel that feedback to a superior is needed, you can say something like, 'I realise that you had to weigh up many pros and cons when you made that decision, but perhaps if there is a next time, I just want to make you aware of...' or 'I'd like to learn more about how we can offer feedback if the team disagrees with you. What's your suggestion?'

And two graceful responses when receiving criticism, 'Thank you. Your observations were really powerful. Just give me a minute to think about what I just heard...' And, 'Thank you. I appreciate being told that. Tell me more...'

Gracious humility first, genuine curiosity second.

But sometimes we need to be cruel to be kind, right?

'But what about those individuals who are really intent on sabotaging our team or organisation?' you might ask. Or, 'What about those people who, regardless of whatever you try, just don't improve or lift their performance? Surely, there are situations in which, as a leader, you must be cruel to be kind?'

Graceful leaders know the uplifting difference between helpful versus harmful feedback. Being mindful in our communication is fundamental when being candid. Not being so can make matters worse. For example, when 'I was just being honest' or 'It's just that I am passionate about this' are used to thinly disguise personal attacks. Or when you reject negative feedback given to you, when your compassionate response should have been to demonstrate humility and curiosity.

In my opinion, there is no such thing as brutal honesty or the need to be cruel to be kind. Apart from the reasons outlined above, being brutal or cruel when giving feedback consumes great energy and generates stress in both the aggressor and the aggressed. I've learned that from a state of kind calmness (low energy use), just a slight rise in energy consumption can be enough to become more assertive, which is often all that is needed to deliver a tough message. This might be through a slightly more solemn glance or a marginally graver voice. In other words, having a default of compassion and coaching, and then becoming just a little bit sterner, for example, in facial expression, verbal and/or body language, is not only energy conserving but also less stressful on yourself and on colleagues. Once colleagues have grown used to the composed workplace climate that can be created through graceful leadership, even the most subtle signs of a leader's disapproval become obvious and will get addressed but with less collective stress and with less energy expended by all involved.

So, if you find yourself thinking 'I need to be cruel to be kind', please hit the pause button and mindfully check your own emotions and intentions (**Practices 1** to **3**), as well as presume positive intent in your colleagues. And how to assume the best in others is our next graceful leadership practice.

Practice 9

Assume the best in others

Beyond work, we are all someone's daughter, son, sister, brother, partner, friend, mum, dad, grandma, granddad and so on. We all want to succeed in these non-work roles, and they generate dreams, challenges and stories that differ for each of us while also shaping how we *show up* at work. Nobody leaves these roles, I think, to come to work to be unsuccessful.

Generous interpretations

My experience has been that everyone shows up at work each day as a *professional*, aiming to be our best self. And all of us want to leave work at the end of each day feeling as if we've made a difference before we return home to our much more important non-work roles. Indeed, our life outside work is *way more important*. That's why I talk about life–work not work–life balancing – life outside work should always be first in this equilibrium.

Let me reaffirm my own experience: no one enters the office door each day *intending to underperform*. As I'll illustrate in **Practice 10**, we must learn to check first for any hidden difficulties when we encounter mistakes, setbacks, performance dips, missed deadlines, absenteeism, communication delays or other challenges with colleagues at work. Generous interpretation here means delaying our managerial urge to quickly judge and blame, and instead hit the leader's pause button to first ask ourselves whether other factors might be driving apparent underperformance. This does not equate to tolerating mistakes that could have been avoided or inexcusable negligence. It just means establishing whether there might be hidden reasons affecting the professional whose performance we're discussing.

But I've also learned that these positive assumptions or generous interpretations must always be wisely balanced with mutually agreed accountabilities. For Dr Monica Worline and Professor Jane Dutton (2017), 'withholding blame and engaging in compassionate conversations that allow generous interpretations about what's happening, while still setting high standards and holding people accountable for consequences, is one of the most skilled forms of workplace interaction we all must learn'.

At the same time, it's crucial to have expectations that empower others and to avoid *over*-expectations that might stress them, even lead to disempowerment, a phenomenon Jean Manzoni, professor of leadership and organisational development, and research professor Jean-Louis Barsoux, both at the International Institute for Management Development, describe as the 'set-up-to-fail syndrome' (Manzoni & Barsoux 2002). Empathising (**Practice 4**) and personising (**Practice 5**) can help leaders understand this 'expectation balancing act'. Trust, respect, civility, mutual accountability and balance epitomise *grace in action*.

As I noted in **Chapter 2**, courage is a vital element of leading with grace. And woven into this particular practice is another dimension of courage – *the courage to openhandedly forgive*. When unintentional mistakes occur or someone just has one of those off days that we all have, generous forgiveness is graceful. But if underperformance continues and no underlying reasons can be found, then we must be compassionately tough (**Practice 8**).

Appreciative inquiry

For the famous humanistic psychologist Professor Carl Rogers, the practice of offering *unconditional positive regard* or UPR – conveying that even when others make mistakes or fail, you will grant them grace and acceptance – was a key to success in client-centred therapy (Rogers 1951). But UPR also became recognised as a vital ingredient in nurturing an individual's growth and in maintaining healthy relationships and social networks (Dames 2021).

As I have noted, a key characteristic of graceful leaders is that they put colleagues first. They always presume that others are turning up to work with good intentions and keep the best interests of individuals and their team or organisation at heart. If we can assume that others will bring their best selves to work, then in turn this helps to build that most precious of team performance transformers – *reciprocal trust*. So, take a chance on people; offer leadership opportunities – however big or small – to anyone. You will usually be pleased. It's what leadership coach Gregg Thompson calls 'appreciative expectation' (Thompson 2007). As motivational speaker Mike Robbins likes to say, 'You'll almost always get exactly what you expect from other people – so expect the best.'

This practice has linkages to *appreciative inquiry* – used in the broader field of organisational change – which aims to develop or redevelop based on what's working rather than trying to fix what isn't (Cooperrider & Whitney 2005). *Appreciative inquiry* seeks to expand creativity, imagination and innovation by asking individuals and teams questions such as, 'What is your/our experience of good performance so far? What might an even better performance be like? What should be your/our version of best performance? What will we need to get there? What will this ultimate performance look and feel like?'

To illustrate briefly, it might be that one of our team comes to us and says, 'You know, our results for the last quarter are way below what we expected.' Instead of asking 'So what was the problem?' or 'What went wrong?', we can positively recast our question as 'Last year, when we had those exceptional results, what went right?' (assuming, of course, that we had exceptional results!). These queries lean into our optimism, drawing a leader's attention to people's strengths and possibilities rather than their weaknesses and faults.

The glowing ember

Finally, purposefully assuming the best in others is a key ingredient if we are to build positive workplace cultures or optimistic team environments that create joy and lead to outstanding performance. My experience has been that if you believe in others, if you adopt an optimistic outlook, no matter the circumstance, and find something positive to say as often as you can, people will feel more comfortable in your company as well as safe enough to tell you what needs to be told.

Discover more about colleagues' non-work roles (**Practice 5**), assume the best in others and frequently reinforce this practice by describing others' motives and successes as positively as possible. Ask yourself, 'How good am I at seeing the positives in others?' And when things don't go so right for them, 'How good am I at giving others a second chance?' Become a source of oxygen that gives others life. Be the breeze that ignites their glowing ember. In the words of designer, healer and kundalini yoga teacher Hannah Duffy, 'Every person, team member, employee, new and old has an ember within them, a higher self that is begging to be recognised. We as leaders need to empower that power and surrender our own egos and worries and believe in these future leaders' (Duffy 2022).

Be an emotional healer

In May 2010, I moved to Kathmandu as the deputy representative or second in charge of the UNICEF team in Nepal. Dr Pankaj Mehta was our chief of health and nutrition. Several years my senior, Pankaj has a twinkle in his eyes and a delightful smile, outlined by a trim, ever-whitening goatee beard. He speaks softly, his words imbued with wisdom forged from experience. Though I was his so-called 'supervisor', I set out to learn as much as I could from him. We struck up a warm, supportive friendship. Personising (**Practice 5**) enabled me to get to know him well.

Pankaj and his wife, Dr Chaya, are both medical alumni of the Christian Medical College (CMC) in Vellore, Tamil Nadu, India. After completing his postgraduate medical degree in preventive and social medicine at CMC, he became a public health consultant and faculty member with M S Ramaiah Medical College in Bangalore, India and later with the Manipal Academy of Health Sciences, Karnataka, India. He is an active member of the Society for Community Health Awareness Research and Action, an independent NGO that promotes a people-centred paradigm for health and development.

Like many, including me, Pankaj began his UNICEF career as a consultant. He started assisting UNICEF India's field office in Madhya Pradesh and later worked at UNICEF India's field office in West Bengal. There he was instrumental in establishing the sick newborn care unit in Purulia, which still gives hope for a healthy future to thousands of mothers and newborns. Pankaj also helped to launch *Akha* or the 'Boat of Hope', which delivers health services to remote island communities in the northern Indian state of Assam, as well as supporting community-managed school initiatives to increase children's access to primary education in the Brahmaputra River Islands. He is highly appreciated in the field of routine immunisation.

Pankaj formally joined UNICEF in Kolkata, India and then moved to Nepal, where our paths crossed. His next move was to Manila, and I was honoured to support his application to become UNICEF Philippines' chief of health and nutrition. He was scheduled to move there on 3 October 2011.

It's 25 September 2011. I'm sitting at home in Kathmandu at the dining table. At around 8.30 am a colleague phones to tell me they've heard there's been a plane crash, and that Pankaj might have been on board. Not believing for a moment he was involved but just to check, I call his mobile.

I shall never forget the next ten seconds.

The ringtone stops and my call connects. 'Hello... Pankaj?' my voice trembles. A distressed voice, crying out in Nepali, is on the other end. All I can decipher are the two heart-stopping English words 'plane crash'. Someone has retrieved Pankaj's cell phone from the carnage.

Flying in dense fog and at 5,000 ft instead of the mandatory 6,000 ft, Buddha Air Flight 103 first hit treetops then a roof in Bisankunarayan village before splitting apart and crashing into foothills several kilometres from Kathmandu's Tribhuvan International Airport, its intended destination. Investigators later determine that pilot fatigue and error were to blame. All 19 passengers and the three Nepalese crew on board the twin-prop Beechcraft died. Of the 19 passengers, ten were Indian, two were from the US, one was Japanese and six were Nepalese.

Double tragedy: I discover that Chaya had perished alongside Pankaj. They had wanted to depart Nepal for the Philippines with memories of the spectacular view of Mount Everest that this Buddha Air special trip offered.

I sit in silence, vividly recalling his glowing smile and soft voice. It takes me many minutes to refocus.

With a very heavy heart, I have many people to inform and agency-related arrangements to commence. The emotions of their family and of the whole UNICEF Nepal team, including me, would need healing.

Pankaj and his family are devout Hindus – a faith firmly believing that each person is intrinsically divine and that the purpose of life is to seek and realise that divinity. Reincarnation is a central tenet – upon death, only the physical body perishes; the soul remains, continuing to recycle, perhaps through many lifetimes, until it settles upon its true nature. With each death, the soul strives to move closer to the Hindu god, Brahma. The nature of each incarnation depends upon a soul's actions during their previous life – the concept of karma.

Upon death, for Hindus the physical body serves no purpose and need not be preserved. Cremation of loved ones is chosen as the quickest way to release the soul and help with reincarnation. Pankaj's and Chaya's remains are recovered, washed, scented with essential oils and wrapped in white sheets. Placed in caskets, they are brought to Pashupatinath Temple, the oldest Hindu temple in Kathmandu, located beside the sacred Bagmati River. It's believed that a Hindu cremated here will be reborn as a human in their next life.

UNICEF staff from our Nepal office as well as from our South Asia regional office, also located in Kathmandu, gather to pay their respects. A Hindu priest, together with the close family, lead us through *mukhagni*, the cremation ceremony, consisting of chants or *mantras*. The sheet-clad bodies are gently placed on specially built pyres of wood. Clouds of incense fill the air. The pyres are lit.

To give others the space to be among the family and fellow mourners, and to not feel out of place in such an intense ceremony since I am not religious, I stand stone still on the

Bagmati riverbank directly opposite their burning pyres.

Throughout the funeral, I remain stooped in silent vigil as many of the team slowly move back across the nearby pedestrian bridge to where I am. We watch on until the fires die, the sun sets and Kathmandu's chill October evening air creeps in. The next day, their ashes are scattered into the Bagmati River.

Traditionally, the Hindu mourning period ranges from 10 to 30 days. Throughout this time, pictures of Pankaj and Chaya, adorned with flower garlands, were displayed in their Kathmandu home. We visited the family during this period and placed a framed photograph of Pankaj, equally adorned and lit up by butter lamps, in our office. On the 13th day of mourning, the grieving family held the *preta-karma*, a ceremony to help release Pankaj's and Chaya's souls for reincarnation.

One year later, on the first anniversary of their deaths, their families hosted a memorial event to honour their lives. Later that same year, I joined a small group of UNICEF colleagues in Bangalore at the wedding of their son Kayur, who became a doctor, like his parents. Their younger son, Dhaval, went on to graduate in environmental engineering in the US. These wonderful young men have followed in their parents' footsteps of being gentle, wise and hard working.

These acts of mourning and remembrance were steps in the healing process for all of us. For several weeks following this tragic plane crash, there were tears in our office, frequently private, often in small groups, sometimes in all-staff meetings. Hanaa Singer, our vibrant and passionately compassionate representative, who had joined the Nepal office just eight weeks before Pankaj's death, led the way in encouraging everyone to keep an eye on and care for one another. Together with Alain Balandi, our gentle and wisely considerate chief of operations, we set about doing our best to heal emotions.

A stewardship journey

Through this experience and many other times when I provided emotional support, I've learned that it's best to view emotional healing as a *stewardship journey* requiring courage, sensitivity and presence. In stressful or traumatic circumstances, the journey's destination is to have helped others mend their broken spirits, recover from anguish and upheaval and to feel *whole* once again – to regain emotional balance, whether as an individual, a team, a community, or an organisation, perhaps even a nation (Powley 2012). Such a journey usually includes at least five leadership steps or phases.

Many times, I've learned that the first three steps are all that is needed; but they are needed. Active listening can help others settle matters for themselves. There are occasions when family members or work colleagues just want someone to walk next to them along the healing journey. In these precious moments, we should just be better listeners, not fixers. This is the powerful capacity to *be* (felt presence) rather than *do* (fix problems) (Jinpa 2015). Simply listening attentively to others, listening with fascination, can ennoble them, and when your dignity is raised, when you feel sensitively legitimised, it can accelerate healing.

> **Step 1.** Being sensitive to the wellbeing and anxieties of others, being perceptive to any change in their behaviour (**Practice 5** and **Practice 8**) and interpreting these small clues that something may be amiss in order to offer help (**Practice 4**) – this first step can be difficult, particularly in busy workplaces where people are preoccupied with results and deadlines that tend to dampen the desire to share personal problems or distract us from noticing suffering in others, or in workplaces where people fear revealing their pain to others (**Practice 6**).
>
> ↓
>
> **Step 2.** From the onset of the shock, mentally preparing to provide support and to tolerate the distress you may feel upon hearing the trauma or stress of others (**Practices 1** and **2**) as well as organising yourself to create the time to assist (**Practice 12**).

181

↓

Step 3. Engaging in patient, non-judgemental, active listening (**Practice 6**). Just sitting with and being present for those suffering. 'We'll get through this together.'

↓

Step 4. Empathetic handling such as calming, comforting, caring and guiding, and perhaps, but only if asked, offering some advice (**Practice 4**). This step can include encouraging those suffering to gently begin to think about what is still positive, worthwhile and hopeful in their lives – beyond the immediate adversity, what do they still have a sense of control over – as well as honouring their potential to self-heal, cultivating positive, while at the same time realistic, beliefs about and expectations of recovery in both the sufferer and the healer.

↓

Step 5. Taking personal or collective responsibility to customise actions in relation to the sufferer's circumstances, whether that be through referral to counselling experts and therapists when needed and/or mobilising social, emotional, financial and administrative support if required – such as buffering the sufferer from having to deal with too much communication, providing meals, reducing their workload during their recovery, organising childcare, reassuring them that their job is secure, collecting donations from colleagues, running errands or facilitating more flexible work arrangements – and then to keep following up or checking in.

Unfinished business

As a leader, you will likely encounter and deal with delicate and/or intractable workplace challenges such as colleagues' burnout, stress, concerns about the future such as job security, frustrations over perceived pay grade discrepancies, career stagnation, perceived and real impacts of discrimination, work-induced emotional lows, the progressive build-up of day-to-day annoyances, complaints, dealings with a micromanager, coping with toxic managers and colleagues, experiences of abuse and harassment, feelings of betrayal following previously lauded yet subsequently unsuccessful efforts to create more humane workplaces that only added to stress levels, unwarranted workloads, unfulfilled expectations and the pressures of staff and resource shortages in the face of constant if not increasing demands. You might be the first to do so.

Individuals and teams may have unresolved situations and conflicts – some stretching back years – that leave them feeling trapped, distressed, remorseful and disconnected. This is 'unfinished business' (Whitehead 2019) and can include:

✦ role ambiguity
✦ the death of a close colleague
✦ unaddressed episodes of insulting, bullying or harassment
✦ chronic exposure to microaggressions – these are indirect or subtle expressions of sexism, heterosexism, racism, religionism, ageism, ableism and/or classism that can degrade *anyone's sense of identity* – no matter their background or professional level (Sue & Spanierman 2020; Washington 2022)
✦ an earlier staff restructure that triggered unresolved grief (see 'Machiavelli's ghost' below)
✦ any performance issue that is left hanging
✦ an unsolved ethical dilemma
✦ a strong feeling of injustice or unfairness
✦ being falsely accused
✦ uncivil grudges
✦ having to wait on a decision or event that impacts one's life in a significant way
✦ an anxiety-provoking conversation yet to take place.

The presence of unfinished business often creates what Michael West and Joanne Lyubovnikova describe as 'pseudo teams' – a team of individuals connected only by lines drawn on an organisational chart (organogram), who *have* to work together yet only care about their own role and what each can selfishly gain. Such teams lack the attributes that define a 'true team' – for example, a shared sense of purpose, open communication, mutual support, psychological safety and a commitment to each other's success (West & Lyubovnikova 2012).

Know the full story

Then there are forms of experience and suffering, external to the workplace, that nevertheless influence individual performance and workplace culture, such as living with a disability, mental health challenges, coping with addictions, exposure to domestic violence, divorce, separation, stresses in family roles and financial difficulties, to name just a few.

As an example, in one of my postings I noticed a team member who seemed to have days when she was very late for work, highly withdrawn and often absent from meetings. Was this a chronic underperformance issue that required a reprimand?

When I observe 'underperformance', first, I always find out whether there could be an underlying reason (**Practice 8**). There usually is. No one sets out to underperform (**Practice 9**). People frequently and understandably suppress information about disease, suffering, loss, uncertainty or grief that is negatively affecting their ability to perform at work because they feel ashamed or because they desire privacy for their personal lives.

Through many compassionate, confidential conversations with her colleagues, I came to learn that my team member was being physically abused by her husband, who was an alcoholic. The days when she seemed 'off key' were after particularly violent assaults the night before. With that knowledge and after once more consulting with other team members, I invited her for a chat. With courage, I just said, 'I know things might be difficult at home. If you ever want me to try to get you some help, just let me know.'

Weeks went by. She said nothing. Then, one day, she came to the office with a black eye. It was the first time there was any visible sign. I relayed the same message through teammates. I was humbled when she accepted our offer to help. We organised for local police and social workers to intervene. She and her child were first moved to a women's shelter. A little later, she felt able to return to her own parents' home and eventually separated from her husband. With further counselling support, her spirit and 'performance' returned.

Covid compassion

Compassion or *karuna* (from a *Sanskrit* word) is a key tenet of Buddha's teaching, one that he believed is something that everyone can learn to offer, even if other parts of his teaching might be difficult to follow. Author and scholar of religions Professor Karen Armstrong has shown that all of the other major religions – Christianity, Hinduism, Islam and Judaism – also have compassion at the heart of their belief systems (Armstrong 2011). Agnostic though I am, I still sense that our entire species, religious or not, underwent a massive rediscovery of compassion during Covid-19.

I was in the Buddhist Kingdom of Bhutan throughout the worst years of the pandemic, so perhaps it's unsurprising to learn that the UNICEF Bhutan team displayed daily compassion to each other throughout the crisis. Together with my gifted deputy representative Marie-Consolée Mukangendo (presently serving with UNICEF Libya), our resolute operations officer Karma Dekar, our thoughtful UNICEF staff association chair, Sonam Wangchuk, the resourceful administrative associate, Chador Tshomo and ever-reliable senior driver, Wangdi Wangdi, we also tried to ensure our colleagues felt supported. Some examples of our collective efforts to heal during those painful lockdowns include getting permission to deliver groceries to every team member's front door when all movement in public was otherwise forbidden, fortnightly virtual gatherings that included online games, and Sonam and I personally phoning everyone once a week just to have a five-minute check-in chat.

By no means were we unique. Countless individuals, teams and groups throughout UNICEF, across other UN agencies and in millions of families, communities, businesses and organisations worldwide carried out similar compassionate acts of care and healing during the pandemic. I guess I'm just curious as to why it takes a once-in-a-century viral plague for most humans, regardless of their religious outlook, to rekindle humanity's finest, universal attribute – kindness.

Machiavelli's ghost

> And let it be noted that there is no more delicate matter to take in hand, nor more dangerous to conduct, nor more doubtful of success, than to step up as a leader in the introduction of changes. For he who innovates will have for his enemies all those who are well off under the existing order of things, and only lukewarm supporters in those who might be better off under the new.
>
> – Niccolò Machiavelli, 16th-century diplomat, historian and
>   author of *The Prince* (circa 1532).

In January 2023, I moved from Bhutan to Cambodia to begin the next chapter of my leadership journey with UNICEF. The team there was in the middle of designing a new five-year programme of support for children and adolescents connected to the government's sustainable development cooperation framework with the broader UN family (2024–2028). This framework was itself aligned with Cambodia's socioeconomic development agenda known as the Pentagonal Strategy-Phase 1 (2023–2028). The stakes were very high.

Before I arrived, the team had commissioned an independent evaluation of UNICEF Cambodia's 2019–2023 programme and completed a comprehensive situation analysis of children, adolescents and women across the country. Both exercises featured extensive consultations with government and non-government stakeholders, including large samples of children and young people together with their families. The design stage of UNICEF's 2024–2028 programme also involved dialogues with a wide range of similar partners. The evaluation, situation analysis and various consultations all called for three key shifts in UNICEF's business model of support to Cambodia.

First, we needed to be much more influential with international, national and sub-national partners so that they increased their *own* investments in child-focused programmes across all relevant sectors such as education, protection, health, nutrition, water and sanitation. This shift acknowledged Cambodia's strong economic performance over the past decade or so, as well as declining levels of donor funds coming directly to UNICEF Cambodia. It was becoming increasingly difficult to mobilise grants for our work and instead we needed to be more effective in securing finances for children (whether or not these were channelled through UNICEF), including, of course, the government's own commitments at all levels.

Linked to this, a second request was to engage more meaningfully with senior authorities in provinces that had the lowest child health and development profiles. We accepted that we could be more consistent, coherent and comprehensive in our provincial partnerships. This meant a move away from 'UNICEF-labelled' assistance offered to local social services via two zonal office teams located in Siem Reap and Kratie, towards helping national ministries to provide 'government-led', child-focused guidance to provincial administrations so that they could then cascade similar support to all decision makers under their jurisdiction. This was in line with Cambodia's decentralisation reforms that were beginning to accelerate.

The third recommendation was the need to expand our promotion of climate action, gender equality and disability inclusion, as well as the holistic development of adolescents and their meaningful engagement in national and local decision making.

These shifts required us to work out how our staffing structure and capabilities could respond to these challenges. To not adapt – to carry on, somewhat complacently, in 'business as before' mode – ran the risk of slowing down, perhaps stagnating, and even worse, reversing hard-won gains for Cambodia's children, many of which were the outcome of UNICEF's earlier catalytic contributions. With the external context changing fast and placing new demands, UNICEF Cambodia had to transform, to unlearn the old and create the new (**Practice 15**).

Leaders can approach such a change scenario with only a staff reconfiguration top of mind and expend all their energy to achieve this new structure as swiftly as possible by repeatedly justifying its organisational value. *Often little attention is devoted to minimising the distress that is always unleashed by such a change.*

This inattention is not necessarily the leader's fault. Certain schools of thought in organisational change (and consultants) advise that when, for example, a downsize is proposed – a planned reduction in staffing, sometimes labelled as a 'necessary evil' or painful action to achieve a greater good – leaders should emotionally disengage, not attend to any suffering and not apologise for any job losses.

But graceful leaders do not follow such suggestions. They are not worried about openly stating that while change offers new beginnings, it can also bring heartache to *every member of the team*, including themselves, as everyone tries to come to terms with losses (eg individual careers) and endings (eg 'but that's how we've always done things'). They know that being open to emotions will not 'stir up trouble' – usually a leader's biggest fear. Instead, they fear that *not* acknowledging people's emotions will stir up even bigger trouble, trouble that can linger for a long time (see 'Prepare for the emotional tsunami' below).

A graceful leader's primary focus is to compassionately help those whose current role could be affected as well as those who will remain after the change to *transition safely, smoothly and, hopefully, successfully through the change* (Avramchuk et al 2013). And by extension, to ensure that every team member, especially every supervisor, also mindfully supports the transition.

Due to the requirements of my professional work prior to joining UNICEF full time in early 2007 (in the Pacific), I had already avidly consumed *Managing Transitions: Making the most of change*, the 1991 bestseller by Professor Bill Bridges, which has been updated in five further editions. To me, this book is a masterclass for leading needed change in a human way, guiding me through every organisational shift I've been involved with, including designing UNICEF programmes of cooperation in the Pacific, Nepal, Iraq, Iran and Bhutan.

On each of these previous occasions, I'd grown familiar with the respective UNICEF team *before* we headed into co-creating the next five-year programme. By contrast, the design of UNICEF Cambodia's next partnership with the government had already begun before I arrived. Despite my positional seniority, I had neither the necessary level of understanding nor levels of trust and respect to immediately agree with and then execute any staff restructuring exercise. But thanks to the recruitment wisdom of my predecessors, Foroogh Foyouzat and Cristian Munduate, I was blessed with two wonderful 'seconds-in-charge' (deputy representatives of programme and of operations, respectively) – Dr Anirban Chatterjee and Devraj Daby.

When Devraj left for UNICEF Myanmar in July 2023, Kimse Leang admirably stepped up as operations officer-in-charge until Devraj's replacement arrived towards the end of 2023 – the astute, warm-hearted Yelena Soldatova. I was equally blessed with a *very human* human resources (HR) team, gracefully led by Marcela Madero and which included the rising star of Theany Ang. We were also fortunate to have earlier internally voted in a perceptive staff association executive committee (the staff representative body within UNICEF Cambodia), the chair of which was the empathetic and entertaining Kimsong Chea. All of them had already built a strong foundation of trust and respect across the UNICEF Cambodia team.

Trust in and respect for leaders are always crucial, but particularly so when a team is dealing with a change that might harm colleagues in some way. Lack of trust and respect makes any psychological transition *much* more complex, and sometimes impossible, by which I mean that while the restructuring might be 'completed', the suffering remains. So, while I set about building my own trusting and respectful connections throughout the team, because of the compassionate nature of my co-leaders (and you need a strong guiding coalition), I had a welcome period of grace during which I could grow more familiar with the context by asking a series of analytical questions (see **Tool E**). This personal analysis improved my understanding of the three requested shifts (described above). Most importantly, I began to feel more reassured that we could adequately address the psychological transition that any staffing reconfiguration might entail.

By April 2023, I believed the whole team was ready to start discussing restructuring options to respond to the requested shifts. If we could reach consensus, this would then be presented to a UNICEF regional committee for their review and hopeful endorsement in September 2023, with our new programme launched in March 2024.

We began internal reflections more than a year ahead, knowing that managing the psychological aspects of a proposed staff reconfiguration would not be easy or resolved swiftly. I was also aware that many colleagues sensed a change was coming – restructuring had been mentioned several times before the Covid-19 pandemic suspended discussion for a couple of years.

After weeks of thorough analysis and intense deliberation across the whole team, we arrived at a proposal to trim 28 positions – 16 posts with the closure of our two zonal offices and 12 posts from our central office in Phnom Penh. Eight new posts were also proposed, so our net reconfiguration was a reduction from 105 to 85 positions. Four of the 28 posts were vacant at the time, which meant that we had 24 colleagues whose UNICEF careers were now on the line. These were the stats. But I was focused on the *souls*.

The proposed reduction was approved by the regional committee in September 2023. At the time of writing, of the 24 staff directly impacted by this change, only one had not secured new beginnings in terms of, for example, re-employment, consultancies, enrolment in further studies or retirement options. In the fourth quarter of 2023, UNICEF Cambodia's 'workplace culture score' – generated from an anonymous survey of all staff across 11 perception measures such as trust in senior management, effectiveness of internal communication, sense of belonging and so on – was two percentage points higher than the 2022 second quarter score (81 per cent versus 79 per cent). I had prepared myself for a *much lower* fourth quarter outcome considering the deep emotions we had all experienced throughout 2023. Undoubtedly this positive result was influenced by Covid-19 no longer being such a burden, and yes, we still had so much more to improve, but to have raised our workplace culture score just a little higher gave me hope.

How was this accomplished? Here are four essential ingredients (we used several others) that were combined and served as we led our needed change in a human way. OK, I'm a keen if very ordinary cook, so please forgive my analogy. We offer our recipe to other leaders and teams who wish to travel through organisational change a little more safely, smoothly and successfully.

1. Recognise and plan for the three phases of transition

If change is to occur, something old must be ended, something new must be started, and there is often a period or gap in between the old and the new that must be safely navigated.

The ending. A psychological transition's first phase is *the ending*, a time of letting go of old identities, earlier routines and previous realities, and for some, terminating association with their current community or organisation. Unless it's the end of a woeful relationship or of a calamitous event such as a conflict or pandemic, endings are generally uncomfortable and disliked. Especially when faced with the prospect of a staff reconfiguration, people will fear a variety of losses, for instance familiar ways of working, valued peer connections, the job or career that gave them dignity, financial security and the possibility of promotion, and even the ending of an era in their organisation's history.

It's not the change itself but *the giving up of old ways* – ways that in the past likely served the team and individuals well – that is most often resisted. Resistance manifests itself through tactics such as tacit non-engagement in and carefully disguised delays or subtle disruptions to the change process itself. More importantly, if this first phase is ignored or mishandled, the rest of the transition will become unmanageable and the proposed change will either end badly or be outright rejected. How a leader communicates is important throughout each transition phase but is critical during the ending.

The neutral zone. The second phase of a psychological transition is *the neutral zone* – an ambiguous phase that's neither the ending of the old nor the beginning of the new. Like a trapeze artist's leap between two suspended swings, this is a period of heightened uncertainty. If not led and managed well, teams can become polarised as they try to cross the gap, with some members wanting to desperately cling to the old ways (the first swing) while others want to jump ahead and grasp the future (the second swing).

A leader's task here is to help the team traverse this emotional chasm. Some leaders don't even realise the neutral zone exists and are surprised when their vision of a new beginning is painfully slow to materialise, or is patchy at best, or worse, never emerges at all. Others might reluctantly acknowledge the neutral zone but either try to rush through it or bypass it completely. Both ill-advised responses can trigger unnecessary staff turnover or severely compromise team morale and thus future performance.

But while the neutral zone is a period of risk and strain, it is also the space within which tremendous transformation can be organised and supported – think of the trapeze artist's graceful acrobatics high above a well-positioned safety net. For example, through individually tailored skills training, job shadowing, work exchanges, mentorships, coaching and so forth, earlier habits can be replaced with ones better suited to future requirements. New internal vacancies might arise during the neutral zone that offer chances for career advancement. Colleagues facing contract termination can be guided through the pros and cons of various options whether that be, for example, applying for one of these new vacancies, transferring to another organisation or taking up a fresh line of work such as becoming a consultant or an expert trainer, pursuing further studies, taking early or full retirement, or just a period of welcome rest.

In UNICEF Cambodia's case, we also used time in the neutral zone to form new cross-sectoral teams to analyse, brainstorm and prepare for the three recommended shifts that lay ahead. These teams set about collectively reflecting on lessons learned, reviewing and revising old procedures and stress-testing future teamwork arrangements and information flows. For example, we constituted a multidisciplinary sub-national working group that developed and prototyped new ways of engaging with provincial authorities, including actual meetings with provincial governors and their administrations. Other special groups started to assemble regularly to advance our promotion of disability inclusion and gender equality, adolescent empowerment and climate action, respectively. These new teams created novel relations among staff, built fresh identities and determined future priorities, replacing old dynamics, changing earlier images of what UNICEF Cambodia symbolises and parking previous priorities.

The neutral zone is always stressful, but if those leading and supporting the transition are well prepared, they can gradually turn the confusion and chaos into calmness and clarity. Again, in the wise words of Professor Bridges, 'Neutral zone creativity is the key to turning transition from a time of breakdown into a time of breakthrough' (Bridges 1991).

The new beginning. Transitions begin with an ending and end with a beginning. The final psychological phase of transition is *the new beginning* and to me it's akin to a fire's release of new seeds that have lain dormant on a forest floor. If the transition has been led gracefully up to this point, then the old has ended well, the ground across the neutral zone has been meticulously cultivated and enthusiasm for the future has been generated. It's time for a new beginning, a fresh start and, for some, perhaps an added sense of renewal, rebirth, a chance to reinvigorate, and even reframe their personal dream and collective purpose.

This final phase is when new identities are crafted, new mindsets emerge and new energies are tapped. Be forewarned, though. Some individuals can get stuck in the neutral zone, unsure and confused (and might still be quietly grieving for the losses they encountered during the ending). Until they complete their journey across the ambiguity of the neutral zone, the team as a whole cannot genuinely make a new beginning. So, careful monitoring, questioning, listening, coaching and emotional support can help to identify and encourage such individuals to safely transition out of this scary wasteland.

UNICEF Cambodia's new beginning was also a time for reprofiling some key staff positions, recruiting quickly to fill new vacancies, formalising our new multi-programme teams (which had started to form during the neutral zone, as mentioned above), reconfiguring how we would conduct programmatic visits to provinces (including with other partners such as line ministry representatives) and signing new implementation agreements with government departments, sister UN agencies and civil society organisations.

In mid-December 2023, we held an all-staff retreat to commemorate the ending, to acknowledge individual staff and teams who had used time in the neutral zone to begin to transform themselves and, significantly, to welcome the new beginning. The retreat imbued everyone with a collective sense of accomplishment, transformation and readiness, helping to reduce feelings of loss, sadness and uncertainty.

In our monthly all-staff meetings from that point on, we talked about the next couple of years being a period of 'trial and error' – setbacks are common when embarking upon any significant change. Mistakes would be made but not considered fatal lapses, simply fruitful learnings. And we kept emphasising the importance of maintaining open minds, remaining curious, challenging ourselves and co-creating new solutions as we forged new ways of working.

One of my favourite sayings is, 'We must build the plane while flying it, but fly we must!' Life seldom bestows upon us the metaphorical luxury to congregate upon a runway, pause and co-construct the 'perfect plane' before it takes off – for 'perfect plane' read perfect life, perfect relationship... family, proposal, project, programme, policy, partnership, investment, global agreement and so on. There are just too many variables, so many unknowns, far too much turbulence along the way. 'Change and disruption are the only constants.' (All right, you guessed it, another of my favourites.)

Of course, mindful sensemaking and using foresight (**Practice 15**) are among the hallmarks of effective leadership but should never stall decisive action when it is needed. *Yet decisive should never be divisive.* So, even though not every detail has been sorted out, if we equip ourselves with a growth mindset shaped by curiosity and humility, new beginnings can, and indeed, must launch *despite uncertainty*. I've always been inspired by archaeological evidence that Pacific island mariners, thousands of years ago, pushed their fragile wooden canoes from familiar shores and left home *forever*. That's courage.

On 29 March 2024, the last working day of our previous programme of cooperation, we had a final celebration with the entire 'old' UNICEF Cambodia team, including almost all of those who were leaving UNICEF for good – some colleagues sadly could not attend as they still had unused annual leave that they wanted to benefit from before their departure. Lessons, stories, appreciation, gratitude, photos, videos, memories, certificates and gifts were warmly exchanged. We announced the official closure of our two zonal offices. There was plenty of laughter and many tears, and that's as it should be.

I continued to offer one-on-one coaching and Marcela's HR team provided ongoing advice to a handful of colleagues who had to leave UNICEF that day. In the meantime, all our UNICEF Cambodia's sectoral units – education, child protection and so on – had some new recruits and therefore organised mini retreats to kick off their own new beginnings. I offered each unit their own six-month team coaching journey.

As we ventured forth, we continued to ask our partners and ourselves this central question, 'What else might help us further optimise the new beginning that we have embarked upon?' A final point to note here. Maintaining a healthy level of humble enquiry helps to avoid one crippling, complacent error often made in organisational change: 'Declaring victory too soon' (Kotter 2012). Planning for and praising small wins is vital. For example, on 15 May 2024, we celebrated the launch of our new sub-national approach together with Cambodia's minister of the interior and minister of education, youth and sports, alongside teams from six provinces – but respectfully, we all recognised the long journey of further learning that lay ahead.

2. Honour a leader's three transitional roles

Envisioning change, managing transition, healing emotions: these three roles interconnect.

Envisioning change involves encouraging multiple inputs from staff and stakeholders to help identify how an organisation can be better, for example, the three shifts requested of UNICEF Cambodia, and then to co-determine the vision of this change (ie our new business model). Ideally, this leadership role is a form of *slow cooking* wherein differing opinions are allowed to simmer and stir on low heat, freeing and deeply infusing diverse new flavours as well as gradually softening tough decisions. Well before I arrived, UNICEF Cambodia had started to ask both itself and partners reflective questions such as, 'Should our next offering be "business as before" or should we pivot, inflect, and be different?' And if the latter, 'What should we do that we have not done before?' Each individual unit slow-cooked these questions, releasing and testing variations of their own 'needed change'.† Over time these *enriched* and *tenderised* reflections were blended into an overall vision, which then needed to be clearly and constantly communicated throughout our transition.

A second leadership role is to help get everyone (those directly and indirectly affected) through the transition safely, smoothly and, hopefully, successfully. Starting with transition preparation: for example, facilitating (slow-cooking) team reflections on recommendations coming out of our previous programme's evaluation as well as discussing how to handle the transition's potential risks and to mobilise the resources needed to support the transition (eg training, counselling and coaching), then leading the team through the three psychological transition phases. And finally, leading them through post-transition.

This role is also educational. Your leadership team needs to ensure that all supervisors and every staff member appreciate the contrast between organisational change and the three phases of psychological transition it sets in motion. You need to explain the different emotions that each phase might stir up and some possible ways of handling them. Managers who understand what affected staff will likely go through are usually better able to relate to and support them. Once prepared for what each phase might entail, directly and indirectly affected staff are, in turn, less likely to attribute how they are feeling to the actual change, and instead focus on labelling and managing their *emotional reactions* to it.

The third leadership role is that of a resilient emotional healer. During many team meetings in Cambodia, I repeated that eliminating the stress of change would not be possible,

† I gratefully acknowledge Anirban for this 'slow cooking' analogy. For their vital role in UNICEF Cambodia's 2023 transition, I'd like to also make special mention of: Annie Nut, Erna Ribar, Hadrien Bonnaud, Hedy Ip, Hiroyuki Hattori, Lisa-Marie Ouedraogo-Wasi, Marianna Garofalo, Michele Paba, Peter Leth, Sophorn Som and Yu Liu.

but we could all try our best to minimise it. If organisational change involves 'downsizing', the focus must be on addressing the often unspoken but nevertheless emotionally debilitating impact of job loss – the *humiliation* felt by those whose posts are proposed for abolishment, *regardless* of whether they are moving on to another post, retiring and so on. This feeling of shame can arise because they perceive that their contribution just did not matter enough. Their darker thoughts might be, 'After all my years of faithful service, all the achievements I've played a part in, and now I'm being told that I no longer have the right skill set, that I'm no longer needed. Where's the recognition? Where's the loyalty to me?'

So, to replace any sense of humiliation with a sense of cherished legacy, it is vital that you share appreciation for the work they've been carrying out – being clear that it mattered a great deal. A graceful leader will transform every affected colleague's potential humiliation into feelings of continued worthiness – a form of *ennoblement*. In addition, many of us cannot openly cope with seeing others in pain or turmoil. A leader's emotional healing role often needs to include caring for those whose posts are not going to be lost but who are nonetheless traumatised by the layoff of long-time friends and colleagues.

3. Prepare for the emotional tsunami

Every organisational change is a neural threat that can trigger many waves of emotion, the impacts of which need to be mindfully managed and healed (Scarlett 2019). Some emotions occur in all three phases of transition, while others rise to the surface in one or two. Endings tend to bring anger, sadness, fear, self-absorption (people looking out for themselves, eg 'Will my job be next?'), distraction, disorientation, hopelessness and depression. Those whose jobs are not directly affected, including managers, can suffer guilt, remorse and regret. Neutral zones (after the ending and before the new beginning) can trigger confusion and increased stress at work as those who remain try to make sense of the change and perceived increase in work demands. New beginnings can excite and bring hope but also anxiety or fear of an uncertain future.

There are brilliant theories that can guide us, such as the five psychological stages of grief (Kübler-Ross & Kessler 2005). Yet the emotional sea swell triggered by organisational change is rarely experienced in a linear, staged fashion. Various passions, stirred up by each transition phase, can be felt all at once. But at least two things do hold steady and must be acknowledged. First, if not directly impacted by an organisational change, your personal world is not at stake and thus it's easy to think that others who are affected seem to be 'overreacting'. They are *not*. They are reacting quite *normally* to endings in *their* world. Their reactions are perfectly natural signs of grieving and require an empathetic ear, patience and compassion. In anticipation of this, we proactively invited Adam Storey, our regional staff counsellor (a chartered counselling psychologist) based in Bangkok, to visit our team twice during 2023 and who offered 'on call' virtual counselling sessions throughout the transition. We also gratefully received wise advice and regular emotional support from two other highly compassionate senior colleagues, our regional director, Debora Comini (a former UNICEF representative in Cambodia) and Dr Myo-Zin Nyunt, our deputy regional director.

Second, *not* managing the emotional rollercoaster of transition well can result in bitter ex-employees and an energetically depleted, downhearted workforce. And this brings me to another emotional wave that is important to prepare for – *the resurrection of old grievances*. Once a transition commences, you might find yourself dealing with earlier battles that may even predate your arrival.

I vividly recall sitting in a meeting with the UNICEF Cambodia team in February 2023. We were reaching the end of a two-day reflection on the three strategic shifts. In the final plenary discussion, one colleague pleaded that if any downsizing of our staff composition was deemed necessary, let it not be mishandled in the same 'inhuman way' as had been the case in a similar exercise conducted more than ten years before. It was Anirban who replied by reassuring our colleague and the team at large that any past experiences would be learned from, and if mistakes had been made, they would certainly not be repeated.

Sometimes the new change is not what people are reacting to but rather it stirs up feelings generated by earlier losses that were either unrecognised or given no time to fully heal. When I heard this colleague's plea, I silently vowed to try to set things right, recalling more inspirational words from Professor Bridges, 'It is never too late to become an organisation that manages its people well. For that reason, the old scar and the unresolved issue are great gifts. They represent opportunities for organisational enhancement' (Bridges 1991).

Transition leadership always focuses on where people currently are in psychological terms, helping them move forward (and occasionally backwards) through the three phases. Yes, every transition has a general 'end state' in mind – to ensure people land safely, smoothly and successfully – but every individual's and team's destination and even final shape is not precisely known in advance, and each phase is not followed in a linear fashion.

Leading a transition is to handle the *horizontal* flow of emotional *energy* with its own bumpy turbulence. Moving with this ebb and flow, your communication style should always be to mindfully connect with people at whatever psychological point they have reached – to meet them where they are. Never rush them towards the planned outcome, no matter how wonderful you think that'll be for them. I doubt a *chef de cuisine* in France would ever announce, '*Assez des entrées et du plat principal, passons aux desserts!*' ('Enough of the entrées and the main course, let's move to the desserts!'). No – a professional cook never coerces customers to relish what they're eating or forces them towards the dessert. Rather they patiently observe and note their customers' reactions *as* they eat *each* dish.

Likewise, employees need time to decide *for themselves* when they're ready to move forward and how good the change's outcome might be (Kotter & Cohen 2002).

4. Imagine you work in air traffic control

This final essential is *la crème de la crème* (the best of all ingredients), culminating in *la pièce de résistance* (the dish of dishes). For me, this ingredient makes or breaks psychological transition and thus organisational change, especially a downsize.

Allow me to recast you from lead chef to leader of an air traffic control tower. In this extreme role, you oversee the movement of all aircraft on the ground and in the air – the transfer of thousands of *souls* – within your designated airspace (usually surrounding an airport's control tower). Using sophisticated technology and two-way communication, your team of controllers must advise all pilots during takeoff and landing and track the position, altitude and speed of their aircraft as they travel across your sky, all the while updating them on various factors, such as weather conditions, that may affect their movement.

Your team is therefore responsible for the smooth flow of air traffic, the maintenance of safe distances between aircraft, the minimising of delays and congestion, and prevention of accidents. When emergencies strike, such as engine failures, mid-air medical situations and other critical events, you and your team must provide rapid, effective assistance. You must also maintain frequent contact with other control towers to ensure secure and efficient air traffic movement between different regions or airspaces. And finally, your team must document every detail of every aircraft's journey and communication, including flight plans, clearances and incidents. The stakes cannot be higher.

You and your team will need tremendous concentration skills; the ability to think rapidly, logically and clearly, sometimes under intense pressure; complex problem-solving skills; the sharpest of judgement and decision-making abilities; meticulous attention to details; excellent verbal communication skills; the ability to work as a cohesive team; capacity to accept criticism; top-notch time and spatial awareness; knowledge of transport methods and their costs and benefits; and a thorough understanding of all your ICT systems. All these competencies will need to be blended to provide uniquely tailored advice to every pilot within your airspace, allowing them to take off, traverse and land safely, smoothly and successfully.

We approached UNICEF Cambodia's transition imagining we worked in air traffic control. We had 24 colleagues directly affected by the approved restructure, whose personal world had literally been 'thrown up in the air' and who needed to regain a sense of control over their future. In essence, they were our 'pilots' and we wanted each to land safely, smoothly and successfully. Well before September 2023 (when the restructure was approved), Marcela and her team had already created a worksheet into which details for each of our likely 'pilots' were entered, allowing us, for example, to identify optimal retirement plans for those nearing certain ages and to monitor progress for all their job applications, within and beyond UNICEF, that we knew of or that they had informed us about.

We offered individually tailored support to exactly match each of their circumstances and regularly fine-tuned it as we tracked where they were in the transition. The types of support included career coaching, life coaching, interview coaching, counselling, job shadowing (eg many zonal office colleagues spent time with certain teams in Phnom Penh to gain more knowledge) and one- to two-week work exposures with a range of international non-government organisations who had agreed to help.

We issued personal recommendation letters and actively connected those who asked to our professional networks. The eight new posts and any new vacancies that arose were first advertised internally (only within UNICEF) so that those in abolished posts who wanted to apply were given the first chance. We fast-tracked all recruitments to potentially minimise breaks in service for any of our affected staff who had applied and were successful. If they were found suitable for a post, they were prioritised in the final selection. Support also comprised a series of HR clinics on topics such as writing CVs, preparing for interviews and understanding your pension (offered to all our staff).

When it came to the highly emotional moment that our 24 colleagues would receive UNICEF's official notice announcing their formal separation, instead of emailing or posting it, we hand delivered their letter, sitting quietly and privately with each of them whether in Siem Reap, Kratie or Phnom Penh. These were personal endings.

Change can be made easier if leaders are attuned to the suffering and attend to any affected colleague with respect, care, support, sensitivity, transparency and fairness. Your ultimate responsibility in leading teams through organisational change is to make sure that all those whose worlds are thrown up in the air, including staff who are indirectly threatened by the change, land safely, smoothly and successfully. Only one of our 24 pilots remains in flight. He's on our radar and we're in regular contact.

A word of caution

A leader who helps to heal emotions can create not just a mentally healthy workforce but also one that possesses more cohesion, collaboration and sustainable relationships among team members (Jit ct al 2017). Having an orientation towards emotional healing has been proven to result in more committed, emotionally balanced and motivated colleagues who, in turn, can enhance a team's or organisation's overall performance. Indeed, some have observed that emotional healing is among the most influential assets of effective leadership (Sturnick 1998).

But a word of caution – this key graceful leadership practice runs the risk of exposing you to 'compassion fatigue' (Brown 2021). Graceful leaders need to help heal emotions in order to ease stress and prevent anguish in others but must do so in such a way that they prevent other people's problems from literally seeping into their own lives and homes. Thus, self-compassion is vital if we are to minimise this very real risk (**Practice 1**). Moreover, it's sometimes leaders themselves who would benefit enormously from emotional healing (**Practices 1, 2** and **3**) in their efforts to exhibit more grace in their leadership.

Use humour and play

I think *too many* leaders take themselves *too seriously*. Showing your humorous, playful side helps others to bond with you and to recognise your humanity (Hughes & Avey 2009). Perhaps a team is already happy, but I still always ask myself, 'How can I transform a team's mood when I enter the room?'

Here, I focus on two leadership elements that can bring joy to work: humour and play.

Humour

The benefits of humour at work

Our workdays can be humourless, often with grinding, serious goals hanging over us. But levity can lighten our load. Research on the effects of moderators (eg the characteristics of leaders and followers such as age, gender, etc), contextual factors (eg culture) and the impact of 'leader humour' is still evolving (Rosenberg et al 2021). Nevertheless, studies conducted over the past two decades have proven that 'leader humour' – conceptualised as an interpersonal communication resource (a form of socioemotional exchange currency) – can, among other benefits, advance wellbeing and psychological empowerment, improve morale, boost engagement and cohesiveness, facilitate interpersonal communication, reduce interpersonal tension, enhance social support, psychological safety and organisational citizenship, build trust and commitment, increase the desire for future interaction and catalyse individual and team performance and productivity, ultimately improving top-/bottom-line results such as profit margins and societal impacts (Robert 2017).

Leaders *with a sense of humour* and *who express it* during interactions with others (even if only a little and even if they're not that 'funny' as judged by co-workers) are more respected and admired, seen as more confident and competent, considered to have clearer communication, viewed as more pleasant, supportive and friendlier to work with, engender greater job satisfaction and are perceived to be more motivational than leaders who are humourless (Bitterly et al 2016).

Use of humour has been proven to boost individual as well as team creativity and spark divergent thinking, helping us to see the big picture (**Practice 15**) (Lehmann-Willenbrock & Allen 2014). As behavioural scientist Professor Jennifer Aaker and corporate strategist Naomi Bagdonas, in their intelligently funny book *Humour, Seriously* (2020), declare, 'Humour encourages a kind of mental gymnastics that reveals connections, patterns and interpretations we'd previously missed. It widens our perspective, makes us feel psychologically safe, and creates fertile ground for creativity to thrive.'

The use of positive, good-natured humour can be a powerful coping tool when you must navigate critical crossroads or get through stressful periods, but negative, mean-spirited humour can make matters worse (Samson & Gross 2012). Healthy humour can help when you need to give tough feedback, make decisions that might negatively impact others and provide much-needed motivation during tense times (Plester 2009). Likewise, you might need to diffuse tension or move forward in a negotiation and in such situations, I always think about how Abraham Lincoln responded to Stephen Douglas in the famous 1858 Lincoln–Douglas debates in the US. At one point, Douglas accused Lincoln of being 'two faced', to which Lincoln replied,

'Honestly, if I were two faced, would I be showing you this one?' In some of the toughest low points I have encountered across my international postings, recounting a joke, recalling a comedic scene from a TV show or film or telling a funny story would lighten the stress myself and my team were under, even if for a few minutes, allowing us to re-gather, re-energise and refocus our attention and effort.

There's a neurochemical foundation to these leader humour impacts. Laughter reduces cortisol (the stress hormone) in our bloodstream by inducing more desirable brain chemicals, for example, dopamine, endorphins, oxytocin and serotonin (Dell 2019). Dopamine boosts learning, motivation, alertness and concentration, while endorphins trigger pleasure. As we've noted already, oxytocin increases our sense of bonding, while serotonin brightens our mood.

Use humour mindfully

Dr Senem Guney, former vice president of Press Ganey, together with Harvard University professor and Press Ganey's chief medical officer Dr Thomas Lee, conducted an extensive analysis of 988,161 survey responses received from patients regarding their interactions with doctors and nurses across the United States during 2020. Using artificial intelligence and natural language processing, 1,270,000 insights were extracted from these responses, with the use of humour by health staff appearing repeatedly.

The analysis demonstrated that the positive impacts of humour included building connections between patients and clinicians, helping patients to feel seen, heard and not alone in their suffering. But crucially, the researchers found that levity's positive impacts *only* occurred when clinicians exhibited authentic and reliable courtesy, respect, empathy, compassion, kindness, helpfulness, attentiveness, patience, pleasantness and emotional support. In short, the use of humour amplified these positive, caring signals. When patients perceived an absence of these behaviours, the use of humour fell flat or, worse, was said to 'add insult to injury'. Senem and Thomas observe, 'Humour offered for no purpose other than providing a distraction is often irritating. Humour in the absence of obvious courtesy and respect can be taken as callous disregard' (Guney & Lee 2021).

Using humour in professional interactions always presents risks and requires mindful communication (**Practice 6**). Research by Dr Brad Bitterly of the University of Michigan's Ross School of Business and Professor Alison Brooks of the Harvard Business School confirms that 'failed humour is quite costly for leaders, making them even worse off than serious, humourless leaders who don't attempt jokes at all. Finding the balance between a benign violation [using humour to show that it's OK to step outside of social norms] and an extreme violation [harming others] can be tricky – even professional comedians routinely face criticism for overstepping – and it takes skill to get it right' (Bitterly & Brooks 2020).

Belittling others must be avoided at all costs, and you need to be careful to avoid committing microaggressions. In one of my duty stations (not mentioned here to respect anonymity), the team was debating flexible work options. One staff member with a young child mentioned that such options would be very useful given their parenting situation. Just for a mindless moment, I lost my sense of compassion and instead replied with what I intended as a comic response. I said, chuckling, 'I agree but we can't just approve this based on _____'s [name of staff member] situation.' The team debate continued but as I scanned the room, I noticed the staff member's eyes had filled with tears. I was gutted. Straight after the meeting, I invited the staff member to a quiet space in our office and profusely apologised for my humour failure. Note to self – *use humour mindfully*.

Generating more humour in the workplace

So, with due mindfulness, how can leaders create more humour in the workplace, even when times are difficult? The first step is to observe and learn about the types and meanings of humour that usually already exist in most workplaces, often fulfilling several functions and reflecting the social architecture as well as political dynamics of a team or organisation. With this understanding, there may be no need to try to 'increase' the use of humour but rather to attempt to channel the use of existing humour in constructive directions. In his seminal book *The Psychology of Humour* (2007), Rod Martin, former professor of psychology at the University of Western Ontario, cautions, 'Improving the quality of humour in the workplace may require efforts to change the overall organisational culture and power structures rather than simply having workers attend a workshop where they learn to tell funny stories and engage in silly activities.'

Professor Martin and co-researchers (2003) proposed four styles in terms of how humour is used both interpersonally and intrapersonally in people's daily lives: affiliative, self-enhancing, aggressive and self-defeating:

+ **Affiliative humour** is the inclination to 'say funny things, to tell jokes and to engage in spontaneous witty banter to amuse others, to facilitate relationships and to reduce interpersonal tensions.' *Self-deprecating humour*, in which one 'conveys an honest and humble look at oneself', is a form of *affiliative humour* and not to be confused with *self-defeating humour* (see below), which can convey a 'depressive and negative view of the self'.
+ **Self-enhancing humour** means to hold 'a generally humorous outlook on life, a tendency to be frequently amused by the incongruities of life, and to maintain a humorous perspective even in the face of stress or adversity'.
+ **Aggressive humour** is 'the use of sarcasm, teasing, ridicule, derision, "put-down" or disparagement humour'.
+ **Self-defeating humour** is used to 'amuse others by doing or saying funny things at one's own expense as a means of ingratiating oneself or gaining approval, allowing oneself

to be the butt of others' humour, and laughing along with others when being ridiculed or disparaged'.

Professor Jennifer Aaker and Naomi Bagdonas (2020) have added to this list of humour styles:

+ **stand-up**, which is to be 'bold, irreverent and unafraid to ruffle a few feathers for a laugh'
+ **sweetheart**, which is to be 'earnest, understated and use humour to lighten the mood'
+ **sniper**, which is to be 'edgy, sarcastic, nuanced – a master of the unexpected dig'
+ **magnet**, which is to be 'expressive, charismatic and easy to make laugh'.

Sweethearts and magnets should be cautious not to damage their reputations by being overly self-deprecating, while stand-ups and snipers must be careful not to be divisive or insulting.

After recognising and understanding what types of humour are already being used, the next step is to get to know your own leader humour style and find as many ways to use it as appropriate. Jennifer and Naomi reassuringly observe that you 'don't have to be a class clown or a comedian to be funny.'

Graceful leaders who express humour are likely to do so in several ways depending on context and after getting to know how their team members use and respond to humour. My experience in many cultural contexts is that people generally appreciate any style of humour apart from, of course, the aggressive kind, which is normally hurtful and offensive. I am personally drawn to an *affiliative/sweetheart* humour style.

I've never been tech-savvy and one of my stories to generate group laughter in a self-deprecating way is the time we ran a simulated earthquake exercise in Nepal. On 30 July 2013, we deployed to several large freight containers located at the back of UN House in Kathmandu. I had a small desk with a laptop and printer set up in one of them. The frenetic four-hour exercise involved responding to a barrage of emails (one almost every 60 seconds) sent to our team by one of our regional emergency experts. Each email contained new information about the imaginary earthquake's unfolding impacts, including aftershocks, the changing status of our response supplies and the actions of humanitarian partners. Simulating that mobile phone towers were damaged, we could only communicate with each other using handheld two-way radios and when team discussions were needed at critical points in the exercise, we would gather in an open space between the containers.

I needed to print several of the emails but each time I hit print, nothing happened. After several hapless attempts to check the laptop–printer connection, I radioed our IT specialist. He ran around to my container and stood beside me. 'Did you check if the printer has paper in it?' he asked innocently. Errrrr... We both laughed and with a ream of paper now loaded, the urgent emails began printing. Ever since, I have used this story to help IT teams understand what's the most they can expect from me.

Dr Brad Bitterly and Professor Alison Brooks (2020) offer a short but handy guide for how and when to use humour as a tool of leadership. They conclude with these inspirational words, 'Be quick to laugh and smile. Delight in the absurdity of life and in the jokes you hear. A life devoid of humour is not only less joyful – it's also less productive and less creative, for you and for those around you. Abundant benefits await those who view humour not as an ancillary organisational behaviour but as a central path to status and flourishing at work.'

Play
What is play at work?
In his riveting book, *Play* (2009), medical doctor and psychiatrist Stuart Brown defines play as a captivating, outwardly pointless amusement that nevertheless induces self-motivating happiness and allows one to suspend time and self-consciousness. We're not just talking about setting up a ping-pong table in the office

common area (though this can be a good start). And while teams and organisations can organise 'play activities' such as team-building games during working hours (which is also great), the main idea here is to consider play at work, not as an activity, but as a *liberating state of mind*.

Play at work can bring all the benefits of humour mentioned above – indeed, one usually feeds off the other – but also a sense of competence, feelings of unity, a team's sense of solidarity, a decreased sense of hierarchy, more sustained social relationships and reduced workplace fatigue and boredom (though more research is needed on this linkage) (Petelczyc et al 2018). Importantly, play at work has a reciprocal relationship with psychological safety. Play can boost psychological safety, and psychological safety can allow the full benefits of play to be realised (**Practice 6**) (Plester & Lloyd 2023). Just like calmness, playfulness can be contagious. I have found that when I am playful, those around me reciprocate with playfulness and that helps us keep matters in perspective and be less defensive. When a leader displays cheerful, buoyant behaviours, colleagues are far more likely to warm to, trust and help the leader.

Play and the brain

It was the late Professor Jaak Panksepp, in a field of research he termed 'affective neuroscience', who showed that play stimulated neurotrophic factors influencing nerve growth in various parts of our brain – literally play sculpts and integrates different parts of our brain thereby improving our memory, attention, emotional regulation and problem-solving skills (Panksepp 2004). Play can also build resilience by allowing us to try things out in a safe way that would otherwise be way too threatening. Literally as I write, our two husky pups, Boopy and Tokyo, are demonstrating this last point as they 'play fight' their way around the living room. Playing our way through imaginary dangers can increase our calmness and resolve when we face real threats, heightening our ability to meet these actual challenges with more grace and composure.

Play and creativity

Because most play takes us to an imaginative world while we are also firmly grounded in reality, we can create new cognitive combinations. Play can help us see the world again through the eyes of a child, helping us to unlearn, gain new perspectives and brainstorm crazy ideas that might just provide breakthroughs (**Practice 15**). It's a well-known fact that many tech companies such as LinkedIn, Google, Facebook, IBM and Sony ensure space and time for employees to play together in activities such as team games, artwork, quizzes, improvisation, skits, karaoke and puzzles, or have space and time to do their 'own thing' unrelated to organisational goals. This 'freedom for fun' can be re-energising as well as trigger some outstanding inventiveness.

Work joyfully, play joyfully

So my invitation is to seek out ways to foster more play at work and thereby liberate our creative minds. It can be as easy as featuring short, playful bonding exercises at the start of team meetings to stimulate the creative right hemisphere of people's brains. For example, inviting each team member to quickly say two things that are true and one thing that is false about themselves, and then seeing if teammates can guess the lie, and other similar quick creative games to kick off the group work. Even asking something as simple as 'Since our last meeting, what positive things have occurred in your life?' can lift spirits. Begin by asking your team, 'What adjustments could we make to foster a more creative and playful work environment?' Consider organising a space in the office where people can step away from tasks to think, socialise and literally play.

Some say, 'Work hard, play hard.' But why be hard on yourself and on others, and through hardness, perhaps cause harm? I prefer to say, 'Work joyfully, play joyfully.'

During our staff retreat in March 2013, the UNICEF Nepal team volunteered to repair and renovate Amarsingh Madhyamik Vidyalaya School in Pokhara. Besides being a form of community service (**Practice 14**), it was a fun way to build team spirit. We split ourselves into smaller work 'crews' composed of colleagues who rarely got to interact with each other back in the office. We had a crew who painted classrooms, a gardening crew, a crew who cooked lunch for the other crews, and so on. I was a member of the gardening crew, but you may have guessed that already.

Practice 12

Embody generosity and gratitude

Back in 2007–2008, the global financial crisis was the most serious economic disaster since the Great Depression of 1929. Predatory lenders in several countries had been targeting low-income homebuyers. At the same time, global financial institutions had taken disgraceful investment risks. Finally, when the US housing bubble burst, a 'perfect storm' emerged, dispersing negative impacts across the entire world.

In many countries, UNICEF began actively tracking the social consequences of the crisis. For the Pacific islands in particular, these were compounded by recent shocks from sharply rising food and fuel prices, not to mention the very real threats and impacts of climate change. At the time, I was chief of policy, advocacy, planning and evaluation, affection-ately known as 'PAPE' (pronounced 'PAP-Y') within the UNICEF Pacific team. Based in Fiji, our economic analysis and advocacy support covered 14 sovereign island states.

My small team, with input from several other UN agencies, rapidly designed and conducted a series of 'pulse' surveys to track in real time how a sample of families in several Pacific island countries were coping – or not – with the economic crisis

(UNICEF 2010). We then relayed this information to national authorities to help shape their early responses, while the Pacific situation was also fed into global monitoring reports (UN Global Pulse 2010). There was still uncertainty about the scope and impact of the economic crisis in the region, but history made it clear that children and women in many island states would likely be among those most severely affected.

The real-time data and personal stories being gathered were grim. But I firmly believed that the region still had a short window of opportunity – due to lag time in the transmission of global impacts to the Pacific – to prepare robust responses to the crisis through, for example, readjusting fiscal and monetary policy, creating an enabling environment in which alternative livelihood opportunities could be found, and developing immediate and longer-term social safety net solutions.

I recalled UNICEF's instrumental advocacy work during the 1980s world recession (one of the ways I came to learn about Jim Grant), captured in the unforgettable study 'Adjustment with a Human Face', which proved how welfare policies can and must become part of national planning even, and especially, when economies are in crisis (Cornia et al 1987). Having consulted with various experts and taking our cue from the 6–7 January 2009 conference held in Singapore on the impact of the economic crisis on children in East Asia, I proposed to the then UNICEF Pacific representative, Dr Isiye Ndombi – another amazingly graceful leader we'll meet again in **Practice 15** – that we should call for a high-level gathering specifically for the island states in order to put the evidence and possible policy options in front of all Pacific governments to contemplate before it was too late. I also suggested that instead of focusing just on children, the debate should be on protecting all vulnerable population groups. Isiye concurred and encouraged me to take the next step.

To set all of this in motion, I feverishly set about writing an advocacy piece, inviting the impressively wise David Abbott, from the UN Development Programme (UNDP) Pacific Centre, and Alastair Wilkinson, from the UN Economic and Social Commission for Asia and the Pacific's (UNESCAP) Pacific Operations Centre, to join me in this bold enterprise (Parks 2009).

A small UN team was simultaneously formed to organise every detail of the conference's preparation, the event itself and the post-conference follow-up, co-led by myself and Carol Flore-Smereczniak, then UNDP Pacific Centre's regional millennium development goal specialist (another wonderful human being).

A short while later, the government of Vanuatu graciously agreed to host the conference and to propose the idea at the 40th Forum for Pacific Island Leaders held in Cairns, Australia, on 5–6 August 2009. The conference aimed to identify effective policy measures and practical responses that Pacific countries could implement to lessen the unwelcome impacts of the global economic crisis, with the longer-term goal of building sustained resilience to future shocks. The Pacific Islands Forum unanimously endorsed Vanuatu's proposal.

Momentum built. Media interest grew. Evidence of initial impacts of the crisis alongside important governance advice began to be transmitted throughout the Pacific. In short, well before the conference was even held, vital conversations about how to protect the most vulnerable had commenced. I know that for some, such convened meetings can be seen as just 'political posturing' platforms rather than a means for garnering decisive action. But, if arranged well, part of the importance of such gatherings is that through the groundwork and mobilisation of partners, numerous, less easily obtained opportunities are created that can galvanise societies and governments. The conference in and of itself is not the departure point nor the endpoint. It is the *journey* before and after that counts way, way more. And this is what happened.

As conference preparations gathered apace, more and more international and regional organisations came on board, refining and amplifying key messages and crucial advice. These included financial institutions, foundations, universities, national and regional bodies, NGOs and UN agencies. With every contact, with every single conversation, vital guidance and ideas were being exchanged, spreading further via their own networks and offices throughout the Pacific region.

Finally, the week of the conference arrived. UNICEF sponsored a pre-conference on 8–9 February 2010 in Port Vila, comprising Pacific youth delegates from across the region to share their views of how the global economic crisis was impacting young people and what they wanted done. Their recommendations were brought forward to the main conference held in Port Vila and attended by the leaders and senior ministers from 13 Pacific island nations and numerous other countries across the world. The top official for the UN was Helen Clark, UNDP's administrator (and former prime minister of New Zealand). Country delegations came from 16 Pacific island nations.

The conference reinforced ongoing country responses and laid out ambitious, forward-looking national agendas for action as well as regional and international agency commitments (UNESCAP 2010).

Many within UNICEF asked me why this conference was not branded with our logo. Why did we opt instead for the generic UN logo? My answer was threefold. First, the evidence showed that this crisis was affecting all age groups, so the conference had to focus on but also go beyond just children across the Pacific. Second, through our negotiation and advocacy, many UN agencies had joined forces; the conference thus, and quite rightly, had become a whole-of-UN effort. Third, it was already clear to many which UN agency had proposed and moved this idea forward from the very beginning. If this was going to be transformed from a conference to a regional movement to protect the vulnerable, we wanted everyone to feel part of something greater than just their own government or agency. And in the process of committing to post-conference action packages, I wanted everyone to gain equal credit.

I'm the first to agree that many times UNICEF's visibility is indeed vital to ensure the voices of children are heard. But in my view, UNICEF both successfully placed children at the centre of Pacific responses to the 2007–2008 global economic crisis while also gaining credibility, not through our branding, but through the gratitude and space we gave to others. Sometimes *we gain credibility through our invisibility*. My belief was grounded in the fact that there was room for everybody to play a role, that it didn't matter who proposed and organised the conference. If it was a success, we would all share in its success. UNICEF would shine if everyone else shined.

What I learned from this was to foster an attitude of abundance. Be an energiser. Generously give others space and help them to achieve. Then celebrate with and acknowledge them when they do.

A mindset of abundance

Embodying gratitude is gracious. You are not in a contest with colleagues to see who can achieve the most or grab the recognition. Graceful leaders give others credit; they don't try to claim it for themselves. Over the years, I've witnessed many colleagues lamenting that they feel underappreciated, even totally unappreciated. I don't know about you, but I have never heard anyone exclaim, 'Damn, I'm feeling too appreciated!' Everyday expressions of thanks can have powerful positive impacts on the performance of others and teams as well as on *yourself*.

So, when things go well, *look out of the window* (rather than in the mirror) to acknowledge others. Ask colleagues frequently, even daily, 'What skills did you gain today that you didn't have yesterday? What challenges are you carefully studying to overcome in the future? What aspects of your work make you feel proud?' And then thank them publicly for their efforts. For some, it may be the only gracious words they hear for weeks on end.

Embodying gratitude also creates wonder and joy for both the giver and receiver. There is clear evidence that gratitude is vital for individual and collective flourishing. As University of California professor of psychology, Dr Robert Emmons (2016) writes, 'Whether springing from the glad acceptance of another's thoughtfulness, appreciation of the splendour of nature, recognition of the good things in life, or from countless other magical moments, gratitude enhances nearly all spheres of our lives. These effects are sustainable and quantifiable.'

Short, personal, handwritten notes of appreciation can be amazingly motivational. When people receive appreciation – a 'thank you' for their efforts – at the team or organisational level, gratitude can enhance employee engagement, job satisfaction, motivation, sense of connectedness and retention, while at the individual level, being thanked releases dopamine (the feel-good neurotransmitter) and can increase personal wellness, self-esteem and optimism, improve sleep habits and metabolism and lessen stress, for *both* the recipient and thanksgiver (**Practice 1**).

I'm constantly scanning the workplace to acknowledge outstanding effort. Complimenting people on every single task can have the reverse effect of lowering the quality of performance, since some might start slipping into comfort zones from where the minimum of effort still receives a leader's praise. *Give praise where praise is due.* So, regularly pause and ask yourself questions such as, 'Who am I appreciative of or thankful for today? What recent contribution or work by others am I grateful for? In what ways has my team earned my admiration? How best can I demonstrate my gratefulness to others?' And ask others, 'What are you grateful for? What's going well right now? How would you like me to appreciate your efforts?'

When things go badly, *look in the mirror* (rather than out the window) and big-heartedly accept responsibility (plus have courage to celebrate these learnings). Such self-examination and admission can challenge even the most stable, humble of egos (**Practices 2** and **3**) so make it easier on yourself by soliciting feedback early by asking, for example, 'How can I do better next time?' or 'What am I not doing to support you?'

Gratiosity

Big-heartedly share your positive energy. Remember that generosity and gratitude propagate – the more you give of yourself and acknowledge others, the more others are inspired to be generous of themselves and appreciative of others. Finally, it's worth noting that this combination of gratitude and generosity – *gratiosity,* as coined by international resilience expert Dr Taryn Marie Stejskal (2023) – is an empirically proven element of how to develop resilience in our lives.

As I have noted several times, building up resilience (the capacity to withstand, thrive in or swiftly recover from adversity) is vital for leaders. By demonstrating beneficence and gratefulness through compassion, kindness, coaching and playfulness, resilience itself can become contagious, adding to the benefits of graceful leadership.

Help people transform

When I took up the role of UNICEF Nepal deputy representative in May 2010, it was the most senior leadership position that I had held so far. I felt blessed. Not only did UNICEF Nepal have at its helm one of the most graceful leaders I've ever met – the representative, Gillian Mellsop – but the team of some 180 staff were recognised as among the most talented and committed. I set about my new leadership role with passion.

But there was a problem. While I had previously been a *manager* of large teams, I had yet to be a *leader*. So, when team members started to come to my office to share the problems or bottlenecks they were experiencing at work, the manager and earlier technician in me wanted to always offer my solutions. They presented a problem; I would 'fix it' for them. Then they would leave, seemingly happy that they had been handed a solution. As word spread, the number of colleagues coming to see me increased. Within a few weeks of my arrival in Kathmandu, every day I would reach my office and there would be a small queue of staff eagerly waiting to get my advice. And then there was the increasing volume of emailed requests for help.

I began to worry. I couldn't sustain this continuous demand for 'fixing' problems. I was being hijacked by and unable to tame my 'advice monster', thereby falling into what Michael Bungay

Stanier later labelled as 'the advice trap' (Bungay Stanier 2020). My wholehearted efforts to help (and offer probably not very useful advice) did not help that much. I was simply rescuing people and simultaneously making them feel incapable. And I was becoming overwhelmed. Something had to change.

I was inspired by the quote attributed to author Peter Lerangis, 'A problem is merely a solution waiting to be found.' So, I came up with what I thought was a neat move, one that would instantly reduce the queues and the emails, thereby allowing me to focus on advocating with the government on behalf of children, strategising, mobilising resources, managing partnerships, preparing for emergencies, coordinating interventions, innovating and all the other tasks a senior UNICEF leader should be concentrating on.

My 'plan' was simple. I would explain to colleagues that instead of bringing me their problems individually or in team meetings, I wanted them to first think through how *they* would go about solving them and then, if they still needed to, share their *solutions* with me. I said I'd be delighted to discuss the pros and cons of any options or ways forward that they had worked out by themselves. I even changed the layout of my office, moving my desk against the wall so that there was no physical barrier between myself and colleagues from behind which I could continue to be perceived as the 'boss with all the answers' and thus still be tempted to nobly hand out *my* advice. Now I could sit alongside colleagues rather than opposite them, making all of us more at ease when I asked questions as they went about explaining *their* advice.

I started to understand the basics of coaching, though back then, I didn't know to call what I was doing 'coaching'. Yes, when people came to see me or I sat in team meetings, I often had some solutions of my own in mind, but I trained myself to suspend my advice or decisions, first by actively listening to what others were telling me, and second, by using what I later realised were coaching questions to get them to reflect and think more deeply.

Sometimes I blissfully had no ideas, so the coaching conversations flowed way more easily since I could just remain curious and 'in the moment', relying on my attentive listening skills (**Practice 6**). If I had ideas and they did not come up in the conversation, I learned to do one of three things depending on the flow of the discussion and the urgency of the situation.

First, after listening to the presented solutions, I might ask, 'What else could you do?' or 'What other options could there be?' or 'What else might be possible?' or 'Is there anything else that we may not have thought of here?' If I was immediately answered with more solutions, then we would continue the conversation until my colleague or the team had landed on their optimal choice, and we would agree to reconvene later to check in on progress. My ideas had not been needed.

Second, if they said, 'Perhaps, but allow me/us more time to think about that,' I was happy and would simply reserve my ideas for another coaching conversation to let my colleagues first try out or work further on their solution. 'Great, pop back to see me once you've tried your current solutions or have some more thoughts.'

And third, if they said, 'No, I/we don't think there are any other options,' I would ask, 'I respect that you know more than me on this, but I have some suggestions. Would you like me to share them?' Usually, the answer was a 'yes' but having just role-modelled the utility of questioning, I would encourage colleagues to push back on my ideas and invite them to ask me questions.

Despite having disseminated my new plan, I'd still be directly (and still am) requested for my advice. For example, colleagues would ask, 'What do you think I should do?' or 'What would you advise in terms of next steps?' and so on. The temptation to give advice was palpable. Mindfully reminding myself of why I needed to avoid the advice trap, I would deploy this kind of response, 'I appreciate the question and do have some suggestions, but before I share them, I'm curious to know what's your thinking on this?' Invariably, colleagues would indeed have their own ideas, to which I then would ask, 'And what else?' And only after squeezing out every last ounce of their creative juice would I proffer my suggestions. 'I'm not sure if this will help, but here are my thoughts...' or 'I may have misunderstood here, but how about...?' or 'Perhaps there's another way of viewing this...'

And this is not a practice that I restricted to face-to-face interactions. Emails, WhatsApp and Microsoft Teams instant messaging became opportunities for coachable moments. For example, I even reduced email responses to a sentence that can fit into the subject line, using simply a coaching question or invitation for comment such as 'What do you think?' or 'Any thoughts?'

I subsequently discovered that there's also a neuroscience angle to this. By encouraging enquiry rather than issuing instructions, coaching significantly boosts the likelihood that our brain's hippocampus encodes the self-learning as a longer-term memory. This is because, once we find solutions on our own, we retain them more effectively than when someone else provides them (Brann 2022).

But back then, I just naïvely thought that by challenging staff to only consult with me once they had identified fixes, workarounds or solutions, followed by all my curious questioning once they had, would decrease the number of colleagues corresponding with me or visiting my office. It increased the numbers. *Empowerment is addictive.*

The graceful power of coaching as a leader

So, it was in Nepal that I came to understand the graceful power of coaching as a leader, and just accepted the need to be hyper-efficient in my task prioritisation, time allocation and energy management *to make space for coaching*. In short, I began *hyperfocusing* (**Practice 1**) so that I could be *more generous* to others with my coaching energy and time.

I also learned that transforming 'problem presenters' into 'solutions seekers' is incredibly ennobling, engaging and empowering – for co-workers and for leaders who coach. The more task efficient I became, the more energy I discovered I had for coaching. In turn, the more I coached, the more energy I found I had to be task hyperfocused. Indeed, in the process, I had transformed my own manager's problem into a leader's solution. And these are uplifting feelings that we all want to have more and more of.

When you genuinely listen to, creatively debate and validate the ideas of others, it can be tremendously transformative for *everyone* involved. It's not about *never* offering advice. It's about not rushing in to offer answers (often when we don't yet know the real problem); instead, it's about leaning into curiosity, getting better at inviting colleagues to create their own solutions and enjoying the experience of helping others self-transform. Track yourself over a day or so and see if you can work out how much time you are investing in questioning from a place of curiosity versus advising from a position of authority – this is your 'ask-to-tell' ratio, and the more it is in favour of asking, the more likely it is that you're embracing a coaching mindset.

Graceful leaders resist the common organisational tendency to assess for talent and then, only post-assessment, provide investments such as executive coaching to only the few labelled as 'having potential'. Instead, graceful leaders assume that anyone can reach their full potential if motivated enough. Such leaders constantly keep an eye out for those who show passion, a strong work ethic and perseverance – in my view, these are the telltale signs of potential. They then invest energy in coaching and mentoring as well as providing other growth opportunities – such as leadership challenges, alternative workplace experiences or staff exchanges, job shadowing, short-term job swapping (for example, while in Fiji, Gillian spent a day as her driver, who spent his day in her role as the UNICEF representative), and stretch assignments – so that anyone, if they are enthusiastic and diligent, can maintain and even increase their motivation, and thereby their performance towards fulfilling their potential.

Coaching as a leader starts by getting to know co-workers' professional or personal goals (**Practice 5**) and then, based upon this understanding, helping them to accomplish those aspirations through using short but frequent coaching conversations. At its core, helping others to grow and succeed is about aiding these individuals to become self-actualised, emboldened, reaching their fullest human potential. Graceful leaders – givers – tend to see the potential in everyone (**Practice 9**) and will do what they can to help others fulfil their potential. This 'growing mindset' (an interest in seeing others bloom or thrive) can become a self-fulfilling prophecy, a virtuous cycle.

Ego-driven leaders – takers – rarely see the potential in and thereby transform others. Anyone with ability represents a threat to disgraceful leaders. This in turn creates a vicious cycle whereby the leader's distrust can constrain the development and motivation of those being led, making them resentful of the leader, which further amplifies the leader's distrust.

Coaching leader principles

In his 2007 upbeat book, *Unleashed!*, executive leadership coach Gregg Thompson puts forward a simple yet, for me, compelling frame of reference for what coaching as a leader entails – one that I have increasingly embraced over the years. His 'Great Expectations Model' – based on the premise that we should both assume the best *in* others and desire the best *for* others (**Practice 9**) – outlines three interdependent principles that leaders can adopt to be more 'coach-like', principles that take them beyond the customary list of leadership skills into the realm of professional coaching – to become a *coaching leader*.

Principle 1: Earn the right to coach

This right does not come with leadership title nor even with coach training and accreditation (though the latter certainly helps). The right to be a coaching leader is earned in two parts. First, we must have an *unquenchable passion* to help 'coachees' (individuals and teams), or as Gregg and co-writer Susanne Biro more fittingly name them, 'the talents'. Second, the talents need to *choose to include us* in their effort to transform. We must be someone they want to be coached by – to invite into their lives.

Coaching can be a 'bumpy road' so their choice matters and will depend on several factors, including whether our behaviour as a leader is *consistent* with the values we espouse – the talent does not need to agree with the leader's values but must witness the following:

✦ consistency
✦ whether we are *authentic* – have unswerving honesty and integrity
✦ whether we possess *self-esteem* – being comfortable in our own skin with no trace of ego, even harbouring the hope that those we coach can reach higher levels of performance than we achieved ourselves
✦ we have *noble intentions* to help – not a shallow need to feel useful, but a deep motivation, even devotion, to assist others to become ever better humans through self-discovery, to genuinely care about *their* success.

Principle 2: A perfect partnership

Having earned the right to coach, this second principle focuses on how a coaching leader begins the coaching relationship by helping the talent (individual or team) to reflect upon their assets, gifts and potentials, even those that the talent may not see in themselves. A great coaching leader then helps the talent develop a legacy of personal power, a sense of ownership and mastery of their own future – partnering with the talent to co-create *their art of possibility* (Zander & Zander 2000).

Another feature of this principle is the coach's ability to challenge the talent with honest, truthful feedback when required, to confront them to reflect on what might be holding them back from being their best – using statements such as, 'It's difficult for me to tell you, but I think you need to know this...' I talked about *compassionate toughness* earlier in the book.

The final part of this principle is the coaching leader holding the talent *accountable to perform at their best or to be the best version of themselves* – to take responsibility for their developmental transformation (as an individual or as a team), noting that they are the only one with the power to do so.

Principle 3: Courageous conversations

The first point to note here is the need for a coaching leader to establish watertight ethical standards with those they are coaching. Unlike external coaches (who must nevertheless be highly ethical), internal coaches can face unique dangers in terms of power dynamics and potential or real conflicts of interest that must be diligently managed. The International Coaching Federation, to which I am accredited, has a very clear code of ethics that I explain whenever commencing any coaching relationship and repeat as necessary (ICF 2021). With every coachee, I clarify the firewalls that I've put in place such as secure storage of any recorded data and strict confidentiality to protect the privacy of coachees as well as to prevent any information being used for anything other than their coaching.

A second point is that coaching conversations can involve challenging subjects and provoke emotional reflections for the talent, even awkwardness at times for both parties. Coaching conversations can be unpredictable. A coaching leader needs to always be hyper-aware of the emotions 'in the room' (including their own), to use their presence, active listening and patient pauses, and to be comfortable with periods of silence. Coaching should always occur within a psychologically safe environment (**Practice 6**).

A final point to this principle is that every coaching conversation and every coaching 'journey' as I call them (consisting of several conversations with the talent) altogether constitute a *flow*, the destination for which is *not* in the hands of the coaching leader. At first, this might feel quite threatening to leaders, particularly if they are used to being the ones in charge of all processes. But as coaching leaders evolve, they come to understand that master coaching is *totally* talent centred and talent driven. Advice or instruction offered by a coach should be the *rarest* of undercurrents or surface features in this flow.

Every overall coaching journey and every coaching conversation within each journey generally transition through three phases:

✦ The *discovery* or awakening of transformative opportunities aligned with fulfilling a meaningful individual or team developmental goal.
✦ The *creation* of and weighing between as many options as possible to achieve this transformation.
✦ The *commitment* to pursue the best option or combination of options through articulation of realistic, actionable next steps.

In essence, coaching is a series of stimulating conversations but only really becomes impactful once the talent (individual or team) starts to take their own action – then the true joy of being a coaching leader begins!

Why are coaching leaders still so rare?

When leaders really know how to coach individuals and teams, it can empower, engage and ennoble – key ingredients for outstanding performance. But coaching as a leader is not without its challenges.

First, we cannot ignore the fact that as a coaching leader you have a degree of authority over the individual coachee or team. Unless the leader adheres to the strictest levels of ethics and integrity (which they should anyway!), their coaching may not reach the depth of rich revelation and sense of confidentiality that conversations with an external coach might. My experience though has sometimes been the opposite – the coaching leader can engage deeper than an external coach because the former is better attuned to the organisation's culture.

Second, any organisation that aspires to foster an internal coaching climate needs to ensure leaders are not set up to fail as coaches. Coaching may not come naturally to some leaders and supervisors who require additional, tailored support. In her invigorating book, *The Transformational Coach* (2022), Clare Norman notes that professional coaches receive training as well as their own coaching supervision and mentoring to maintain the quality standards of coaching, continued learning, unlearning and problem solving and emotional health. Developing leaders as effective coaches requires no less.

Third, even if they are super as a coach, being coached by your leader is not everyone's cup of tea. Some colleagues might prefer to receive advice in a more directive style – 'Enough of the questions already. Just tell me what to do!' Some might require less of a coaching intervention and more of a therapeutic approach (**Practice 10**), while some may indeed benefit from coaching but prefer to be coached by an external coach.

Finally, many leaders I've spoken with, while fully recognising the benefits that coaching could bring to their leadership repertoire and thus their teams' performance, nevertheless claim they have 'no time to coach'. Chris Whitehead (2019) holds a mirror to this claim. It has, he notes, 'an element of Catch-22 about it: Why can't you find time to coach? Because I'm too busy firefighting. Why are you too busy firefighting? Because I don't have time to coach my team so that they can think for themselves.'

How can we encourage more leaders at every level to use coaching in their daily work? David Creelman, CEO of Creelman Research, Dr Anna Tavis, associate professor of human capital management at New York University, and Michael Bungay Stanier, founder of Box of Crayons, offer some pointers (2018):

✦ **Change perceptions of what coaching entails.** Based on what we might ourselves have experienced or heard about, many of us assume 'coaching' must involve several hours of intense sessions spread over several months. But short conversations using coaching questions are often all that's needed to progressively unleash people's talent.

- **You don't have to be a coach, just more coach-like.** Some may think that coaching requires extensive training or accreditation. While this can certainly provide leaders with a deeper level of confidence and mastery, it's much less about certification and more about enhancing our curiosity. Empowering conversations can be simply built around coaching questions and resisting the temptation to give advice or provide instruction.
- **Coaching others benefits all.** Obviously when a leader coaches, the coachee (whether individual or team) and ultimately the organisation benefits. Usually, coachees experience increased trust, increased autonomy and personal growth. It helps the organisation by creating more reflective teams that are adaptive, quick learners and capable of working without direct supervision from their line manager. And adopting a coaching style of leadership across an organisation can facilitate the development of a more transparent and participatory culture. But how does the coaching leader gain? Examples might include reducing the stress that comes with feeling that you have to have all the answers, and therefore spending less time 'firefighting' because your colleagues and teams will become more self-sufficient, resilient and able to solve their own bottlenecks and problems. As a result, you and your team will have more space and energy to hyperfocus on solving problems that really matter.

The gardener leader

Research shows that when leaders adopt an optimistic, transformative approach it brings positive personal outcomes for those being gracefully led. In short, knowing that their leader believes in their potential helps people to believe in their own potential, and thus perform better. In a thorough meta-analysis of 17 investigations encompassing almost 3,000 employees from a broad range of business sectors, associate professor in management Brian McNatt showed that when managers were randomly assigned to see employees as having potential or to view them as 'bloomers', employees bloomed by comparison with employees whose managers were randomly assigned to not see them as having potential (McNatt 2000).

This graceful leadership practice of cultivating others' potential is analogous to gardening. I think Jim Carroll, brand strategist and former chairman of advertising agency Bartle Bogle Hegarty UK, superbly describes the analogy in a 2016 blog. 'Surely, we need leaders who can plant and nurture; tend and grow. Modern leadership is not about power; it's about empowerment. It's not about controlling; it's about cultivating' (Carroll 2016).

So, my invitation to you here is to try approaching every conversation like a coach. Use reflective questions such as:

+ How can I help you become your best self?
+ How can I best help with your career?
+ What adjustments could we make to foster a more creative and talented work environment?
+ What does this team want to be known for?
+ How can we better mould this team into the greatest?

In my experience, holistic investment in others gives a positive return – those people I've coached want to invest themselves back in their team, organisation or community.

Learn to recognise and use 'coachable moments' in daily work (and family) interactions, for instance, when:

+ chances for innovation, task improvement or a career move arise
+ colleagues need motivation, are strategising or gaining new knowledge and skills
+ you detect a behaviour that's impeding an individual's or team's performance
+ preventable errors or troublesome delays occur
+ others are seeking an immediate solution.

These are moments when you can lean into curiosity and ignite choice in others by asking situational coaching questions (see **Tool F**).

When leaders are able to adopt a coaching mindset in their daily interactions, it can sometimes change an organisation's entire approach to performance appraisal and management. For example, when Ashleigh Walters (2020) took over as president of the family-run Onex Company, she did away with employee annual performance reviews. Ashleigh recalls, 'Instead of waiting until the end of the year to review what was over and done – what was really good or really bad in someone's performance – we are having conversations in the moment they are relevant. We have created a coach approach.'

Recognise the talent and coach the potential that lies within, praise others, share your advice with them, link them to your networks. Provide opportunities for empowerment or responsible freedom – the freedom to be independent, make decisions and be self-reliant. Empowerment builds confidence and capacity. This practice is Professor Jinpa's third pillar of compassionate leadership, namely 'motivational connection' – tangibly demonstrating that you want success for others, that you have their best interests at heart (Jinpa 2015).

In the moving words of 19th-century physician and poet, Oliver Wendell Holmes Sr, 'Many people die with their music still in them.' Leaders who coach set about ensuring that the lives of those entrusted to them are lived with the music of their soul played completely, right to the end, *full range, full volume.*

Practice 14

Create value for the community

Graceful leaders intentionally and purposely give back to their own and/or to the local community in which they are working. Lalit Johri, a senior fellow in international business at the Saïd Business School, University of Oxford, conducted an exploratory study of 47 senior leaders from 27 countries (a mix of emerging and developed economies). These leaders worked in a variety of organisations, including private sector, civil service, government-owned companies, social enterprises and not-for-profit organisations. Yet despite the different contexts and roles, these leaders all shared similar stories about how they created value for their local communities. 'The kindness acts,' writes Lalit, 'are in the forms of doing relief work when natural disasters hit a community, launching skill development programmes to help the local community to augment its income and improve people's quality of life, and building social infrastructure to cater to basic needs of the communities' (Johri 2018).

The five-minute and 100-hour rules

I've seen many leaders engage in regular philanthropy, for example by participating in sponsored walk-a-thons or volunteering at their place of prayer, cleaning a local riverbank or supporting their company's corporate social responsibilities, such as helping to construct a local school. Then there are leaders who take on unpaid roles in public and social welfare boards, think tanks, employee associations, trade unions or community organisations. Others help out at their children's school, for example, by being a sports coach or a backstage assistant at the annual pantomime.

Still more use their personal resources to help others in what have become known as 'reciprocity rings', wherein work colleagues can ask for help whether that entails someone forwarding them a contact, putting in a good word on their behalf, mentoring or coaching them, or just offering an ear to listen (Tomasulo 2013). For me, volunteering over the years has included being a cheerleader, accountability partner, reference writer and personal board advisor to others (**Practice 1**), as well as a mentor to young UNICEF staff and coaching dozens of colleagues and teams inside and outside UNICEF. I've learned the power of liberally sharing networks and knowledge. Our networks should add and create value for everyone; we should not reserve them selfishly for our own benefit.

Five minutes

Do you have five minutes to lend a hand to someone else? When I read his optimistic book, *Give and Take* (2013), I was struck by Professor Adam Grant's observation of Adam Rifkin, co-founder of the successful start-up KnowNow, whose lifetime of constantly offering help to others is underpinned by a simple rule, 'You should be willing to do something that will take you five minutes or less for anybody.' It's the *anybody* that matters.

So, in the workplace, try to use actions and words that clearly demonstrate to colleagues that their concerns are your top priority, way ahead of your own. Though this may mean breaking from your own tasks to assist others with theirs, please do so as much as you can – create daily 'wriggle room' to accommodate these important requests (**Practice 1**).

Alongside compassion, kindness and playfulness, the act of giving to others with no expectations is contagious. Experiencing or seeing acts of others freely giving can elicit 'elevating' emotions that motivate us to give to others as well (Algoe & Haidt 2009). But remember, just as you offer others your time, energy and space, don't forget to maintain space for yourself. This means being generous to others with your attention, coaching and mentoring, for example, but doing so wisely to prevent your own burnout (also **Practice 1**).

One hundred hours

When it comes to voluntarily giving your time, a minimum of 100 hours a year or two hours per week seems to be a magic number (Grant 2013).

The science suggests that when and where circumstances permit, graceful volunteering – involving yourself in local activities and inspiring others to volunteer for community work – brings multiple benefits to not only those who receive but also to those who give. In addition, this practice enables you to connect the compassionate vocations of yourself and your team or organisation with the everyday realities of the wider community. It can also help you to refocus and re-energise, even to unlearn old frames of reference by taking you beyond your comfort zone (see **Practice 15**). Building a sense of community or actively contributing to a community's goals can enhance one's sense of life purpose and meaning.

Evolving communities, organisations and networks of grace

Communities of research, practice and training on elements of what I call graceful leadership are evolving, and an increasing number of organisations are appearing that have compassion and kindness (to both people and planet) as an aspiration as well as forming networks to amplify these aims around the world (see **Tool G**). The advent of communities, organisations and networks cultivating and promoting more compassionate, coaching, distributed leadership parallels the increasing call for more caring, collaborative, distributed ownership of 'commons' – environmental resources (eg air, water, a habitable planet) and cultural assets (eg art, music, digital information) that need to be equally accessible to all members of society.

For MIT faculty members and co-founders of the Presencing Institute, Dr Otto Scharmer and Dr Katrin Kaufer, this attention to shared stewardship of commons is part of the needed global transformation from ego-systems to ecosystems. In their terrific book, *Leading from the Emerging Future* (2013), they warn, 'The present time is a profound moment in our evolutionary path: We can either wake up and redirect ourselves, or we can ignore what's going on and stay on a collision course that will cause catastrophic failures affecting billions of people just in our lifetime.'

Challenged by ever-fluctuating possibilities of peace and polycrisis, we must strengthen our collective systems thinking and creative capabilities. For this, we would benefit from graceful leaders able to help us focus on the big picture.

Practice 15

Focus on the big picture

The World Economic Forum's Future of Jobs Report (2023) identified analytical thinking and creative thinking as the two most important workplace skills. In this final graceful leadership practice, I'll consider two core skills that can help us to step back, look up and focus on the big picture: systems thinking and collective creating. From the wide field of systems thinking, I'll highlight *sensemaking*, *presencing* and *foresighting*. And for creating, I'll touch on the importance of *unlearning*, *innovating* and *leading for sustainability*.

The world entire

Both the *Qur'ān* and the *Talmud* scriptures contain a similar expression, the essence of which is, 'Whoever saves one life, saves the world entire.'

When crises or complexities confront us, we yearn for mindful clarity, compassion and calmness – we all seek grace (Baldoni 2023). On the dehumanising frontlines of north-east Iraq during the week of 9 August 2014, around 100,000 families (some 400,000 individuals, half of them children) were being mercilessly pursued by ISIS insurgents towards Duhok Governorate (OCHA 2014). With its border protected by *Peshmerga* (expert military units of the autonomous Kurdistan region of Iraq), UNICEF had pre-positioned humanitarian supplies in several warehouses within the governorate a few weeks before (see **Chapter 3**).

On first news of this massive population movement, we immediately deployed our emergency team from Erbil to reinforce our field office colleagues already based in Duhok's capital. But it was obvious that the measures we had put in place alongside other UN agencies in Zakho, Shariya, Khanke, Bajed Kandala and elsewhere were about to be overwhelmed by the sheer number of internally displaced people (IDPs).

As we drove in a small convoy of armour-plated UN cars towards this chaotic situation, I pondered what words of comfort, vision and strategy I could possibly offer our team. We were all extremely anxious, even the seasoned among us. Parking outside our office as the sun set on the evening of 10 August, I urged the whole UNICEF team to get some rest and requested that we meet in our makeshift conference room at 7.00 the next morning. But what could I say to allay everyone's fear?

That night I stood for hours on a small balcony outside my guest room looking across the city as columns of cars, horns blaring into the night sky, alerted the people of Duhok to the oncoming wave of terrified citizens and the armed extremists who hunted them. I tried to make sense of what was happening. I breathed deeply. In the darkness, that expression from the *Qur'ān* and the *Talmud* rang deep within me. I recalled all those who had influenced my life up to that point. I wanted to honour them. I couldn't sleep.

The sun rose and the UNICEF team gathered in our office. There was a flip chart in a corner of the meeting room. As I walked in and headed towards it, I announced, 'Colleagues, let me share with you our purpose for today and for the coming days.'

I took up a marker pen, turned to a blank sheet of flip chart paper and wrote:

SAVE ONE CHILD

Simply this. 'Each of us needs to just save one child and then move on to the next child, and then on to the next, and the next,' I said, adding that each child was the world entire. I gently put the pen down and turned back to the team. 'How do we want to go about this?' I asked. 'What are our options?'

The room burst open with ideas, concerns and shared responsibilities. By 8.30 am, we had reached consensus on our next steps, completed security procedures, divided into smaller teams and dispersed to various road junctions, IDP reception centres, settlements and temporary encampments to work alongside our government, civil society and UN partners, while our operations team got busy packing and trucking humanitarian supplies to all these locations.

For the rest of that day in Duhok Governorate and during the weeks that followed, UNICEF and our partners greeted thousands of displaced children and their families with emergency relief (water, food, soap, first aid, psychological support, toys and so on), then registered and referred them to IDP shelters and camps. All the while, we kept listening, observing, learning and modifying our interventions. I could not have asked my UNICEF colleagues for more compassion, dedication, unswerving courage and relentless energy.

The team later revealed that as I approached the flip chart that August sunrise, they were anticipating something far more erudite – some sort of multi-layered, inter-sectoral IDP rescue and recovery plan. But these three words sufficed. 'Save one child. This simple sentence gave focus, made sense of the chaos and kept reminding us of our core purpose,' I was told.

How to focus on the big picture? Here are three initial reflections (written with the benefit of hindsight).

✦ **Spark possibility:** There's nothing remarkable in what I did. I just took the risk to simplify our mission in the face of adversity, not to be melodramatic or to dumb down the solution, but simply to help my team sense the small steps that could be taken – to imagine *possibilities* within an unfolding catastrophe. I then welcomed their wisdom. We embraced the risks and remained adaptive.

✦ **Channel humanity:** I didn't discover their wise words until quite recently, but Dr Frank LaFasto, former senior vice president of organisation effectiveness at Cardinal Health Incorporated, and Dr Carl Larson, professor emeritus of human communication studies at the University of Denver, in their compassionate research on humanitarian leaders four years earlier had already noted, 'The narrowing of focus, from a problem to a person, is critical to energising a pragmatic optimism. When we focus on the person it allows possibilities because we don't have to grapple with the whole problem' (LaFasto & Larson 2011). When inspiring hope, we focus on the person, not the problem. When co-creating solutions, we focus on the problem, not the person (see **Practice 4**).

✦ **Activate agency:** While these three words helped us cope with uncertainty, perhaps they also elicited a familiar calling to protect 'family'. In her soul-stirring book *Imaginable* (2022), Dr Jane McGonigal, director of games research and development at the Institute for the Future, wrote the following words eight years later that far more eloquently state my intention that dawn in Duhok, 'If we are given a clear purpose within the first minute of imagining the future – here is a choice you have to make right now – we feel more engaged... The future starts to feel a little more familiar, like a place where we could find our way, discover something new, help others, and achieve our goals.'

Systems thinking

To see a world in a grain of sand
And a heaven in a wild flower
Hold infinity in the palm of your hand
And eternity in an hour.
– 'Auguries of Innocence' by William Blake, 19th-century poet
  and painter.

I believe systems thinking is both an art and a science.

It's an 'art' in the sense that leaders and teams must be:

+ physically, mentally, emotionally and spiritually attuned to the circular, interconnected nature of the world around us
+ hyper-perceptive of the influence that deep-rooted structures and sociocultural norms have in generating the living conditions and triggering the complexities that we experience and witness every day
+ able, if possible, to predict the intended and unintended consequences of our actions.

It's a 'science' in the sense that leaders and teams must be:

+ disciplined in using precise, reflective questions to decipher why problems are occurring and not leap to possibly biased, incomplete or mistaken conclusions that reactively trigger pre-judged, insufficient and perhaps even harmful action
+ skilled in systematically moving from mere observations and collecting surface-level intelligence and on-the-spot data to discerning deeper, richer patterns and associations over time (should time allow)
+ capable of judiciously discovering allusive linkages, seeing things from unconventional angles and purposively enlarging the options available to us from which we can craft sustainable solutions – some of which may be unpopular.

Within the vast realm of systems thinking approaches (Stroh 2015), here I'll just focus on *sensemaking*, *presencing* and *foresighting* as they have proved the most valuable during my professional journey.

Sensemaking

Although there is no agreed definition of *sensemaking*, it's generally accepted to be a process that enables individuals, teams or groups to make sense of unclear, ambiguous or complex situations and events. For example, UNICEF teams use periodic analyses, known as SITANS, to gather and decipher qualitative and quantitative information on the situation of children, adolescents and women in every country in which the agency operates. This analysis then helps to shape UNICEF's multi-year programmes of cooperation with national authorities. Comprehensive SITANS are usually conducted every five years and updated annually to guide our programming.

In crises, UNICEF deploys rapid data collection techniques, for instance through mobile phone applications, to generate daily or weekly situation reports or SITREPS, which capture essential facts to guide our humanitarian responses. In some circumstances, as highlighted in **Practice 12**, we conduct real-time monitoring or periodic pulse surveys – often a mix of interviews, focus group discussions and other data sources – to track the situation of especially vulnerable groups during an emergency. All this helps the organisation to make sense of the multiple, often overlapping challenges confronting children and their families.

During situation analyses, I've always been a great fan of 'the 5 Whys'. Developed in the 1930s by Sakichi Toyoda, the Japanese industrialist, inventor and founder of Toyota Industries, the 5 Whys technique was popularised in the 1970s. It simply involves seeking ever-deeper answers to the question 'Why?' when asked five times in sequence.

Here's an example. Sarina's mother is a seamstress. Her father is a farmer and part-time mechanic. Although they both want Sarina to continue her education, she drops out of secondary school. Why? Because in this culture, continuing school is generally perceived as a threat to a girl's virginity, which will be important when Sarina gets married. Why? Because the bride's price paid by a groom will be much higher and it is now urgently needed to alleviate her family's situation. Why? Because Sarina's father has been crippled after stepping on an old anti-personnel mine that became exposed when topsoil was washed away by recent, unusually severe flash flooding. Why? Because his land had not been cleared of mines left from an earlier war due to the funding for the mine clearance programme being slashed. Why? Because another conflict with a neighbouring country has started and the government is diverting its financial resources to purchase more military equipment.

I've deliberately chosen an outlandish case linking a girl's education to social norms surrounding child marriage to subsistence farming to climate change to de-mining expenditure cuts to a new war, to illustrate how the 5 Whys technique can identify underlying factors that might need to be addressed but which will not be apparent if we only conduct a superficial analysis – in the radical example above, addressing school dropout rates by only trying to change traditional values associated with early marriage. But while the 5 Whys helps to reveal root causes, if not combined with other sensemaking tools, its 'why-because' linearity can lead to singular solutions or a limited number of solutions. To take my extreme illustration, de-mining investment won't by itself shift child marriage social norms (if at all).

With complex problems (and failures), we need to zoom out to take a balcony view of the multiple, frequently overlapping webs of causality to identify potential patterns, contributions and interconnected possibilities. We need analytical perspectives that mimic how rhizomes grow beneath the soil – the constant creation and readjustment of multi-nodal networks with no clear beginning or end. Rhizomatic *sensemaking* helps us to detect what *could* be done, not what should be done or what's been done before.

Leadership style matters here. Often our 'advice monster' (we met mine in **Practice 13**) desperately wants to command and control both the enquiry as well as the course of action, especially during a crisis. But *sensemaking*, even in emergencies, is best conducted in transdisciplinary teams or groups so that no one specific technical perspective or singular world view dominates or biases the interpretation of incoming data. Instead, the team or group benefits most when there is diverse thinking and joint creation of a solution 'bank' containing multiple innovations.

Faced with a complex challenge, we need to engage our spiritual intelligence (**Practice 3**) and tap into the collective and diverse wisdom of our teams. Organisational psychologist and executive coach Frank Uit de Weerd, together with team coach and CEO of CRR Global, Marita Fridjhon, describe this combination as *systems inspired leadership*, 'Sensing and knowing what wants to emerge, tapping into the collective wisdom, and creating from the system are very different and new ways to engage with the challenge' (Uit de Weerd & Fridjhon 2021).

Besides techniques such as the 5 Whys, effective *sensemaking* involves collectively identifying and then posing even more *powerful questions* that can trigger exploration, inspire reflective discussion, provoke creative thinking, reveal hidden presumptions, awaken imagination, fuel momentum, direct focus, deeply resonate with listeners, induce further questions and connect multiple perspectives (see **Tool H**) (Vogt et al 2003).

Presencing

For Dr Otto Scharmer and Dr Katrin Kaufer (2013), *presencing* is a combination of sensing future possibilities while being fully present in the here and now. They illustrate this with examples of a sports team playing 'in the zone' (where the combined focus and brilliance of play becomes an irresistible flow) or a jazz band 'finding its groove' (where the harmonious melody and propulsive rhythm unite in a life of their own).

Presencing is to connect to our highest self, to our spiritual intelligence. For Professor Danah Zohar and the late Dr Ian Marshall (2012), this represents a transition from thinking and acting from the peripheral level of self (personal ego), through a mid level (associative and interpersonal), to a central level of self (transpersonal). Obtaining such ecosystem awareness demands that leaders and teams also acquire the ability to view issues from the viewpoint of others (**Practice 4**). It's a move away from 'either/or' (limited, ego-level analysis) to 'both/and' (expansive, transpersonal-level analysis).

Presencing also facilitates unitive or integrative thinking, creative originality, seeing things from unconventional angles and forming associative or allusive links between ideas or events. Let me quickly share one example.

While with UNICEF in Nepal, I was privileged to be among *presencing* thinkers – such as Nafisa Binte Shafique, UNICEF Nepal's chief of adolescent development and participation (who would later become a brilliant representative for UNICEF in The Gambia), Dr Amjad Rabi, a mathematician as well as an economist and then chief of social policy, and Dr Alok Rajouria, a specialist in social welfare systems. One autumnal morning in November 2013, we were travelling by minibus to a workshop through the busy streets of Kathmandu. Our energetic conversation turned to the 'wicked' issue of child marriage.

Despite domestic laws against it dating back to 1963, Nepal still has one of the highest rates of child marriage in Asia for both girls and boys (UNICEF 2019). No matter how it's debated, child marriage is a human rights violation, restricting children's choices, changing their life paths, curtailing their formal education, exposing young girls in particular to the risks of serious pregnancy-related complications, and significantly increasing children's chances of being sexually abused and violently assaulted.

In Nepal, as elsewhere, there are several complicated causes for child marriage. In addition to the caste system and patriarchal culture, other contributing factors include poverty, low regard for daughters, elopement and lack of access to education. While we discussed these root causes on our way to the meeting, it occurred to me that despite years of rights-based advocacy and numerous communications for social and behaviour change campaigns, no one in Nepal had ever put forward a financial argument against child marriage. 'What's child marriage costing the national economy?' I asked.

The bubbly, out-of-the-box mind of Dr Amjad immediately set to work. Brainstorming with multiple partners and collecting data from diverse sources, he designed a simulation model that tracked a cohort of married girls aged 15 to 19 over the next 36 years, estimating the national economic loss in terms of potential cash flow from the labour market that could have been generated had girls delayed their marriage until the age of 20 and thereby continued their education to enhance their labour market skills. Measuring only from a labour market standpoint and using conservative assumptions (for instance, the model does not account for important costs in the areas of health, mortality and psychological deprivation), the model estimated Nepal's economic loss due to child marriage to be around NPR74,500 million or US$762 million, representing 3.9 per cent of its GDP back in 2014 (UNICEF 2014a).

The study's launch by the government of Nepal in front of a range of stakeholders and the press sent out a ripple that created new dialogues and possibilities. For example, UNICEF's advocacy as the study was being designed encouraged the government to pledge to end child marriage at a high-level Girl Summit held in London on 22 July 2014, jointly hosted by the government of the United Kingdom and UNICEF. The study's findings were later presented at the first-ever panel discussion on child marriage, organised by the UN General Assembly in New York on 5 September 2014.

At the same time, UNICEF, together with UNFPA (United Nations Population Fund), strengthened our partnerships with inter-faith leaders to focus on the negative aspects of child marriage, resulting in religious leaders throughout the country denouncing child marriage through their regular sermons (UNICEF 2014b). The research contributed to a landmark National Strategy to End Child Marriage and a costed action plan involving 13 government ministries, civil society organisations and other UN agencies, which was launched in 2016 (Girls Not Brides). Momentum continued when, on 23 March 2016, the First Nepal Girl Summit – 'Girls are the Future of Nepal' – was inaugurated by Bidya Devi Bhandari, the president of Nepal, and the UK's Prince Harry to support the country's commitment to end child marriage by 2030.

A comparison between nationally representative survey data from 2014 and 2019 in Nepal indicated a decline in the prevalence of child marriage among women aged 20 to 24 of 15.7 percentage points (from 48.5 per cent in 2014 to 32.8 per cent in 2019) (UNFPA & UNICEF 2021). But while this decrease is promising, child marriage remains a wicked issue. Nationwide advocacy and awareness-raising continues, much of it now championed by young people themselves. I like to think that our *presencing* conversation during that November 2013 minibus ride played a small part in Nepal's ongoing journey to end child marriage.

Foresighting

Over the years, I've learned enormously from UNDP colleagues, especially the use of strategic foresight or 'the discipline of exploring the future to anticipate changes, to develop possible transition pathways and to withstand shocks, to "help us act in the present to shape the future we want"' (UNDP 2022). Policies and programmes can be made much more resilient to surprises and flexible to changing tides by employing foresight to proactively detect new risks and opportunities. Foresight is also used by most businesses involved in production when plans are set in motion to modify or replace a product even if it's still high on its success curve. Organisational *foresighting* is somewhat similar to the personal use of *episodic future thinking*, which refers to an individual's ability to project the self forward in time to pre-experience an event (Schacter et al 2017).

The goal of *foresighting* is not to forecast what will happen but rather to future-test our planning assumptions, broaden our risk appetite, enhance our organisational agility and to warn us of possibly concealed or impending events that could trigger positive possibilities or negative consequences. According to UNDP, strategic foresight can help us to:

+ embrace and deal with uncertainty and emerging risks
+ better anticipate emerging opportunities and future challenges
+ spark novel ideas about how best to address these potential opportunities and challenges
+ expand the range of alternative futures to plan for
+ stress-test our strategies to make them more adaptive against a range of future shocks.

Foresighting tools include:

+ **horizon scanning** – determining and compiling early warnings of change, or developing signals, that could, if they materialise, have a substantial impact
+ **driver mapping** – identifying which change-influencing factors are most important in forming, transforming or having the potential to influence a system
+ **trend analysis** – spotting relationships, correlations and patterns that emerge between situations or problems to determine potential pathways of change
+ **futures wheel** – visualising how current events, trends and decisions might evolve and turn out in the future prior to developing solutions (eg by asking, 'What if?')
+ **futures triangle** – creating a range of plausible scenarios depending on the various ways that the drivers from the past, present and future interact
+ **scenarios** – crafting realistic narratives of the future to stress-test present programming, policies and strategies

(using **wind tunnelling**, see below) to check they can withstand whatever scenario arises

+ **three horizons framework** – unpacking (and reframing if needed) current assumptions about the future by assessing the balance between the needs of today (Horizon 1), the future (Horizon 3) and the steps needed to get there (Horizon 2)

+ **inclusive imaginaries** – a participatory tool to encourage the collective visualisation of more contextualised and regionally driven futures, which can guide the creation of policies with a strong cultural foundation

+ **backcasting** – envisioning a future in which our strategic objectives and goals have already been achieved, then retracing the actions that got us there

+ **wind tunnelling** – stress-testing strategies against a range of future scenarios. One wind tunnelling technique is to hold a 'pre-mortem' whereby a team begins with the assumption that their decision/project will fail and then explores why it will fail. This process usually uncovers hidden flaws and leads to a better decision/project (Klein 2007)

+ **roadmapping** – laying out the set of laws, policies, plans, measures and resources required to bring about a desired future.

All these tools generate useful ideas about the future, giving us time to try to prevent a catastrophe, helping us to prepare for challenges before they arise or motivating us to immediately make positive changes in our daily lives and communities.

While in the Islamic Republic of Iran (2015–2019), there was an extended period throughout which I had to intensively use a combination of horizon scanning, trend analysis, futures wheel and triangle, scenarios and wind tunnelling. Let me explain.

On 8 May 2018, after many months of political positioning, the United States finally announced its withdrawal from the 2015 Joint Comprehensive Plan of Action (JCPOA) or 'the Iran nuclear deal'. Six months later, on 5 November, the United States fully reimposed sanctions that had been lifted or waived under the JCPOA. Back then, these were the toughest USA sanctions ever imposed on Iran, targeting critical parts of the national economy, including the energy, financial, shipping and shipbuilding sectors.

For the UN and for UNICEF in particular, the potential impacts of sanction 'snapbacks' had already been part of our 2016 *foresighting* conducted during the design of a new programme of cooperation with Iran (2017–2021). We had anticipated that the most vulnerable in the country, who would not be the target of sanctions – some 10 million people living below the national poverty line and an additional 15 million living just above it – would be increasingly at risk of not receiving the necessary protection in terms of effective social safety nets and quality social services. Economic pressure due to sanctions would likely be transmitted to the most vulnerable through, for example, scarcities in imports including medicines, lower salaries, increased unemployment, decreases in household purchasing power and overall income, higher prevalence of social harms and crime, and increased social protection needs.

From November 2018 onwards, I led a small team within our office – including my talented deputy, Christine Weigand (currently the UNICEF representative in Armenia), and our operations manager, the highly experienced Sana Roumani (presently with UNICEF Lebanon) – together with colleagues from our Amman-based regional office, in producing monthly 'briefs' based on a handful of *foresighting* tools as noted above. Assimilating data from the government, NGOs and regular reports issued by the Economist Intelligence Unit, International Monetary Fund, World Bank, Assynt and other sources, each brief focused on the current situation and plausible futures in Iran over the next two to four years.

Together we tracked trends and projections across the following: Iran's economy; foreign investment; national politics; Iran's natural environment; social harms (such as substance use and crime rates); regional geopolitics; and a series of issues directly affecting children, including health, nutrition, HIV, education, protection, climate change impacts, emergencies and child poverty rates. Based on our tracking analysis, we created four scenarios or cases (best, medium, worst, very worst), monitored their likelihood and regularly stress-tested UNICEF's programming, in-country operations, and staff security and wellbeing against all four scenarios.

Given the sensitivity of information contained in each, I will just share snapshots of only the best and medium cases we developed:

✦ Best case (unlikely): the European Union (EU) manages to buffer Iran's economy from the impact of US sanctions. China and Russia engage more strongly in Iran's economy. Iran continues global reintegration and economic growth. Domestic economic and social reforms continue. Iran's economy dips but avoids recession.
✦ Medium case (most likely): the EU manages to buffer some but not all of Iran's economy from the impact of US sanctions. China and Russia engage even more strongly in Iran's economy. Iran's global reintegration stagnates. Domestic economic and social reforms narrow. Iran's economy enters recession.

Foresighting helped us to fine-tune our efforts to assist the children and families of Iran through these troubled months that, sadly, have since turned into years.

Systems thinking is not a cure-all that magically solves complex problems. But it can help us to reveal their root causes, discern associative patterns, recognise if something is off track, embrace uncertainty, look beyond horizons and start to co-create remedies and possibilities.

Collective creating

Confronted by ever more complexity, volatility, misinformation and uncertainty, we need teams, organisations and societies fuelled by curiosity, diversity and passion to unlearn old ways, take risks, learn from failures and create multifaceted, enduring solutions at a rate equal to or quicker than the speed of change. For me, 'collective creating' is the coalescence of at least three powers: *unlearning, innovating* and *leading for sustainability*.

Unlearning

It might seem odd to begin a personal reflection on 'creating' as a leader with the suggestion that this can be boosted by first *unlearning* some of what you already know. Surely, both individual and collective 'progress' and 'success' are fuelled by and founded upon the gradual *accumulation* of skills, knowledge and experience? Well... yes and no. For example, evolution, ecology, philosophy, neuroscience and horticulture (in honour of my late mum) all point out that further growth comes through acquisition of the new but also from the re-sculpting, pruning and shedding of the old. I would contest that those who wish to maintain a growth mindset – as opposed to those with a fixed mindset who feel they have nothing new to learn – need to embrace a healthy amount of *unlearning*. But what's *unlearning*? I think it has at least three interwoven dimensions.

While he did not use this term, one dimension of *unlearning* is aptly captured in the title of the world-famous executive coach Dr Marshall Goldsmith's book *What Got You Here Won't Get You There* (2007). In this classic exposé, he examines how so-called 'successful' managers can transform into what I would call graceful leaders – a metamorphosis accomplished only after they've 'broken' (ie *unlearned*) at least 20 highly ubiquitous workplace habits.

As I read through Dr Goldsmith's top 20, I couldn't help but glance back to my description of 'disgraceful leadership' near the beginning of this book. Falsely revered yet ultimately self-limiting managerial norms that should be unlearned include, for example, the need to win at all costs and in all situations; the overwhelming desire to always have to speak (especially in meetings); needless microaggressions that we foolishly believe make us appear witty; reacting in anger; the ego-driven, knee-jerk impulse to say, 'No, that won't work'; the reluctance to acknowledge and thank others for their contribution; not giving attention or actively listening to those who seek our help; stealing credit when others have done the work; and blaming everyone else but ourselves when things go wrong.

All these entrenched habits require rich, deep *unlearning*. Earlier, I shared the analogy of swimming out to and back from an orange buoy anchored out at sea, shedding the ego. So, one way to think about *unlearning* is the willingness to discard unhelpful, possibly even harmful behaviours. Can you identify any outdated beliefs or professional habits that you've outgrown yet still cling to? What springs to mind?

For me, a second dimension of *unlearning* is about striving to see situations and events anew, from a different, perhaps unusual set of angles, always *presencing* in the moment with an eye on the future – to pause, slow down, hold our biases in check and to freshly ask, 'What else could be emerging here? What might the other group be thinking?' If possible, to steer clear of our pre-judgements entirely. Not to do so can mean, regardless of what's ahead of us, we plough on with an entrenched belief of success or that what we're doing is 'right' based on past assumptions (that may have served us well but in other times and places) only to tragically realise it's now too late to change course. To visualise what I'm implying here, perhaps just the word *Titanic* suffices.

Within this second dimension of *unlearning*, I find it useful to occasionally remind myself of the observation made by Charles Baudelaire, a 19th-century poet and writer, 'A child sees everything in a state of newness' (Baudelaire 1863). Twentieth-century visual artist Henri Matisse (his legacy inspired the choice of my daughter's first name) echoed this thought when he said, 'We must learn to see the world again, as through the eyes of a child.'

Lifelong learning through embracing a growth mindset is vital. But learners who can also *make the familiar unfamiliar*, who remain agile unlearners, who try to observe things in an unrestrained state of newness, with a sense of deep curiosity, are doubly blessed. You can spot unlearners – they'll be the ones challenging social norms and traditions head on by questioning their origins and motives. Unlearners regularly ask, 'Why is this the way it is? Why do we do things this way? Why should it have to be this way? Why can it not be different? What other perspectives and ways of doing this could there be?' They interrogate the *status quo*. We need many more of them. Become one.

A third dimension of *unlearning* is less intense but no less liberating. Here *unlearning* simply means to let go of something old to make room for something new. It's about humbly accepting that most of us only have so much cognitive space – I'm guessing tech experts might talk about the overall size of our storage and processing capacity if our brains were the same as a computer's mainframe (Johnson 2023).

In sum, for me, *unlearning* is a rich blend of personal actions along three interconnected dimensions: first, getting rid of unhelpful habits that could even be harmful (taming our ego and advice monster); second, awakening our inner child by probing the *status quo* in a refreshing way (maintaining a healthy critique of existing models, theories, ways of doing things and frames of reference, even our own); and third, pruning old thinking to offer space for innovations (using our inherent neuroplasticity to unclutter our minds so that novel ideas can be uploaded).

So, this leads logically, I hope, to the next question. How does one go about *unlearning?*

We encountered *unlearning* before. For example: unlearning reactivity (leaning into the 'magic of the pause'); unlearning the myth of 'multitasking' (replacing with 'singletasking'); unlearning the fear of mistakes (celebrating 'failure'); and unlearning negative thinking (shifting to 'positive self-talk').

Unlearning must always be a deeply personal journey. There's no blueprint or 'how-to' manual. And it's not quick nor easy since it involves seeking and sometimes rediscovering your best self. Finding and changing thought and belief patterns that have been passed down over generations and ingrained in you requires time and determination.

Unlearning also requires humility. As Dr Jane McGonigal (2022) observes, we must be willing 'to let our assumptions and beliefs go when they no longer serve us, especially if we get new information that makes us rethink our original position.' One can possess strong opinions, Jane notes, but hold them *lightly* and don't be afraid of letting them go when that can better serve your team, organisation and, ultimately, humanity. Thought leaders in team performance Jon Katzenbach and Douglas Smith came to the same conclusion in their classic research, namely that the wisdom of a high-performing team is always greater than an individual's, no matter their level of expertise (Katzenbach & Smith 1993).

Thinking back, I realise that I've been *unlearning* in my own peculiar way all my life. For instance, the neurological restructuring I experienced when I transitioned from biology to social anthropology in my university days (back then I joked that it felt like a 'meltdown'). And as I shifted my know-how through various specialisations – from medical anthropology to public health to evaluation to planning to participatory research to social change communication to economic policy to programme management – and once again when I left management for leadership. Even now, I'm *unlearning* leadership – moving away from believing that I must give instructions and advice towards co-creating and coaching.

One important clarification to make here is that *unlearning* is not about negating what's gone before. It's not about dismantling and destroying all that we have experienced up till now. It's about exploring what might be holding us back in the present or could derail us in the future, seeking and removing possibly redundant attitudes, viewpoints or habits, while retaining, maintaining and reassembling those that continue to serve us well, for now.

Unlearning aims to improve our future, not ignore our past. It's about constantly pruning back the exterior to unleash new growth – our set of core values, ie our fiercely compassionate inner warrior remains intact (so be sure this warrior serves you well!). Even if our brains (I noted in **Practice 2** that each of us has more than one) hang on to certain memories and perspectives just in case they might come in handy, when we remain curious and childlike, passionately reconfiguring new ways of looking at the world, through neuroplasticity's magic even once handy recollections and outlooks can eventually vanish.

Unlearning is best accompanied by *innovating*, which I consider next.

Innovating

Innovation blends deep curiosity, creativity and courage. Its neurological foundation is fascinating. Our head-brain's two hemispheres function in complementary ways. The left works in a methodical, arboreal (analytic) and time-conscious manner, drawing conclusions from logical inferences – similar to the 5 Whys questioning technique. The right hemisphere is more rhizomatic (fluid) by nature, skilled in both vision and space, with an increased ability to perceive several objects simul-taneously and connect the pieces to the whole – a bit like the *presencing* technique. The right is more likely to solve problems through rapid, intuitive jumps and unexpected revelations than the left, which is more linear and time focused.

Sparked by curiosity, innovation seems to require engaging both hemispheres through a cognitive oscillation, a neurological dance if you will, from initial *insight* (right hemisphere) to *saturation* of data gathered from multiple sources (left hemisphere) to *imaginative contemplation* or diving through the data (right hemisphere) followed by *illumination* or the 'Aha!' moment (right hemisphere again) and ending with *verification* where the breakthrough idea is rationalised (left hemisphere) (Edwards 1988). A dance instructor might say, 'Right and left, then right, and right again, then left...'

Often the right hemisphere's creative genius works when we're *not* consciously, proactively looking for solutions or outcomes but when we're taking a break from analysing, perhaps spending time in our galleries and sanctuaries (**Practice 1**). This might have been the case when the Ancient Greek mathematician and inventor Archimedes supposedly proclaimed 'Eureka!' after he had stepped into a bath and suddenly realised that the volume of water displaced matched the volume of the body portion he had submerged.

There are many wonderful books about how to innovate (eg Anthony et al 2020). One that continues to inspire me is *Idea Work* (2012), by Associate Professor Arne Carlsen, Professor Stewart Clegg and Dr Reidar Gjersvik. One reason this book gripped me was because they don't focus on what makes individuals creative, nor do they provide advice on how to develop one's unique innovation potential. Instead, they focus on the *collective elements* and *culturally rooted forms* of innovation practised by teams. Their four-year study explored how innovation occurred within six diverse Scandinavian organisations – an architectural firm, an exploration unit of a major oil company, a law firm, an alliance of savings banks, a supplier of trading analytics and a weekend magazine.

Carlsen and colleagues define *Idea Work* as 'activities concerned with generating, selecting, realising, nurturing, sharing, materialising, pitching and communicating ideas in organisations'. And they weren't interested in just any kind of *idea work* but in ideas that were capable of powering breakthroughs; in short, ideas that became innovations. Their research identified ten ways through which high-value ideas are generated and realised in organisations. I share them here as teams I've been part of have benefited from using several:

✦ **prepping** – running information through a rigorous process of preparation, construction and revitalisation to optimise its potential for use at the moment of creation (a process similar to UNICEF's situational analyses)

✦ **zooming out** – letting go of specifics, adopting a big-picture approach and searching for the essential concepts instead of becoming immersed in data or engrossed in detail (sensemaking)

✦ **craving wonder** – the amazing feeling of being in a mystery, the juxtaposition of being shocked and searching with a passion (powerful questioning)

✦ **activating drama** – posing the question 'What's at stake here?' while urging others to embrace adventure and engage their fullest potential (negotiation)

✦ **daring to imagine** – stepping out bravely into uncharted terrain by fostering a language of possibilities, handling setbacks and offering support (celebrating failure)

✦ **getting physical** – bringing ideas to life and making them visible through artefacts, images, touching, drawing, gesturing and moving around while working on ideas (playing)

✦ **double rapid** – quick prototyping, testing and refinement of partially developed concepts to facilitate early sharing and support of these ideas (building the plane as we fly it)

✦ **liberating laughter** – methods for igniting co-creation with improvisation, comedy and jokes to foster social connections, lighten the mood, loosen mental restrictions and promote novel combinations of information (using humour)

✦ **generative resistance** – recognising uncertainty, conflict and criticism as tools to challenge the *status quo* and foster creativity rather than as distracting noise to be avoided or ignored (celebrating team diversity and wind tunnelling)

✦ **punk production** – acting boldly and taking decisive action to organise against conventional methods, exposing and bringing to life original concepts of potential worth.

Entrepreneurial spirits

This last quality of extraordinary idea work labelled provocatively (and I think, ingeniously) by Carlsen and colleagues as 'punk production' took me a while to get my head around. But it started to make sense when, in June 2018, after two years of careful groundwork, UNICEF set about engaging with Iran's private sector in ways that we had not done before. Until then, we had conventionally considered partnering with the private sector to align with their corporate social responsibility interests (such as sponsoring the construction of schools and hospitals) and sometimes as a source of potential financial resources.

But, ably assisted by the UNICEF team in Iran, especially the dedicated Vida Montakhab, alongside colleagues from UNICEF's Office of Innovation, notably the effervescent Chris Fabien, we teamed up with the Iran Chamber of Commerce to launch the country's first-ever UNICEF business innovation platform with the goal of discovering, incubating and delivering new ways to accelerate sustainable results for children in Iran (UNICEF 2018). The idea was to link children's creativity with the ingenuity of entrepreneurs and business leaders to co-create radical solutions to pressing development challenges. The initiative has blossomed ever since, with annual innovation challenges being just one of the new evolutions (UNICEF 2023).

When an innovative solution is proposed, many times we might hear others around us say 'But that's outside our policy' or 'We don't have enough resources to support this' or 'No, we've always done that this way.' But a graceful leader will reflect on the big picture, check whether the innovation is really solving the problem that it's targeting and, having first ensured colleagues will be safe, take the risk to try something new. I am forever inspired by more of George Bernard Shaw's words, 'You see things; and you say "Why?" But I dream things that never were; and I say "Why not?"' Having the courage to think and act outside the box also reminds me of Australia's Northern Territory tourism catch cry from the early 1990s, 'You'll never, never know, if you never, never go!'

Let wild grasses grow

Hypothetical question (I sincerely hope): Earth's fragile ecosystems have finally collapsed, overwhelmed by the unrelenting, overlapping impacts of climate change, pollution, biodiversity loss, poverty, epidemics and war. Via lottery, you and your loved ones have been lucky enough to win a ticket that allows you to escape to another planet and begin human enterprise afresh. You've been nominated and later voted in as a *leader* of this future civilisation. But this is your first-ever leadership role. The shuttle's cabin space is limited so you're allowed to hand-carry only a couple of leadership books to guide you on the new planet. Which two books would you choose?

If I could only grasp two books on leadership, one tightly held in each hand as I run to the launch pad, which two would I be holding? Standing inside this imaginary space centre in front of bookshelves stacked high with so many incredible leadership texts, I'm loath to answer my own question. But it's an intriguing exercise that I hope you might want to think through, if only to distil what your core leadership colours represent.

OK, enough stalling. If I really had to pick, one would certainly be former President Nelson Mandela's *Long Walk to Freedom* (1994). Heartbreaking at times, it's an inspirational goldmine of real-world leadership wisdom. In my one hand, I therefore clasp a gracious forgiveness of the past, of *what was but must never be again*. I'm sure many would opt for this autobiographical masterpiece as they clamber on board their escape vessel from our dying planet.

My second book was far more difficult to select. *Long Walk to Freedom*'s first release was in 1994. Even before that and increasingly in the past three decades, leadership publications have become breathtakingly numerous and diverse. Yet for me (not just because UNICEF gets a mention), London Business School professor Gary Hamel and Dr Michele Zanini, co-founder of the Management Lab, have richly crafted an uplifting possibility of how human potential can be unleashed by organisations – *Humanocracy: Creating Organisations as Amazing as the People Inside Them* (2020).

You know you're reading a great book when on virtually every page there's something quotable. So it is with *Humanocracy*. In my other hand, I thus grip a human-centric, elevating glimpse of the future, *an emancipatory vision of what every organisation can become*. Many more great books on leadership will doubtless materialise, but if our planet were to fail tomorrow and the evacuation ship's engines were running, I hope many would consider grabbing *Humanocracy* on their desperate way through the departure terminal in the hope of building better organisations on our new world. Yet to simply wait until the Earth might have to be abandoned is entirely defeatist. What Professor Hamel and Dr Zanini offer is a manifesto to radically transform organisations right *now*. Before I highlight some of their revelations, what's the reason they believe organisations need to change?

Bureaucracy.

Their observation is bleak. 'Across the world, organisations are disabled by bureaucracy – they are inertial, incremental, and inhuman. This is a problem not just for CEOs, but for all of us. Ponderous, inflexible institutions misuse society's resources and reduce productivity. They squander imagination, suppress initiative and bungle the future' (Hamel & Zanini 2020). The authors argue that most bureaucracies dehumanise workers, 'Ironically, it seems that human-built organisations have scant room for exactly those things that make us furless bipeds special – things like courage, intuition, love, playfulness and artistry.'

Confronted by polycrises, even perhaps entering an era of permacrisis, we need our organisations to change. It seems that bureaucratic governance cultures that evolved over centuries to solve societal problems are now becoming a societal problem. No single leader is to blame – rather, it's how bureaucracy prefers conformity over creativity, gives too much emphasis on the few at the expense of the many, assigns people to limiting positions, strips them of autonomy and views them as nothing more than resources. The quality of systems thinking and the speed of innovation needed to run large organisations are beyond such archaic managerial hierarchies.

And who's really transforming the world? According to *Humanocracy*, it's largely activists such as Malala Yousafzai, the Nobel Prize-winning Pakistani teenager, who, after escaping a Taliban attempt on her life, began a global initiative to increase girls' access to education. Or Greta Thunberg, another teenager at the time, whose demonstration at the Swedish parliament prompted more than a million children from 125 nations to skip school and urge their governments to take immediate action to combat climate change.

Like these global movements, we need organisations that are horizontal, many-to-many, emergent forms of collaboration rather than vertical, a few-to-many, engineered forces of competition. We need to move from bureaucracy to *humanocracy*.

For Professor Hamel and Dr Zanini, bureaucracy's central question is, 'What's the best way to enable people to work more effectively for the organisation?' Whereas the question at the heart of humanocracy is, 'What kind of organisation brings out and inspires the finest that humans have to offer?' How can our organisations create environments that support innovation by all? How can we rethink our management procedures so that they boost everyone's innovative spirit rather than limit it?

If we are to create self-renewing organisations that take risks and succeed in our increasingly complex world, then everything boils down to willing, enthusiastic, joyous employee engagement. Giving staff the chance to *be* more, rather than pressuring them to *do* more, is the essence of humanocracy.

We need workplaces that allow every team member to fully express their problem-solving and business-building abilities. We need organisations that *let wild grasses grow*.

Does this all sound too good to be true? Do such humanocratic entities exist?

Professor Hamel and Dr Zanini analyse several post-bureaucratic pioneers – Buurtzorg, Haier, Morning Star, Nucor, Spotify, Svenska Handelsbanken, Vinci, and W L Gore, among others – revealing that it's absolutely possible to run large, complex organisations with super-flat structures, distributed leadership, cellular approaches to problem solving and swarms of self-managing 'micropreneurs' who are gladly prototyping dozens of parallel experiments to enhance performance and outcomes.

I genuinely welcome the authors' invitation to embrace the principles and practices of humanocracy. Every organisation will be able to succeed in a world that is vastly different from the one that gave rise to bureaucracy, plus every worker will get the chance to thrive. Please don't wait to grab this book if you're lucky enough to be on that last escape shuttle from Earth. We need leaders and organisations right here, right now, able to help us address the world's wicked problems by releasing our individual and collective artistry, ingenuity and grace.

Leading for sustainability
Collective leadership

In her inspiring book, *The Art of Leading Collectively* (2016), Dr Petra Kuenkel identifies six competencies that leaders need to combine if they are to meaningfully interact in co-creative partnerships that produce sustainable results: a sense of future possibilities, engagement, innovation, humanity, collective intelligence and of wholeness. These connect with many of the graceful leadership qualities and practices I have explored here. I highly recommend her book.

None of the wicked issues facing humanity, whether poverty, climate change, epidemics, discrimination, inequality, economic crises or violence and conflict, to name just a few, can be tackled in isolation. We need new types of leadership and enabling infrastructures, humanocracies, that support people to co-sense and co-develop multiple solutions using their entrepreneurial spirit (Hull et al 2020). Polycrises demand 'polyresponses' forged out of shared, rhizomatic systems thinking. Over time, if we are deeply attentive, co-creative, resourceful and adaptive enough, I believe the 'poly' can begin to be taken out of 'polycrises'. Throughout my career, I've sought ways to build collective leadership at scale. I have constantly encouraged teams and partners to ask, 'Whose voice is missing? Who else needs to be at the decision-making table?'

Put another way, our complex problems will never be solved by reactive, singular, rigid, isolationist, surface-level, 'either/or' interventions or decisions. Instead, these wicked issues require reflective, multi-directional, flexible, connective, deep-rooted flows of 'both/and' prototypes or trial-and-error solutions that test out portfolios of possibilities and seek out resilient inter-connections – an innovative, flexible, constantly rejuvenating ecosystem like the humble rootstalks of ginger, turmeric, bamboo, lotus, mint and iris.

While we might be tempted to think that the largest single living organism is the majestic blue whale, based on area, it's actually a 4,500-year-old stretch of seagrass located off Western Australia, covering approximately 200 km2 – equal to around 28,000 soccer fields or more than 450 times bigger than Vatican City, our world's smallest country (Edgeloe et al 2022).

And in terms of weight and age, it's a soulful grove of quaking aspen trees in Utah's Fishlake National Forest. Nicknamed 'Pando' or the 'Trembling Giant', this forest consists of some 47,000 stems or ramets that appear as individual trees yet are joined by a single root system spanning 106 acres. Weighing in at around six million kilograms (adding together all the individual trunks, branches and leaves), with an estimated age of at least 14,000 years, Pando is the heaviest and oldest living thing on Earth (Ding et al 2017).

The scalability, durability and sustainability of these two *single-bodied* organisms are due to their incredibly interconnected, non-hierarchical, non-linear, hyper-adaptive root systems that can regenerate multiple new stems above the surface at any point. Tragically, both fascinating species face uncertain futures due to climate change and other human-induced environmental intrusions, diminishing our chances to learn more about their extraordinary resilience and problem-solving capabilities (Evans et al 2018; Morelli & Carr 2011).

So, if provoked by complexity and when striving for sustainability, *invite your teams and partners* to collectively step back; breathe deeply; suspend judgement; listen and observe attentively; accept ambiguity; embrace contradiction; reframe the problem (several times if needs be); nurture mental spaciousness; invoke diverse opinions; free-associate ideas; scan for larger patterns, unexplored relationships, concealed connections and novel combinations; and co-create with fellow collaborators a range of adaptive, ever-adapting options (Plan A, Plan B, Plan C, etc)... then communicate with simplicity.

Kaleidoscope

Over the years, I've thought deeply about creating a handy frame of reference through which both humanitarian and developmental challenges could be viewed and addressed. In November 2008, I travelled to the Federated States of Micronesia, the Republic of the Marshall Islands and the Republic of Palau alongside Dr Isiye Ndombi, the then Pacific representative for UNICEF – luckily for me, the first of several graceful leaders I was to encounter in the organisation. Kenyan by birth, he is an incredibly wise soul with a calm, statesmanlike presence and deep-oak, melodic voice. Now enjoying his retirement, Isiye remains for me the UN's equivalent of the outstanding, multi-award-winning actor, Morgan Freeman (we'd often laugh about my Hollywood analogy).

On that trip, Isiye and I met with high-level officials in each country to discuss children's rights and to explore how UNICEF could improve our technical assistance to the northern Pacific. Given the flight connections back then, it was a long journey, but we spent our downtime between meetings passionately debating and distilling what we thought might become a useful integrative template for programme analysis, planning and mobilisation. I've tinkered with it since those enriching conversations, but it has remained pretty much as we co-created (see below).

Alongside systems thinking and unlearning (to help reduce bias and pre-judgement), this frame of reference became the light-splitting, reflective prism through which I've worked with many teams and multiple partners in numerous countries and cultural contexts to unpack human-centred challenges and to stimulate and design possible 'polyresponses'. It's not intended to be fixed nor comprehensive and, depending on the challenge at hand, sometimes more items are added while occasionally a handful are removed.

Like a kaleidoscope – a popular toy during my childhood – this shiftable frame of reference has offered me an endless set of new perspectives, reflections and options. It reminds me of the three-way flows between policies, services and communities necessary for important accountabilities to be shared and for often precious resources to be protected and optimised. The underlying principle is to always start with the most vulnerable first. Some terms in this frame of reference have already been defined in other parts of the book. While for others, like a kaleidoscope's shifting patterns, I prefer to leave them open to interpretation. Several abbreviations are explained below.

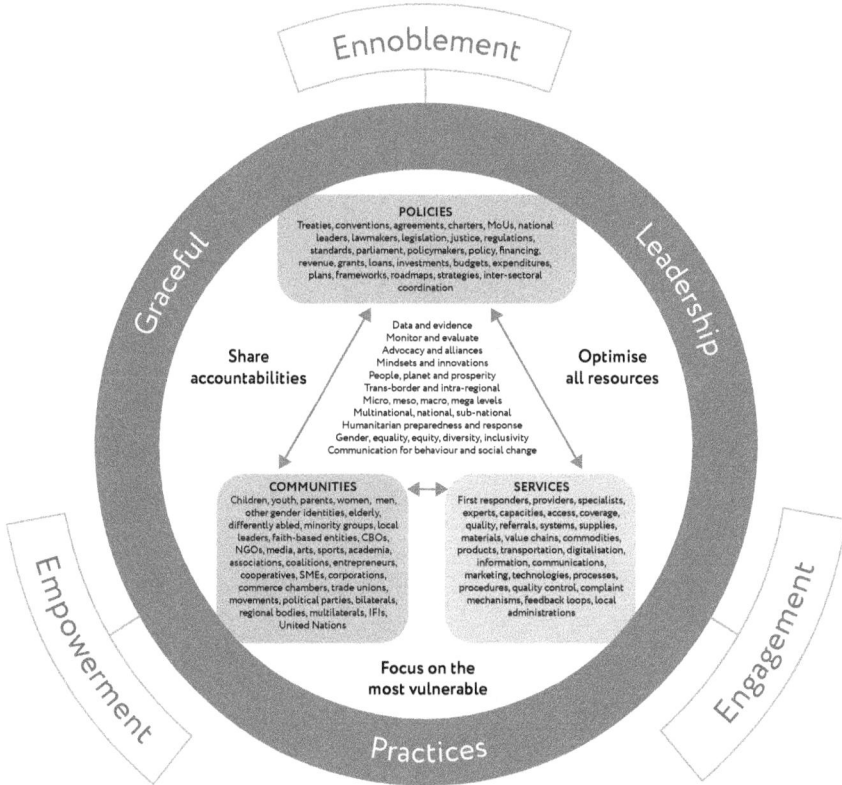

Ennoblement

Graceful

Leadership

Empowerment

Engagement

Practices

POLICIES
Treaties, conventions, agreements, charters, MoUs, national
leaders, lawmakers, legislation, justice, regulations,
standards, parliament, policymakers, policy, financing,
revenue, grants, loans, investments, budgets, expenditures,
plans, frameworks, roadmaps, strategies, inter-sectoral
coordination

Data and evidence
Monitor and evaluate
Advocacy and alliances
Mindsets and innovations
People, planet and prosperity
Trans-border and intra-regional
Micro, meso, macro, mega levels
Multinational, national, sub-national
Humanitarian preparedness and response
Gender, equality, equity, diversity, inclusivity
Communication for behaviour and social change

Share
accountabilities

Optimise
all resources

COMMUNITIES
Children, youth, parents, women, men,
other gender identities, elderly,
differently abled, minority groups, local
leaders, faith-based entities, CBOs,
NGOs, media, arts, sports, academia,
associations, coalitions, entrepreneurs,
cooperatives, SMEs, corporations,
commerce chambers, trade unions,
movements, political parties, bilaterals,
regional bodies, multilaterals, IFIs,
United Nations

SERVICES
First responders, providers, specialists,
experts, capacities, access, coverage,
quality, referrals, systems, supplies,
materials, value chains, commodities,
products, transportation, digitalisation,
information, communications,
marketing, technologies, processes,
procedures, quality control, complaint
mechanisms, feedback loops, local
administrations

Focus on the
most vulnerable

Abbreviations: CBOs (community-based organisations), NGOs (non-government organisations), SMEs (small and medium enterprises), IFIs (international financing institutions), MoUs (memoranda of understanding)

True north

Dr Petra Kuenkel emphasises the importance of maintaining a 'collective leadership compass' that connects leading as an individual task with leading as a collective task. Her compass helps leaders to prepare for collaborative journeys; locate where they are and identify available information as well as knowledge gaps; set a course, navigate and adjust as they proceed; and convince others that if we are to sustainably transform the world, creative, collective leadership will be key.

And I've found that guidance along this communal, outer journey of thought and action towards sustainable development is best combined with a personal, inner exploration steered by what I call a 'compass of inner purpose' or, as businessman and Harvard professor Bill George and emerging leader Zach Clayton put it – one's 'true north' (George & Clayton 2022).

Combining outward, whole-of-systems, creative, collective action with inward, value-based, mindful reflection to sustainably address our world's wicked problems resonates with *conscious full-spectrum responses* as explained by Professor Monica Sharma, Tata Institute chair and former director of leadership and capacity development at the United Nations, in her dynamic book *Radical Transformational Leadership* (2017). For Professor Sharma, a conscious full-spectrum response is based on transdisciplinary, multidimensional, shared thinking and joint action to solve not only immediate problems (surface symptoms) but also to transform unworkable systems and cultural norms that give rise to or perpetuate the problems in the first place (root causes). She challenges, 'Do you truly recognise the magnitude and underlying factors of our problems today? Will you choose to understand and act upon what is equitable and transformative and integrate it into your daily life and work? And are you called to step up and offer your learning and action in service of humanity and our planet?'

So, throughout my journey in international development, what's been my true north? My personal compass of inner purpose is to daily ask myself three simple questions:

✦ Am I unleashing talent? (Ennobling)
✦ Am I creating joy? (Engaging)
✦ Am I transforming performance? (Empowering)

These are derived from my *life purpose*, which I referred to at the beginning of this book. If I answer 'yes' to all three questions – it's been a great day! And if I answer 'no' to any, I challenge myself at the close of the day, 'What could I have done better? What do I need to do tomorrow to realign with my life purpose?' Mindfully, such inner questions invoke a return to self-compassion, to **Practice 1**, keeping my flywheel of effort to become a graceful leader in unending, exponential motion.

Final thoughts

I ended my interviews with Mohamed, Gillian, Hamida, Peter and Ugochi by asking, 'Knowing what you know now about leadership, what would you tell your younger self?' Here's what they said.

Mohamed: 'I would say to any young person getting into the path of leadership, "Never undermine your values. Your integrity is very important." Because early on, I was in a leadership position at the National School of Medicine, leading the student association there. And at the time we were really fighting the government to get things changed. I remember getting called by the president through somebody else to come and take money for us to slow down. And I refused. And I think my path would have been different today if I'd have taken the money. I would have disgraced myself. So, I think your integrity, your values should never be compromised. Although we are now in a world in which morals are not looking the best, people still want a leader to have those values. So, I would say, don't let your values get compromised.'

Gillian: 'When I look back to my first UNICEF representative's posting in the Pacific, I wish I had been more compassionate and understanding of staff. My expectations were quite high, and I was not being cognisant that for many staff, English was not their first language. They were often the first members of their family who had had a university education, and I was expecting them to operate in a Western organisational model. I would do that quite differently now. I would be more compassionate, more understanding of where staff come from. And undertake more coaching of staff than I did in my first role in the Pacific.'

Hamida: 'I think it's extremely important to have humility. Because there are leaders I have seen who are down to earth and not really wanting to just do things because they want to be seen themselves and their importance to be known. I always feel that we should not claim for all the achievements and say, "Yeah, I did this. I did that." So, humility is extremely important because you gain respect out of that as well when people see that you care for others, you think of others, you really put others first and you come after, especially when it comes to recognition. And you know being humble doesn't mean you are stupid, that you don't know. Some people really want recognition. But for me, let other people recognise what you have done. By promoting yourself, it doesn't give them a lot of confidence in you.'

Peter: 'I've learned, you know, learned from the horrendous times, learned from the good times, learned from the mediocre times. And I've been lucky. And I'm grateful for it. But it doesn't stop me from fighting for tomorrow. So, I would say to the younger Peter, "Keep going. Just keep going. Just do it. And there's nothing stopping you." I often say that it's like being a goalkeeper. And the first five minutes of your biggest match ever, the ball goes through your legs and into the net. What do you do? You've got to clean your face. You've got to go forward. You cannot dwell on what happened. You learn from what happened. Close your legs or position yourself differently or whatever it is but you've got another 85 minutes of the biggest match of your life. That's what life is about. It's inevitable. You'll have your emotional crises. It's how you handle it and how you take it forward.'

Ugochi: 'One, do not let anyone define you. You define yourself. Because that's your grounding. Two, know your stuff. Because when I'm prepared, I'm confident. This is your fountain of confidence. Three, always make sure you make people feel seen, heard, valued and respected. And that kind of leads to the fourth: the trust of my team. Because with the trust of my team, we can weather any storm. They will go above and beyond. So, invest in building trust. And finally, whatever position you're in, the terms of reference or TOR that you have are the floor, not the ceiling. You set your own ceiling. You must *have a ceiling that is much higher than your TOR. One that is going to drive you every day to get out of bed and to think about what more it is that I can do or that needs to be done.'*

The age of compassion and coaching

There will likely be more VUCAH years ahead. As I noted at the beginning of this book, we are entering the era of *polycrisis*; some even talk about *permacrisis*. A leadership mindset of coaching united with wise compassion is the most effective, humane way to support people through unstable, difficult times. As we brace for these challenges together, we would gain enormously if there were compassionate, coaching leaders at all levels of communities and organisations, and compassionate, coaching leadership shared at every level.

A bedrock of graceful leaders serving as role models of compassion and coaching can ennoble, engage and empower employees and community members; attract, boost and retain top talent; bring tremendous benefits, including wellbeing and joy, to individuals, families, teams, communities, organisations and even societies; and optimise individual and team cohesion, collaboration and thus performance, accelerating an organisation's results, all the while generating and sustaining psychological safety.

Keep in mind: leading with compassion and coaching is contagious – graceful leadership can trigger a chain reaction of kindness and goodness. The more grace you embody, the more graceful your colleagues will be. Through neurochemistry, pretty much all the practices described in this book are *contagious*. If leaders at all levels can embrace and embody these practices, contagion will likely do the rest. That is why I am convinced that it is possible to move from more graceful individuals to more graceful teams to more graceful organisations to more graceful communities, ultimately serving and advancing humanity *with grace*.

As I reflected upon my personal journey, researched for and wrote this book, time and again I sensed an alternative leadership approach *coming of age*, at all levels and in all varieties of teams and organisations, profit and non-profit, as well as, humbly, in myself. It's not perhaps a 'revolution' like the one UNICEF's Jim Grant bravely launched for the world's children. But with a sense of grounded optimism, I believe we are witnessing an 'evolution' – a determined departure from leadership epitomised by command and controlling others towards leadership exemplified by compassion and coaching others.

The ending

Wednesday 21 October 2015. We are midway through UNICEF's winterisation campaign – an urgent effort to protect tens of thousands of families displaced to north-east Iraq due to ongoing attacks by ISIS militia from winter temperatures that vary between 24°F and 63°F (-4°–17°C). With the help of multiple donors, as a stopgap survival measure, UNICEF distributes thousands of 'family winter boxes' that hundreds of volunteers have hand-packed with sets of warm clothes for all age groups.

On that damp Wednesday morning as I stand handing out such boxes, my left palm is clutched by the hand of a small Yazidi boy. He looks up into my eyes. It's been a year since he escaped the horrific genocide by ISIS in Sinjar. Without words, I clutch a box, and we walk together to where his family stands patiently. Small gestures, but they express how trust and compassion can transcend the boundaries of ages and of cultures. I remembered myself as a small boy standing beside my pedal car. A lifetime ago and a world apart, yet here we were.

Dalal internally displaced people's camp, Duhok Governorate, autonomous Kurdistan region of Iraq. Photo: UNICEF Iraq.

I opened this book with the heartbreaking earthquake and subsequent tsunamis in Solomon Islands on 2 April 2007. Leaning into an analogy, geophysicist Professor Xavier Le Pichon, famous for his research on the Earth's tectonic plates, drew an intriguing parallel between the fragility of our planet and that of humanity (Le Pichon 2009). Within the Earth's deeper rock layers where the temperature is high, when natural defaults in the plates become active, the rocks deform without fracturing – they absorb the energy released by literally 'flowing' in fusion with each other. But in the last few miles nearer to the Earth's surface, where it is much colder, these higher rock layers are more fixed and cannot flow together when a tectonic fault line shifts. Instead, the abrasive energy released in these rigid, upper layers triggers earthquakes and volcanic eruptions, both often generating tsunamis.

And so, with leaders of humanity. When we can deeply empathise with others, warmly support and kindly care for people, cultivate talent, accommodate human delicateness in all its various forms, build meaningful relations and foster mutual understanding, leaders come to embody compassion and coaching – daily leadership then becomes a natural flow of positive energy. But when we remain indifferent to others, interested only in ourselves and in shallow results such as profit and not in nurturing those who produce the results, leaders obsess about commanding and controlling others – daily leadership then becomes ossified, unable to handle diversity, stress and fragility, too often spewing forth negative energy.

The leadership transformation the world urgently needs is for all leaders to dynamically expand their mindset from surface-level, cold, fixed, reactive friction to deep-layer, warm, fluid, creative fusion.

Leadership should be a liberating dance. For me, *graceful leadership is an ennobling, engaging, empowering flow.*

So, my final questions for you are as follows. How are you going to begin your own journey into leading with grace? And if you've already started practising graceful leadership, what are your next steps? How will you enrich your grace? At and on whatever stage you find yourself, how will you make this splendid leadership torch that you've got hold of just for the moment burn as brightly as possible?

Graceful leadership toolbox

Tool A

Questions to help define your life purpose

+ Who am I when I'm at my best?
+ What do I really want to do with my life?
+ Who do I really want to be?
+ What is my 'why'?
+ What makes me come alive?
+ What feeds my life?
+ What do I consider my special skills, strengths and best contributions?
+ What motivates and brings me the most satisfaction?
+ What do I care deeply about?
+ What is my highest love?
+ What is sacred to me?
+ What do I believe in so much that I would gladly do it for free or even pay to do it?
+ What gives me the most energy?
+ What am I grateful for?
+ What is essential for me?
+ What and/or who am I serving?
+ How would I describe my ideal self?
+ Who am I now relative to who I really want to be?
+ What areas of my life are there where my ideal self is already aligned with my real self?
+ What areas of my life are there where my ideal self is not yet aligned with my real self?
+ What does it mean to live true to myself?
+ Do I feel that my life is aligned with what matters to my heart?
+ Am I living true to myself – today?
+ What is at risk if I truly live my passion?

Tool B

Wigglesworth's quadrants of spiritual intelligence

Quadrant 1: Self/self-awareness ↗

This quadrant contains five skills:

1. Awareness of your own world view: 'How do I view the world acknowledging that this is just a particular view, not *the* view?'
2. Awareness of life purpose: 'Why am I here?'
3. Awareness of values hierarchy: 'How will I choose what matters to me, to my values?'
4. Complexity of inner thought: 'Do I handle the complexity of life? Can I embrace both/and thinking instead of either/or thinking?'
5. Awareness of ego self/higher self: 'Who is driving my life, ego or higher self?'

Among other leadership benefits, this quadrant *builds our knowledge of self; illuminates our mission in life and what's closest to our heart; gives us courageous comfort to hold or stay with ambiguity and complexity; and helps us to follow the wise voice of higher self as opposed to only reacting from the ego.*

↓

Quadrant 3: Self/self-mastery →

This quadrant contains five skills:

12. Commitment to spiritual growth (gain deeper understanding of my world view): 'What can I keep learning from my belief system of origin, whether that is faith or non-faith based?'
13. Keeping higher self in charge: 'Am I consistently able to rapidly recognise, interrupt and overcome ego moments, especially in times of high stress?' And 'What is my soul's perspective on this situation?'
14. Living your purpose and values: 'Am I able to stand by my values even if at significant personal cost?'
15. Sustaining faith skill: 'During challenges, how willing am I to trust that, in the long run, life is purposeful?'
16. Seeking guidance from higher self: 'In this moment what would the wisest, most honest person I have known tell me to do?'

This quadrant builds on awareness skills (Quadrants 1 and 2), especially self-awareness, helping leaders to move well beyond ego towards self-mastery, *by learning how to live according to the mission and values you have chosen; and staying centred and composed in the face of difficulty and turmoil.*

⬐ **Quadrant 2:** Universal awareness

This quadrant contains six skills:

6. Awareness of interconnectedness of life: 'Do I deeply revere the natural world? Do I consider the consequences of my choices on ecosystems and future generations?'
7. Awareness of world views of others: 'When I disagree with others, do I still aspire to truly understand their perspectives?'
8. Breadth of time perception: 'Do I pause to reflect upon the thousands of years of leading up to this moment?'
9. Awareness of limitations/power of human perception: 'How well do I suspend initial perception/bias and permit wiser, multi-perspective intuition to kick in?'
10. Awareness of universal principles: 'Am I living aligned with universal ethics, morals and spiritual laws that explain what to do and how to live in harmony and with internal peace?'
11. Experience of transcendent oneness: 'Have I ever experienced a joyful realisation of my place and association with the cosmos?'

This quadrant helps leaders *to ponder the impacts of their actions in space and across time; to more profoundly comprehend others' viewpoints; to revere the universe's longevity; to seek more informed interpretations; to live from a deeper set of universal principles; and to discover a sense of ultimate performance flow, creative peak and wider connectedness to something larger than themselves.*

⬇

Quadrant 4: Social mastery and spiritual presence

This quadrant contains five skills:

17. Being a wise and effective teacher/mentor of spiritual principles: 'How can I activate the inner learner in others? Am I role modelling calmness, compassion and wisdom, even in times of high stress?'
18. Being a wise and effective leader/change agent: 'Am I able to deeply understand the needs of others and patiently reach win–win solutions? If an initiative fails, do I learn from the experience to become a better change agent?'
19. Making compassionate and wise decisions: 'Am I using my leadership power carefully, kindly, steadily, effortlessly, wisely, even with those who wish to harm me? Was there a wiser, more compassionate option?'
20. Being a calming, healing presence: 'Do I remain caring, centred and poised even if others are agitated or the situation is disturbing? Do people feel more at ease or peaceful in my presence?'
21. Being aligned with the ebb and flow of life: 'Am I in touch with my own levels of energy and in tune with what is happening around me? Do I instinctively know what might be emerging and able to apply just the right amount of action when it is needed to positively aid the process?'

This quadrant builds upon all three other quadrants, helping leaders to *invoke curiosity in others and demonstrate graceful leadership; use empathy to co-create welcomed change and learn from failures; use authority wisely and compassionately; remain calm and transfer that calmness to others; be present in the flow of daily life but know exactly when to add their touch to help or creatively transform.*

Tool C

Questions when analysing psychological safety data

✦ What is this team's purpose?
✦ What is it like to work in this team?
✦ What might keep you from 'being yourself' with your team or group or social setting?
✦ Imagine yourself in an everyday situation at work. And ask yourself: what keeps me from being 100 per cent?
✦ How often in the past month did you not speak up about something you felt wasn't right?
✦ How easy is it for each of you to be vulnerable to your team colleagues? (How often in the past month have you not allowed your vulnerability to show?)
✦ How often have you held back on offering a suggestion to a team colleague for fear of offending the other person or 'treading on their toes'?
✦ What can we count on each other for?
✦ What do you trust each of your team colleagues for most and least?
✦ What's holding us back? What are we avoiding? What are the 'unspeakable topics' (elephants in the room) for this team?
✦ What could you do to raise the level of trust? What would this look/feel like?
✦ What could you do to create a psychologically safe place for this team?
✦ How can we cultivate a team culture of inquiry that welcomes courageous, uncomfortable and disruptive questions?
✦ What would be the result of having psychological safety for this team?
✦ As a team, what reputation do you aspire to have?
✦ What do we need to do differently to achieve that reputation and fulfil our purpose?

Tool D

Questions to create a learning conversation when mistakes occur

◆ We're all disappointed but multiple factors could be at play here. Can we all perhaps uncover what they are?

◆ What have we done right?

◆ Where might we have gone off course?

◆ What can we do to fix this?

◆ What influence did we each have in this?

◆ How do we want to deal with this?

◆ What can we all learn from what's just happened?

◆ What might we each have done differently?

◆ How could we have assisted each other to respond and interact with more compassion?

◆ If we encounter this situation again, what do we each need to do differently in terms of our individual contributions?

◆ How can we all make sure this goes better next time?

◆ What is our deeper learning here?

◆ What can we create from this?

◆ How can we grow from this?

◆ How could this help trigger innovation?

◆ What possibilities do we now see?

◆ What needs our immediate attention going forward?

◆ What would be our ideal future solution?

◆ What would it take to create change on this issue?

◆ How can we support each other in taking the next steps?

◆ What unique contribution can we each make next time?

Tool E

Questions when preparing for organisational change

✦ Is this change necessary and, if so, why? And why now? Who believes so and upon what basis?

✦ If it does not occur now, what are the consequences?

✦ Are the requested shifts and possible staff reconfiguration considered valid and necessary by most of the team?

✦ Is the change going to effectively solve real problems or do colleagues suspect that it is being rolled out with ulterior motives?

✦ Does the team acknowledge that it is time to modify or let go of, and why?

✦ Who must let go of what if the change is to succeed?

✦ Are the possible losses (eg employment) and endings (eg traditional ways of working) being discussed openly?

✦ What is the new beginning going to require of us? And of myself?

✦ How might people's behaviours and attitudes change, especially if we form new teams?

✦ What must we stop doing, start doing, do more of, do less of?

✦ Who might gain and who might lose something from the change?

✦ Could restructuring end up polarising the workforce ecosystem?

✦ Are old scars of previous, perhaps poorly managed reconfigurations creating uncertainty and mistrust?

✦ Is there sufficient trust in the current leadership team?

✦ Does the leadership team realise that the psychological transition triggered by the change will need to be managed far beyond the apparent completion of the restructuring?

✦ Will we be able to offer affected and non-affected staff alike adequate support eg training, mentoring and coaching to handle new roles or pursue new career pathways or life options?

✦ Will affected employees be left to fend for themselves or has a core group been assigned to ensure the transition is handled with care and does that group have the necessary resources to do so?

✦ And will we be able to set up a means to closely monitor the transition?

Tool F

Situational coaching questions

+ How would you respond to/answer this?
+ What do you think can be done?
+ How would you solve this problem?
+ What options do we have?
+ What do you recommend?
+ What's the real challenge here for you?
+ What would you do if resources were not a concern?
+ If you could move one obstacle out of your way, what possibilities could that reveal?
+ Pause a moment and picture the wisest, most honest person you have ever met. Ask them, 'What would you do?' Hear their familiar voice. What is their reply?
+ What do you think would be a good first step?
+ Tell me what resources would be helpful. How or where might you acquire those?
+ How might you broaden your current line of thinking?
+ What will being fully committed to this idea look like/feel like?
+ In saying 'yes' to this, what are you saying 'no' to?
+ What did you learn about yourself during this process?
+ What was most valuable for you in this conversation?

Tool G

Communities, organisations and networks of grace

Examples of communities of research, practice and training

✦ Center for Compassion and Altruism Research and Education at Stanford University: ccare.stanford.edu
✦ Center for Courage and Renewal: couragerenewal.org
✦ Center for Creative Leadership: ccl.org
✦ Center for Empathy in International Affairs: centerforempathy.org
✦ Center for Mindful Self-Compassion: centerformsc.org
✦ Center for Positive Organizations: positiveorgs.bus.umich.edu
✦ Collective Leadership Institute: collectiveleadership.de
✦ Compassion Institute: compassioninstitute.com
✦ Solutions for the Human Animal: humananimal.earth
✦ Greater Good Science Center at the University of California: ggsc.berkeley.edu
✦ Innovative Dynamic Education and Action for Sustainability (IDEAS) programme: mitsloan.mit.edu/global-programs/ideas-asia-pacific
✦ International Center for Compassionate Organizations: compassionate.center
✦ International Foundation for Original Play: originalplay.eu
✦ Institute for New Economic Thinking: ineteconomics.org
✦ Institute for Organizational Science and Mindfulness: iomindfulness.org
✦ Kiel Institute for the World Economy: ifw-kiel.de
✦ Max Planck Institute for Human Cognitive and Brain Sciences: cbs.mpg.de/en
✦ Search Inside Yourself Leadership Institute: siyli.org
✦ u-school for Transformation: u-school.org
✦ Wisdom Labs: wisdomlabs.com

Examples of organisations and networks

- B Team: bteam.org
- Business Network International: bni.com
- Center for Compassionate Leadership: centerforcompassionateleadership.org
- Center for Nonviolent Communication: cnvc.org
- Charter for Compassion: charterforcompassion.org
- CEO Action for Diversity and Inclusion: ceoaction.com
- Climate and Development Knowledge Network: cdkn.org
- Coalition for Inclusive Capitalism: coalitionforinclusivecapitalism.com
- CompassionLab: compassionlab.com
- Compassionate Leadership Academy: compassionateleadership.academy
- Compassionate Mind Foundation: compassionatemind.co.uk
- Conscious Capitalism: consciouscapitalism.org
- Global Alliance for Banking on Values: gabv.org
- Global Compassion Coalition: globalcompassioncoalition.org
- Globally Responsible Leadership Initiative: grli.org
- Go-Giver Movement: thegogiver.com/movement
- Integrating Spirituality and Organizational Leadership Global Foundation: isolglobalfoundation.org
- Kickstarter: kickstarter.com
- Kindness Offensive: thekindnessoffensive.com
- Kindness organisation: kindness.org
- KindSpring: kindspring.org
- Kiva: kiva.org
- Life Vest Inside: lifevestinside.com
- Net Impact: netimpact.org
- Operation HOPE: operationhope.org
- Purpose Institute: thepurposeinstitute.com
- Random Acts of Kindness Foundation: randomactsofkindness.org
- Reboot the Future: rebootthefuture.org
- TED talks: ted.com/talks
- Wellbeing Economy Alliance: weall.org
- Women of the Future Programme: womenofthefuture.co.uk
- Women for Women International: womenforwomen.org
- World Economic Forum's New Champions: newchampions.org
- World Kindness Movement: theworldkindnessmovement.org

Tool H

Powerful questions for sensemaking

✦ What might have happened in the past that led up to this event?
✦ Who and what else is affected by this?
✦ What else is or could be going on here?
✦ What's surprising?
✦ What early warnings are we detecting?
✦ What patterns and themes do we see across sources?
✦ What's the real question underneath all this data?
✦ What are we not seeing?
✦ What questions are we not asking about this situation?
✦ What assumptions or beliefs are we holding that are the key to the insights we are having here?
✦ What would this circumstance look like if we were looking at it from a different perspective?
✦ What are our partners and stakeholders saying about it?
✦ What analogies or stories will help us share this with others?
✦ What's been the major learning or discovery so far?
✦ What can we unlearn from this?
✦ What's the possibility we see in this situation?
✦ What alternative courses of action are available?
✦ What haven't we thought of that could make a difference?
✦ What new connections are we making?
✦ Is/are the solution/s we've arrived at acceptable from a range of perspectives?
✦ What's the next level of thinking we need to do?
✦ What implications does this have for our future plans and work?
✦ If our success was completely guaranteed, what bold steps might we choose?
✦ What are the future implications of the actions we might take now?

- ✦ What other challenges might come our way and how might we meet them?
- ✦ If we had the chance to build our policies and programming systems from scratch to better address this issue, what kind of structures and processes would we create?
- ✦ What seed might we plant together today that could make the most difference to the future?
- ✦ What conversation, if begun today, could ripple out in a way that creates new dialogues and possibilities?

References

The beginning

Fifield, A (2015) *A Mighty Purpose: How Jim Grant sold the world on saving its children*. Other Press.

Jolly, R (ed) (2001) *Jim Grant: UNICEF visionary*. UNICEF Innocenti Research Centre.

Part 1

Brown, G, El-Erian, M et al (2023) *Permacrisis: A plan to fix a fractured world*. Simon and Schuster.

Tooze, A (2023) URL: weforum.org/videos/experts-explain-adam-tooze-what-is-the-polycrisis

Chapter 1

Bettencourt, S, Croad, R et al (2006) 'Not if but when: Adapting to natural hazards in the Pacific Islands Region'. World Bank.

Legu, M, McAvoy, D & Eloga, A (2008) 'Solomon Islands April 2nd 2007 earthquake and tsunami disaster: An evaluation of UNICEF's response in the emergency and initial recovery phases'. UNICEF Pacific Office.

Miskelly, R, Parks, W et al (2009) 'Monitoring the early response to a humanitarian crisis: The use of an omnibus survey in the Solomon Islands'. *Journal of Emergency Management* 7(5).

Chapter 2

Axtell, P (2021) *Compassionate Leadership: 16 simple ways to engage and inspire your team at work*. Simple Truths.

Bachelder, C (2018) *Dare to Serve: How to drive superior results by serving others*. Second edition. Berrett-Koehler Publishers.

Baldoni, J (2019) *GRACE: A leader's guide to a better us.* Indigo River Publishing.

Bloom, P (2016) *Against Empathy: The case for rational compassion.* HarperCollins.

Boyatzis, R & McKee, A (2005) *Resonant Leadership: Renewing yourself and connecting with others through mindfulness, hope, and compassion.* Harvard Business School Press.

Boyatzis, R, Smith, M & Blaize, N (2006) 'Developing sustainable leaders through coaching and compassion'. *Academy of Management Learning and Education* 5(1).

Boyatzis, R, Smith, M & Van Oosten, E (2019) *Helping People Change: Coaching with compassion for lifelong learning and growth.* Harvard Business Review Press.

Bradley, A (2020) *The Human Moment: The positive power of compassion in the workplace.* MID.

Brown, B (2018) *Dare to Lead: Brave work. Tough conversations. Whole hearts.* Random House.

Brush, K A (ed) (2022) *Heart-Centered Leadership: Unique pathways, approaches and strategies to soul-aligned success.* Exalted Publishing House.

Burnison, G (2022) *The Five Graces of Life and Leadership.* John Wiley and Sons.

Cabeen, J (2019) *Lead with Grace: Leaning into the soft skills of leadership.* Times 10 Publications.

Chapman, B & Sisodia, R (2015) *Everybody Matters: The extraordinary power of caring for your people like family.* Penguin Random House.

Clifton, J & Harter, J (2019) *It's the Manager: Moving from boss to coach.* Gallup Press.

Collins, J (2001) *Good to Great: Why some companies make the leap and others don't.* Harper Business.

Covey, S (1989) *Principle Centered Leadership.* Simon and Schuster.

Crowe, D (2023) *The Heart-Centered Leadership Playbook: How to master the art of heart in life and leadership.* Manuscripts LLC.

Curry, O S, Rowland, L A et al (2018) 'Happy to help? A systematic review and meta-analysis of the effects of performing acts of kindness on the wellbeing of the actor'. *Journal of Experimental Social Psychology 76.*

Dalai Lama & Hougaard, R (2019) 'The Dalai Lama on why leaders should be mindful, selfless, and compassionate'. *Harvard Business Review.*

Dhiman, S K & Roberts, G E (eds) (2023) *The Palgrave Handbook of Servant Leadership.* Palgrave Macmillan Cham.

Drucker, P F (1995) 'Introduction to Mary Parker Follett: Prophet of management'. In Graham, P (ed) *Mary Parker Follett – Prophet of Management: A celebration of writings from the 1920s.* Harvard Business School Press.

Drucker, P F (2002) *Managing in the Next Society.* Truman Talley Books.

Follett, M P (1924) *The Creative Experience.* Longmans.

Follett, M P (1949) 'The Essentials of Leadership'. In Urwick, L (ed) *Freedom and Co-ordination: Lectures in business organization.* Garland.

Gautam, K C (2018) *Global Citizen from Gulmi: My journey from the hills of Nepal to the halls of United Nations.* Publication Nepalaya.

Goleman, D (2000) 'Leadership that gets results'. *Harvard Business Review.*

Goleman, D (2005) *Emotional Intelligence: Why it can matter more than IQ.* Tenth anniversary edition. Bantam Books.

Hargreaves, P (2021) *The Fourth Bottom Line: Flourishing in the era of compassionate leadership.* SRA Books.

Hargreaves, S (2021) *The Compassionate Leader's Playbook: How to lead with compassion and ensure your people thrive.* Independently published.

Haskins, G, Thomas, M & Johri, L (eds) (2018) *Kindness in Leadership.* Routledge.

Higgins, S (2020) *Power of Love Leadership: 7 proven strategies to drive success, maximise results and inspire compassion and trust.* SRA Books.

Hopkinson, M (2014) *Compassionate Leadership: How to build an engaged, committed, and high performing team.* Piatkus.

Hougaard, R & Carter, J (2022) *Compassionate Leadership: How to do hard things in a human way*. Harvard Business Review Press.

ICF (2024) 'ICF, the gold standard in coaching'. URL: coachingfederation.org.

Kiechel, W (2012) 'The management century'. *Harvard Business Review*.

Maxwell, J C (2011) *The 5 Levels of Leadership: Proven steps to maximize your potential*. Centre Street.

Metcalf, H C & Urwick, L (eds) (1940) *Dynamic Administration: The collected papers of Mary Parker Follett*. Harper and Row.

Monteiro, G (1990) 'Hemingway's notion of "grace"'. *Studies in American Fiction* 18(1).

Papworth, K (2023) *Compassionate Leadership: For individual and organisational change*. De Gruyter.

Patnaik, D (2009) *Wired to Care: How companies prosper when they create widespread empathy*. FT Press.

Ross, K (2022) *The Kind Leader: A practical guide to eliminating fear, creating trust, and leading with kindness*. CRC Press.

Sorensen, D with Kohler, V (2016) *Big-Hearted Leadership: Five keys to create success through compassion*. Wise Ink Creative Publishing.

Thomas, M & Rowland, C (2014) 'Leadership, pragmatism and grace: A review'. *Journal of Business Ethics* 123.

Thompson, A (2020) *The Power of a Graceful Leader*. Lioncrest Publishing.

Tramuto, D with Corwin, T B (2022) *The Double Bottom Line: How compassionate leaders captivate hearts and deliver results*. Fast Company Press.

Tripathi, D, Tripathi, S & Priyadarshi, P (2023) 'The role of servant leaders in sustainable development'. In Dhiman, S K & Roberts, G E (eds) *The Palgrave Handbook of Servant Leadership*. Palgrave Macmillan Cham.

Van den Brink, J (2021) *The Three Companions: Compassion, Courage and Wisdom: The powerful keys to happier work and a fulfilled life*. SRA Books.

West, M A (2021) *Compassionate Leadership: Sustaining wisdom, humanity and presence in health and social care.* The Swirling Leaf Press.

Whitehead, C (2019) *Compassionate Leadership: Creating places of belonging.* Solopreneur Publishing.

Worline, M & Dutton, J E (2017) *Awakening Compassion at Work: The quiet power that elevates people and organizations.* Berrett-Koehler Publishers.

Woudstra, G (2025) *Mastering the Art of Team Coaching: An emergent approach to unleashing the potential in teams.* Second edition. Right Book Press.

Younger, H R (2021) *The Art of Caring Leadership: How leading with heart uplifts teams and organizations.* Berrett-Koehler Publishers.

Chapter 3

Al Khateeb, F (2021) 'Returning Iraqis face dire conditions following camp closures'. UNHCR 27 May. URL: unhcr.org/news/stories/returning-iraqis-face-dire-conditions-following-camp-closures

Center for Preventive Action (2024) 'Instability in Iraq'. 13 February. URL: cfr.org/global-conflict-tracker/conflict/political-instability-iraq

Stanley, T J (2000) *The Millionaire Mind.* Bantam.

UNICEF (2015) '5 questions: The rapid response mechanism'. 11 October. URL: medium.com/stories-from-unicef-in-iraq-english/5-questions-the-rapid-response-mechanism-59b9b8cdb3f0

UNICEF (2016) 'A heavy price for children: Violence destroys childhoods in Iraq'. URL: unicef.org/mena/media/7441/file/IRQ-Heavy%20Price%20-%20En.pdf

Chapter 4

Barsade, S & O'Neill, O A (2016) 'Manage your emotional culture'. *Harvard Business Review.*

Boedker, C, Vidgen, R et al (2011) *Leadership, Culture and*

Management Practices of High Performing Workplaces in
Australia: The High Performing Workplaces Index. Society for
Knowledge Economics.

Boyatzis, R & McKee, A (2005) op cit.

Business in the Community (2018) 'Mental Health at Work
Report: Seizing the momentum'. 23 October. URL:
affinityhealthhub.co.uk/d/attachments/mental-health-at-
work-survey-report-2018-23oct2018new-1540366141.pdf

CIPD (2019) 'Health and well-being at work'. URL: cipd.org/
globalassets/media/comms/news/iihealth-and-well-being-
at-work-2019.v1_tcm18-55881.pdf

Dalai Lama & Hougaard, R (2019) op cit.

Diener, E & Biswas-Diener, R (2008) *Happiness: Unlocking the
mysteries of psychological wealth*. Blackwell.

FirstCare (2018) 'Change at work: How absence, attitudes and
demographics are impacting UK employers'. URL: astutis.com/
astutis-hub/news/workplace-absence-costs-uk-economy

Fredrickson, B L & Losada, M F (2005) 'Positive affect and
the complex dynamics of human flourishing'. *American
Psychologist* 60.

Gelles, D (2015) *Mindful Work: How meditation is changing
business from the inside out*. Profile Books Ltd.

Hougaard, R & Carter, J (2018) *The Mind of the Leader: How
to lead yourself, your people, and your organization for
extraordinary results*. Harvard Business Review Press.

Hu, J & Liden, R C (2011) 'Antecedents of team potency and
team effectiveness: An examination of goal and process
clarity and servant leadership'. *Journal of Applied Psychology*
96(4).

Kaye, B & Jordan-Evans, S (2014) *Love 'Em or Lose 'Em: Getting
good people to stay*. Berrett-Koehler Publishers.

Lilius, J M, Worline, M C et al (2008) 'The contours and
consequences of compassion at work'. *Journal of
Organizational Behavior* 29(2).

Maalouf, G Y (2019) 'Effects of collaborative leadership on
organizational performance'. *International Journal of Multi-*

disciplinary *Research and Development* 6(1).

McKee, A & Wiens, K (2017) 'Prevent burnout by making compassion a habit'. *Harvard Business Review*.

McKinsey Health Institute (2022) 'Addressing employee burnout: Are you solving the right problem?'. 27 May. URL: mckinsey.com/mhi/our-insights/addressing-employee-burnout-are-you-solving-the-right-problem

Mehta, P K & Shenoy, S (2011) *Infinite Vision: How Aravind became the world's greatest business case for compassion.* Berrett-Koehler Publishers.

Organ, D W, Podsakoff, P M & Bradley, S (2005) *Organizational Citizenship Behavior: Its nature, antecedents, and consequences.* Sage Publications Inc.

Parmar, B (2016) 'The most empathetic companies, 2016'. *Harvard Business Review*.

Shanock, L & Eisenberger, R (2006) 'When supervisors feel supported: Relationships with subordinates, perceived supervisor support, perceived organizational support, and performance'. *Journal of Applied Psychology* 91(3).

Sisodia, R, Sheth, J N & Wolfe, D (2014) *Firms of Endearment: How world-class companies profit from passion and purpose.* Pearson FT Press.

Srinivasan, A, Meinhardt, R & Staehr, H (2020) 'Sight to the world: How Aravind improves access to care for millions'. URL: marketing.webassets.siemens-healthineers.com/1800000007508241/246fa201adb2/siemenshealthineers_Insights_Series_13_Sight_to_the_world.pdf

Trzeciak, S. & Mazzarelli, A (2019) *Compassionomics: The revolutionary scientific evidence that caring makes a difference.* Studer Group.

Walumbwa, F O, Hartnell, C A & Oke, A (2010) 'Servant leadership, procedural justice climate, service climate, employee attitudes, and organizational citizenship behavior: A cross-level investigation'. *Journal of Applied Psychology* 95.

Zaki, J (2016) 'Kindness contagion: Witnessing kindness inspires kindness, causing it to spread like a virus'. *Scientific American*, 26 July.

Part 2

Harris, M A, Brett, C E et al (2016) 'Personality stability from age 14 to age 77 years'. *Psychology and Aging* 31(8).

Ibarra, H & Scoular, A (2019) 'The leader as coach: How to unleash innovation, energy and commitment'. *Harvard Business Review*.

Mitchell, T (2017) *The Yoga of Leadership: A practical guide to health, happiness and inspiring total team engagement*. Independently published.

Thompson, A (2020) op cit.

Weng, H Y, Fox, A S et al (2013) 'Compassion training alters altruism and neural responses to suffering'. *Psychological Science* 24(7).

Practice 1

Bailey, C (2018) *Hyperfocus: How to work less to achieve more*. Macmillan.

Boyatzis, R & McKee, A (2005) op cit.

Brach, T (2003) *Radical Acceptance: Embracing your life with the heart of a Buddha*. Bantam Books.

Brach, T (2019) *Radical Compassion: Learning to love yourself and your world with the practice of RAIN*. Penguin Life.

Cirillo, F (2018) *The Pomodoro Technique: The acclaimed time-management system that has transformed how we work*. Crown.

Davidovich, C (2023) *Five Brain Leadership: How neuroscience can help you master your instincts and build better teams*. Page Two Press.

Elliott, J (2023) *Think Yourself Resilient: Harness your emotions. Build your confidence. Transform your life*. Thread.

Emmons, R A (2016) *The Little Book of Gratitude: Create a life of happiness and wellbeing by giving thanks*. Gaia Books.

Gelles, D (2015) op cit.

Germer, C K (2009) *The Mindful Path to Self-Compassion: Freeing yourself from destructive thoughts and emotions.* The Guilford Press.

Gilbert, P (2009) *The Compassionate Mind: Compassion focused therapy.* Constable and Robinson.

Gillions, A, Cheang, R & Duarte, R (2019) 'The effect of mindfulness practice on aggression and violence levels in adults: A systematic review'. *Aggression and Violent Behavior* 48.

Keller, G with Papasan, J (2013) *The One Thing: The surprisingly simple truth behind extraordinary results.* John Murray Press.

Klug, K, Felfe, J & Krick, A (2022) 'Does self-care make you a better leader? A multisource study linking leader self-care to health-oriented leadership, employee self-care, and health'. *International Journal of Environmental Research and Public Health* 19(11).

Kotler, S (2014) 'Is the secret to ultimate human performance the F-word?' *Forbes*, 8 January. URL: forbes.com/sites/stevenkotler/2014/01/08/the-research-is-in-a-four-letter-word-that-starts-with-f-is-the-real-secret-to-ultimate-human-performance

Kreitzman, L (2009) 'Guest column: Larks, owls and hummingbirds'. *New York Times*, 21 April. URL: archive.nytimes.com/opinionator.blogs.nytimes.com/2009/04/21/guest-column-larks-owls-and-hummingbirds

Lieberman, M (2013) *Social: Why our brains are wired to connect.* Oxford University Press.

Loehr, J & Schwartz, T (2003) *The Power of Full Engagement: Managing energy, not time, is the key to high performance and personal renewal.* The Free Press.

Madore, K P & Wagner, A D (2019) 'Multicosts of multitasking'. *Cerebrum: The Dana Forum on Brain Science.*

Mcfadden, J P (1997) 'Turkel [sic] Brings Life to Ed School Stage'. *The Harvard Crimson*, 2 December. URL: thecrimson.com/article/1997/12/2/turkel-brings-life-to-ed-school

Moore-Ede, M (1993) *The Twenty-Four-Hour Society.* Addison-Wesley.

Neff, K D (2009) 'The role of self-compassion in development: A healthier way to relate to oneself'. *Human Development* 52(4).

Neff, K D (2015) *Self-Compassion: The proven power of being kind to yourself.* William Morrow Paperbacks.

Niezink, L & Train, K (2020) 'The self in empathy: Self-empathy'. *Psychology Today*, 13 July. URL: psychologytoday. com/intl/blog/empathic-intervision/202007/the-self-in-empathy-self-empathy

Reivich, K & Shatte, A (2002) *The Resilience Factor: How changing the way you think will change your life for good.* Broadway Books.

Robbins, M (2007) *Focus on the Good Stuff: The power of appreciation.* Jossey-Bass.

Robertson, I H (2000) *Mind Sculpture: Unlocking your brain's untapped potential.* Fromm International.

Rock, D (2020) *Your Brain at Work, Revised and Updated: Strategies for overcoming distraction, regaining focus, and working smarter all day long.* HarperCollins.

Sturt, D & Nordstrom, T (2015) 'Do what you love? Or, love what you do?' *Forbes*, 13 March. URL: forbes.com/sites/davidsturt/2015/03/13/do-what-you-love-or-love-what-you-do

Watson, J & Strayer, D (2010) 'Supertaskers: Profiles in extraordinary multitasking ability'. *Psychonomic Bulletin and Review* 17.

Wood, J, Oh, J et al (2020) 'The relationship between work engagement and work-life balance in organizations: A review of the empirical research'. *Human Resource Development Review* 19(3).

Mindfulness apps:

workmindfulness.com/mindfulness-using-s-o-b-e-r-technique

'Search inside yourself: Google's life-changing mindfulness course' (businessinsider.com/search-inside-yourself-googles-life-changing-mindfulness-course-2014-8)

healthline.com/health/mental-health/top-meditation-iphone-android-apps

Practice 2

Brann, A (2022) *Neuroscience for Coaches: How coaches and managers can use the latest insights to benefit clients and teams.* Kogan Page.

Brierley, S & Costa, M (eds) (2016) *The Enteric Nervous System: 30 years later.* Springer.

Cooper, R K (2000) 'A new neuroscience of leadership: Bringing out more of the best in people'. *Strategy and Leadership* 28(6).

Delizonna, L (2017) 'High-performing teams need psychological safety. Here's how to create it'. *Harvard Business Review.*

Denny, B, Inhoff, M et al (2015) 'Getting over it: Long-lasting effects of emotion regulation on amygdala response'. *Psychological Science* 26(9).

DiGangi, J (2023) *Energy rising: The neuroscience of leading with emotional power.* Harvard Business Review Press.

Dimitriadis, N & Psychogios, A (2021) *Neuroscience for Leaders: Practical insights to successfully lead people and organizations.* Second edition. Kogan Page.

Doty, J R (2016) *Into the Magic Shop: A neurosurgeon's true story of the life-changing magic of compassion and mindfulness.* Hodder and Stoughton.

Freedman, J (nd) *Practicing Emotional Intelligence.* URL: 6seconds. org/practicing-eq-ebook

Fuchs, E & Flügge, G (2014) 'Adult neuroplasticity: More than 40 years of research'. *Neural Plasticity* 5.

Kahneman, D (2011) *Thinking, Fast and Slow.* Farrar, Straus and Giroux.

LeDoux, J (2019) *The Deep History of Ourselves: The four-billion-year story of how we got conscious brains.* Viking.

Lieberman, M, Eisenberger, N et al (2007) 'Putting feelings into words: Affect labeling disrupts amygdala activity in response to affective stimuli'. *Psychological Science* 18(5).

MacLean, P D (1990) *The Triune Brain in Evolution: Role in paleocerebral functions.* Plenum Press.

Pert, C B (1997) *Molecules of Emotion: The science behind mind-body medicine.* Scribner.

Quinn, R E, Fessell, D P & Porges, S W (2021) 'How to keep your cool in high-stress situations'. *Harvard Business Review.*

Radecki, D, Leonie, H et al (2021) *Psychological Safety: The key to happy, high-performing people and teams.* The Academy of Brain-based Leadership.

Siegel, D (2011) *Mindsight: Transform your brain with the new science of kindness.* Oneworld Publications.

Tan, C (2015) 'Just 6 seconds of mindfulness can make you more effective'. *Harvard Business Review.*

Taylor, J B (2006) *My Stroke of Insight: A brain scientist's personal journey.* Viking.

Verduyn, P & Lavrijsen, S (2015) 'Which emotions last longest and why: The role of event importance and rumination'. *Motivation and Emotion* 39(1).

Weng, H Y, Lapate, R C et al (2018) 'Visual attention to suffering after compassion training is associated with decreased amygdala responses'. *Frontiers in Psychology* 9.

Practice 3

Covey, S (2004) *The 8th Habit: From effectiveness to greatness.* Simon and Schuster.

Janosky, J (2017) *Show Your Self: Authentic compassionate leadership.* AugustSolutionsGroup LLC.

McGehee, P (2016) 'Spirituality is the deep human longing: Interview with Dr J Pittman McGehee'. *Consciousness NOW TV* 44(30) cited in Brown, B (2018) op. cit.

O'Donnell, K (1997) *Endoquality: The emotional and spiritual dimensions of the human being in organizations.* Editora Casa da Qualidade.

Rossiter, A (2006) *Developing Spiritual Intelligence: The power of you.* John Hunt Publishing Ltd.

Wigglesworth, C (2012) *SQ21: The Twenty-One Skills of Spiritual Intelligence.* SelectBooks.

Wigglesworth, C (2014) 'Deep intelligence: The critical

intelligences for leadership success in the 21st century'. URL: deepchange.com/Wigglesworth_Deep_Intelligence_white_paper.pdf

Zohar, D (1997) *ReWiring the Corporate Brain: Using the new science to rethink how we structure and lead organizations.* Berrett-Koehler Publishers.

Zohar, D & Marshall, I (2012) *Spiritual Intelligence: The ultimate intelligence.* Bloomsbury.

Practice 4

Argyris, C (1982) *Reasoning, Learning and Action: Individual and organizational.* Jossey-Bass.

Berridge, G R (2022) *Diplomacy: Theory and practice.* Sixth edition. Palgrave Macmillan.

Cooper, A F, Heine, J & Thakur, R (eds) (2015) *The Oxford Handbook of Modern Diplomacy.* Oxford University Press.

Fisher, R & Ury, W (1981) *Getting to Yes: Negotiating agreement without giving in.* Houghton Mifflin.

Forlè, F (2024) 'The sense of we-agency and vitality attunement: Between rhythmic alignment and emotional attunement'. *Phenomenology and the Cognitive Sciences* 23.

Fosha, D, Siegel, D J & Solomon, M F (eds) (2009) *The Healing Power of Emotion: Affective neuroscience, development and clinical practice.* W W Norton and Company.

Garvin, D A (2013) 'How Google sold its engineers on management'. *Harvard Business Review.*

Germer, C (2020) 'The near and far enemies of fierce compassion'. Center for Mindful Self-Compassion, 3 September. URL: centerformsc.org/the-near-and-far-enemies-of-fierce-compassion

Grant, A (2013) *Give and Take: A revolutionary approach to success.* Weidenfeld and Nicolson.

Jinpa, T (2015) *A Fearless Heart: How the courage to be compassionate can transform our lives.* Avery.

Kline, N (1999) *Time to Think: Listening to ignite the human mind.* Ward Lock.

McLaren, K (2013) *The Art of Empathy: A complete guide to life's most essential skill.* Sounds True.

Schwartz, T & McCarthy, C (2007) 'Manage your energy, not your time'. *Harvard Business Review.*

Singer, T & Klimecki, O (2014) 'Empathy and compassion'. *Current Biology* 24. Emphasis added.

Stone, D, Patton, B & Heen, S (2010) *Difficult Conversations: How to discuss what matters most.* Penguin.

UN Human Rights Council (2024) 'Universal periodic review'. URL: ohchr.org/en/hr-bodies/upr/upr-home

UNICEF (2016) 'Country Programme Document. Islamic Republic of Iran'. URL: unicef.org/executiveboard/country-programme-documents

UNICEF (2023) 'UNICEF Executive Board: An informal guide'. URL: unicef.org/executiveboard/media/14411/file/2023-EB-Informal_Guide_2023-EN-2022.12.19.pdf

UNOHCHR (2024) 'Reporting guidelines: Committee on the Rights of the Child'. URL: ohchr.org/en/treaty-bodies/crc/reporting-guidelines

Ury, W (1991) *Getting Past No: Negotiating your way from confrontation to cooperation.* Bantam Books.

Worline, M & Dutton, J E (2017) op cit.

Practice 5

Bazerman, M H (2014) *The Power of Noticing: What the best leaders see.* Simon and Schuster.

Berscheid, E (2003) 'The human's greatest strength: Other humans'. In Aspinwall, L G & Staudinger, U M (eds) *A Psychology of Human Strengths: Fundamental questions and future directions for a positive psychology.* American Psychological Association.

Davidovich, C (2023) op cit.

Earley, P C & Mosakowski, E (2004) 'Cultural intelligence'. *Harvard Business Review.*

Edmondson, A C (2012) *Teaming: How organizations learn, innovate, and compete in the knowledge economy.* Jossey-Bass.

Fiske, S T (2013) 'Controlling other people: The impact of power on stereotyping'. *American Psychologist* 48.

Pentland, A (2012) 'The new science of building great teams'. *Harvard Business Review.*

Rosales, R M (2016) 'Energizing social interactions at work: An exploration of relationships that generate employee and organizational thriving'. *Open Journal of Social Sciences* 4.

Schein, E H & Schein, P A (2018) *Humble Leadership: The power of relationships, openness, and trust.* Berrett-Koehler Publishers.

Stephens, J P, Heaphy, E D & Dutton, E J (2012) 'High-quality connections'. In Cameron, K & Spreitzer, G (eds) *Handbook of Positive Organizational Scholarship.* Oxford University Press.

Yammarino, F J & Dansereau, F (2002) 'Individualized leadership'. *Journal of Leadership and Organization Studies* 9(1).

Practice 6

Anathan, G (2021) 'Psychological safety: What it is & why it matters'. *Coach Transformation Academy Webinar Series.*

Argyris, C & Conant, J B (1991) 'Teaching smart people how to learn'. *Harvard Business Review.*

Barzun, M (2021) *The Power of Giving Away Power: How the best leaders learn to let go.* HarperCollins.

Bongino, D (2023) *The Gift of Failure (And I'll rethink the title if this book fails!).* Liberatio Protocol.

Bowden, M & Thomson, T (2018) *Truth and Lies: What people are really thinking.* HarperCollins.

Brown, B (2018) op cit.

Bungay Stanier, M (2016) *The Coaching Habit: Say less, ask more and change the way you lead forever.* Box of Crayons Press.

Clark, T (2020) *The 4 Stages of Psychological Safety: Defining the path to inclusion and innovation.* Berrett-Koehler Publishers.

Covey, S (1989) *The 7 Habits of Highly Effective People: Powerful lessons in personal change.* Simon and Schuster.

Duhigg, C (2016) 'What Google learned from its quest to build the perfect team'. *New York Times Magazine,* 28 February. URL: nytimes.com/2016/02/28/magazine/what-google-learned-from-its-quest-to-build-the-perfect-team.html

Dweck, C S (1986) 'Motivational processes affecting learning'. *American Psychologist* 41.

Edmondson, A C (2018) *The Fearless Organization: Creating psychological safety in the workplace for learning, innovation, and growth.* John Wiley and Sons.

Edmondson, A C (2023) *Right Kind of Wrong: Why learning to fail can teach us to thrive.* Cornerstone.

Frazier, M L, Fainshmidt, S et al (2017) 'Psychological safety: A meta-analytic review and extension'. *Personnel Psychology* 70(1).

Helbig, K & Norman, M (2023) *The Psychological Safety Playbook: Lead more powerfully by being more human.* Page Two Press.

Madden, L, Duchon, D et al (2012) 'Emergent organizational capacity for compassion'. *Academy of Management Review* 37(4).

Nichols, M P & Straus, M B (2021) *The Lost Art of Listening: How learning to listen can improve relationships.* Third edition. Guilford Press.

Parks, W (2021) 'Promoting mental well-being among children and young people in Bhutan'. *Druk Journal* 7(2).

Radecki, D, Leonie, H et al (2021) op cit.

Roberts, J & David, M E (2017) 'Put down your phone and listen to me: How boss phubbing undermines the psychological conditions necessary for employee engagement'. *Computers in Human Behavior* 75.

Rogelberg, S G (2019) *The Surprising Science of Meetings: How you can lead your team to peak performance.* Oxford University Press.

Schein, E H & Bennis, W G (1965) *Personal and Organizational Change through Group Methods: The laboratory approach.* John Wiley and Sons.

Shannon, J (2023) *Lead Engaging Meetings: A practical guide to maximize participation and effectiveness*. Independently published.

Sinek, S (2014) *Leaders Eat Last: Why some teams pull together and others don't*. Penguin Random House.

Smutny, M (2021) *THRIVE: The facilitator's guide to radically inclusive meetings*. Emerald Lake Books.

Stone, D, Patton, B & Heen, S (2010) op cit.

Tsheten, T, Chateau, D et al (2023) 'Impact of COVID-19 on mental health in Bhutan: A way forward for action'. *The Lancet Regional Health – Southeast Asia* 11.

UNICEF (2021) 'The State of the World's Children 2021: On My Mind: Promoting, protecting and caring for children's mental health'. URL: unicef.org/reports/state-worlds-children-2021

Washington, M C, Okoro, E A & Cardon, P W (2014) 'Perceptions of civility for mobile phone use in formal and informal meetings'. *Business and Professional Communication Quarterly* 77(1).

Practice 7

Cabeen, J (2019) op cit.

Kanov, J M, Maitlis, S et al (2004) 'Compassion in organizational life'. *American Behavioral Scientist* 47.

Kuensel (2017) 'The people's king'. 21 February. URL: kuenselonline.com/the-peoplex27s-king

Kuensel (2021) 'The compassionate king'. 21 February. URL: kuenselonline.com/the-compassionate-king

Ministry of Health, Royal Government of Bhutan & World Health Organization (2022) 'The people's pandemic: How the Himalayan Kingdom of Bhutan staged a world-class response to COVID-19'. URL: moh.gov.bt/wp-content/uploads/ict-files/2022/09/The-Peoples-Pandemic-How-the-Himalayan-Kingdom-of-Bhutan-staged-a-world-class-response-to-COVID-19.pdf

Pasricha, A (2021) 'Bhutan scripts rare COVID-19 success

story'. *Voa News*, 1 August. URL: voanews.com/a/
south-central-asia_bhutan-scripts-rare-covid-19-success-
story/6209022.html

Simas, D (2020) 'Compassionate management. LinkedIn CEO
Jeff Weiner interviewed by Obama CEO, David Simas'. URL:
youtube.com/watch?v=HUubrI-h1ss; news.linkedin.com/
compassionaward

Weiner, J (2017) 'Jeff Weiner on managing compassionately'. 31
January. URL: linkedin.com/learning/jeff-weiner-on-
managing-compassionately

Worline, M & Dutton, J E (2017) op cit.

Practice 8

Avolio, B J (2016) 'Candor and transparency: Aligning your
leadership constellation'. *People and Strategy* 39(4).

Chapman, S (2009) *The No Gossip Zone: A no-nonsense guide to a
healthy, high-performing work environment*. Sourcebooks.

Davey, L (2023) 'Hold your team accountable with compassion,
not fear'. *Harvard Business Review*.

Dutton, J E & Heaphy, E D (2003) 'The power of high-quality
connections'. In Kim S, Cameron, K S et al (eds) *Positive
Organizational Scholarship: Foundations of a new discipline*.
Berrett-Koehler Publishers.

Frost, P (2003) *Toxic emotions at work: How compassionate managers
handle pain and conflict*. Harvard Business School Press.

Frost, P & Robinson, S (1999) 'The toxic handler: Organizational hero – and casualty'. *Harvard Business Review*.

Gallo, A (2016) 'How to manage a toxic employee'. *Harvard
Business Review*.

Housman, M & Minor, D (2015) 'Toxic workers'. *Harvard
Business School Working Paper*.

Lewis, C (2021) *Toxic: A guide to rebuilding respect and tolerance in
a hostile workplace*. Bloomsbury Business.

Pearson, C & Porath, C (2009) *The Cost of Bad Behavior: How
incivility is damaging your business and what to do about it*.
Penguin Books.

Purushothaman, D & Stromberg, L (2022) 'Leaders, stop rewarding toxic rock stars'. *Harvard Business Review*.

Rimm, A (2013) 'To guide difficult conversations, try using compassion'. *Harvard Business Review*.

Scott, K (2019) *Radical Candor: How to get what you want by saying what you mean*. Pan Books.

Stone, D, Patton, B & Heen, S (2010) op cit.

Sutton, R I (2017) *The Asshole Survival Guide: How to deal with people who treat you like dirt*. Harper Business.

Whitehead, C (2019) op cit.

Practice 9

Cooperrider, D L & Whitney, D (2005) *Appreciative Inquiry: A positive revolution in change*. Berrett-Koehler Publishers.

Dames, S (2021) *Root Strength: A health and care professional's guide to minimizing stress and maximizing thriving*. Elsevier.

Duffy, H I (2022) 'Empower the ember and honor the human'. In Brush, K A (ed) *Heart-Centered Leadership: Unique pathways, approaches and strategies to soul-aligned success*. Exalted Publishing House.

Manzoni, J F & Barsoux, J (2002) *The Set Up to Fail Syndrome: How good managers cause great people to fail*. Harvard Business School Press.

Rogers, C R (1951) *Client-centered Therapy: Its current practice, implications and theory*. Houghton Mifflin.

Thompson, G with Biro, S (2007) *Unleashed!: The leader as coach*. SelectBooks.

Worline, M & Dutton, J E (2017) op cit.

Practice 10

Armstrong, K (2011) *Twelve Steps to a Compassionate Life*. Anchor Books.

Avramchuk, A S, Manning, M R & Carpino, R A (2013) 'Compassion for a change: A review of research and theory'. *Research in Organizational Change and Development* 21.

Bridges, W (1991) *Managing Transitions: Making the most of change*. Addison-Wesley.

Brown, H (2021) 'What is compassion fatigue? 24 causes and symptoms explained'. Positive Psychology, 13 September. URL: positivepsychology.com/compassion-fatigue

Jinpa, T (2015) op cit.

Jit, R, Sharma, C S & Kawatra, M (2017) 'Healing a broken spirit: Role of servant leadership'. *The Journal for Decision Makers* 42(2).

Kotter, J P (2012) *Leading Change*. Harvard Business Review Press.

Kotter, J P & Cohen, D S (2002) *The Heart of Change: Real-life stories of how people change their organizations*. Harvard Business School Press.

Kübler-Ross, E & Kessler, D (2005) *On Grief and Grieving: Finding the meaning of grief through the five stages of loss*. Simon and Schuster.

Powley, E H (2012) 'The process and mechanisms of organizational healing'. *Journal of Applied Behavioral Science* 49(1).

Scarlett, H (2019) *Neuroscience for organizational change: An evidence-based practical guide to managing change*. Kogan Page.

Sturnick, J A (1998) 'Healing leadership'. In Spears, L C (ed) *Insights on Leadership*. John Wiley and Sons.

Sue, D W & Spanierman, L (2020) *Microaggressions in Everyday Life*. John Wiley and Sons.

Washington, E F (2022) 'Recognizing and responding to micro-aggressions at work'. *Harvard Business Review*.

West, M A & Lyubovnikova, J (2012) 'Real teams or pseudo teams? The changing landscape needs a better map'. *Industrial and Organizational Psychology* 5.

Whitehead, C (2019) op cit.

Practice 11

Aaker, J & Bagdonas, N (2020) *Humour, Seriously. Why humour is a superpower at work and in life. And anyone can harness it. Even you*. Penguin Random House.

Bitterly, B, Brooks, A W & Schweitzer, M E (2016) 'Risky business: When humour increases and decreases status'. *Journal of Personality and Social Psychology* 112(3).

Bitterly, B & Brooks, A W (2020) 'Sarcasm, self-deprecation, and inside jokes: A user's guide to humour at work'. *Harvard Business Review*.

Brown, S with Vaughan, C (2009) *Play: How it shapes the brain, opens the imagination, and invigorates the soul*. Avery.

Dell, P (2019) *Why We Laugh: The science of giggles (decoding the mind)*. Compass Point Books.

Guney, S & Lee, T H (2021) 'When is humour helpful?' *Harvard Business Review*.

Hughes, L W & Avey, J B (2009) 'Transforming with levity: Humour, leadership, and follower attitudes'. *Leadership and Organization Development* 30(6).

Lehmann-Willenbrock, N & Allen, J A (2014) 'How fun are your meetings? Investigating the relationship between humour patterns in team interactions and team performance'. *Journal of Applied Psychology* 99(6).

Martin, R A, Puhlik-Doris, P et al (2003) 'Individual differences in uses of humour and their relation to psychological wellbeing: Development of the Humour Styles Questionnaire'. *Journal of Research in Personality* 37.

Martin, R A (2007) *The Psychology of Humour: An integrative approach*. Elsevier Academic Press.

Panksepp, J (2004) *Affective Neuroscience: The foundations of human and animal emotions*. Oxford University Press.

Petelczyc, C A, Capezio, A et al (2018) 'Play at work: An integrative review and agenda for future research'. *Journal of Management* 44(1).

Plester, B (2009) 'Healthy humour: Using humour to cope at work'. *Kōtuitui: New Zealand Journal of Social Sciences Online* 4(1).

Plester, B & Lloyd, R (2023) 'Happiness is "being yourself": Psychological safety and fun in hybrid work'. *Administrative Sciences* 13(10).

Robert, C (2017) *The Psychology of Humour at Work: Current issues in work and organizational psychology.* Routledge.

Rosenberg, C, Walker, A et al (2021) 'Humour in workplace leadership: A systematic search scoping review'. *Frontiers in Psychology* 12.

Samson, A C & Gross, J J (2012) 'Humour as emotion regulation: The differential consequences of negative versus positive humour'. *Cognition and Emotion* 26(2).

Practice 12

Cornia, G A, Jolly, R & Stewart, F (eds) (1987) *Adjustment with a Human Face: Volume I: Protecting the Vulnerable and Promoting Growth.* Clarendon Press.

Emmons, R (2016) op cit.

Parks, W with Abbott, D & Wilkinson, A (2009) 'Protecting Pacific island children and women during economic and food crises: A working document for advocacy, debate and guidance'. UNICEF Pacific, UNDP Pacific Centre, and UNESCAP Pacific Operations Centre. URL: childimpact. unicef-irc.org/documents/view/id/51/lang/en

Stejskal, T M (2023) *The 5 Practices of Highly Resilient People: Why some flourish when others fold.* Hachette Go.

UN Global Pulse (2010) 'Voices of the vulnerable: Recovery from the ground up'. URL: ids.ac.uk/download.php? file=files/dmfile/VoicesoftheVulnerable0.pdf

UNESCAP (2010) 'Outcome of the Pacific Conference on the Human Face of the Global Economic Crisis'. URL: unescap. org/sites/default/d8files/event-documents/E66_INF7.pdf

UNICEF (2010) 'Voices of the vulnerable in the Pacific: Summary note'. URL: childimpact.unicef-irc.org/ documents/view/id/52/lang/en

Practice 13

Brann, A (2022) op cit.

Bungay Stanier, M (2020) *The Advice Trap: Be humble, stay curious & change the way you lead forever.* Box of Crayons Press.

Carroll, J (2016) 'Leadership: Are you a gardener or a mechanic?' 18 May. URL: jimcarrollsblog.com/blog/2016/5/18/leadership-are-you-a-gardener-or-a-mechanic

Creelman, D, Tavis, A & Bungay Stanier, M (2018) *The Truth and Lies of Performance Management.* Box of Crayons Press.

ICF (2021) 'ICF Code of Ethics'. URL: coachingfederation.org/app/uploads/2021/01/ICF-Code-of-Ethics-1.pdf

Jinpa, T (2015) op cit.

McNatt, D B (2000) 'Ancient Pygmalion joins contemporary management: A meta-analysis of the result'. *Journal of Applied Psychology* 85.

Norman, C (2022) *The Transformational Coach: Free your thinking and break through to coaching mastery.* The Right Book Press.

Thompson, G with Biro, S (2007) op cit.

Walters, A (2020) *Leading with Grit and Grace: A journey in organizational culture change.* Independently published.

Whitehead, C (2019) op cit.

Zander, R S & Zander, B (2000) *The Art of Possibility: Transforming professional and personal life.* Harvard Business School Press.

Practice 14

Algoe, S B & Haidt, J (2009) 'Witnessing excellence in action: The 'other-praising' emotions of elevation, gratitude, and admiration'. *Journal of Positive Psychology* 4.

Grant, A (2013) op cit.

Johri, L (2018) 'Kindness in leadership: A global perspective'. In Haskins, G, Thomas, M & Johri, L (eds) *Kindness in Leadership.* Routledge.

Scharmer, O & Kaufer, K (2013) *Leading from the Emerging Future: From ego-system to eco-system economics.* Berrett-Koehler Publishers.

Tomasulo, D J (2013) 'What is the reciprocity ring? What can happen when you ask for what you really want?' *Psychology Today*, 29 August. URL: psychologytoday.com/intl/blog/the-healing-crowd/201308/what-is-the-reciprocity-ring

Practice 15

Anthony, S D, Cobban, P et al (2020) *Eat, Sleep. Innovate: How to make creativity an everyday habit inside your organization.* Harvard Business Review Press.

Baldoni, J (2023) *Grace Under Pressure: Leading through change and crisis.* Savio Republic.

Baudelaire, C (1863) *The Painter of Modern Life and Other Essays.* Translated and edited by Jonathan Mayne. New York Graphic Society Publishers Ltd.

Carlsen, A, Clegg, S & Gjersvik, R (2012) *Idea Work: Lessons of the extraordinary in everyday creativity.* J W Cappelens Forlag AS.

Ding, C, Schreiber, S G et al (2017) 'Post-glacial biography of trembling aspen inferred from habitat models and genetic variance in quantitative traits'. *Scientific Reports* 7(1).

Edgeloe, J M, Severn-Ellis, A A et al (2022) 'Extensive polyploid clonality was a successful strategy for seagrass to expand into a newly submerged environment'. *Proceedings of the Royal Society B.*

Edwards, B (1988) *Drawing on the Artist Within: A guide to innovation, invention, imagination and creativity.* HarperCollins Publishers.

Evans, S, Kingsley, G et al (2018) 'Seagrass on the brink: Decline of threatened seagrass *Posidonia australis* continues following protection'. *PLOS ONE* 13.

George, B & Clayton, Z (2022) *True North: Leading authentically in today's workplace, emerging leader edition.* John Wiley and Sons.

Girls Not Brides (nd) 'Child Marriage Atlas'. URL: girlsnotbrides.org/learning-resources/child-marriage-atlas/atlas/nepal

Goldsmith, M with Reiter, M (2007) *What Got You Here Won't Get You There: How successful people become even more successful.* Hachette Books.

Hamel, G & Zanini, M (2020) *Humanocracy: Creating organizations as amazing as the people inside them.* Harvard Business Review Press.

Hull, R B, Robertson, D P & Mortimer, M (2020) *Leadership for Sustainability: Strategies for tackling wicked problems.* Island Press.

Johnson, D (2023) *The Unlearning Curve: How to break free and unlock your potential.* Independently published.

Katzenbach, J R & Smith, D K (1993) *The Wisdom of Teams: Creating the high-performance organization.* Harvard Business Review Press.

Klein, G (2007) 'Performing a project premortem'. *Harvard Business Review.*

Kuenkel, P (2016) *The Art of Leading Collectively: Co-Creating a sustainable, socially just future.* Chelsea Green Publishing.

LaFasto, F M J & Larson, C (2011) *The Humanitarian Leader in Each of Us: 7 choices that shape a socially responsible life.* Sage Publications Inc.

Mandela, N (1994) *Long Walk to Freedom: The autobiography of Nelson Mandela.* Little Brown and Company.

McGonigal, J (2022) *Imaginable: How to see the future coming and be ready for anything.* Bantam Press.

Morelli, T L, & Carr, S C (2011) 'A review of the potential effects of climate change on quaking aspen (*Populus tremuloides*) in the Western United States and a new tool for surveying sudden aspen decline'. General Technical Report 235. USA Department of Agriculture, Forest Service, Pacific Southwest Research Station.

OCHA (2014) 'Iraq IDP Crisis Situation Report No 7'. 15 August. URL: reliefweb.int/report/iraq/iraq-idp-crisis-situation-report-no-7-9-august-15-august-2014

Schacter, D L, Benoit, R G, & Szpunar, K K (2017) 'Episodic future thinking: Mechanisms and functions'. *Current Opinion in Behavioral Sciences* 17.

Scharmer, O & Kaufer, K (2013) op cit.

Sharma, M (2017) *Radical Transformational Leadership: Strategic action for change agents.* North Atlantic Books.

Stroh, D P (2015) *Systems Thinking for Social Change: A practical guide to solving complex problems, avoiding unintended consequences, and achieving lasting results.* Chelsea Green Publishing.

Uit de Weerd, F & Fridjhon, M (2021) *Systems Inspired Leadership: How to tap collective wisdom to navigate change, enhance agility, and foster collaboration.* Independently published.

UNDP (2022) 'UNDP RBAP: Foresight Playbook'. United Nations Development Programme.

UNFPA & UNICEF (2021) 'Global Programme to End Child Marriage. Nepal 2020 Country Profile'. URL: unicef.org/media/111391/file/Child-marriage-country-profile-Nepal-2021.pdf

UNICEF (2014a) 'Cost of inaction: Child and adolescent marriage in Nepal'. URL: girlsnotbrides.org/learning-resources/resource-centre/cost-inaction-child-adolescent-marriage-nepal

UNICEF (2014b) 'UNICEF Nepal Annual Report'. URL: sites.unicef.org/about/annualreport/files/Nepal_Annual_Report_2014.pdf

UNICEF (2018) 'Iranian experts from public and private sectors come together'. URL: unicef.org/mena/stories/iranian-experts-public-and-private-sectors-come-together

UNICEF (2019) 'Nepal country profile'. URL: unicef.org/media/88831/file/Child-marriage-Nepal-profile-2019.pdf

UNICEF (2023) 'UNICEF innovation challenge 2022'. URL: unicef.org/iran/en/stories/unicef-innovation-challenge-2022

Vogt, E E, Brown, J & Isaacs, D (2003) *The Art of Powerful Questions: Catalyzing insight, innovation, and action.* Whole Systems Associates.

World Economic Forum (2023) 'Future of Jobs Report. Insight, May'. URL: www3.weforum.org/docs/WEF_Future_of_Jobs_2023.pdf

Zohar, D & Marshall, I (2012) op cit.

The ending

Le Pichon, X (2009) 'The fragility at the heart of humanity'. An interview by Krista Tippett. 25 June. URL: onbeing.org/programs/xavier-le-pichon-the-fragility-at-the-heart-of-humanity

Gratitude

To my *Anam Ċara*, Ranjana, whose graceful presence in my life personifies everything I seek. 'Namaste' – I bow to you.

To Henry, Oliver, Matisse and Yashna – you'll never know how much I'm blessed with your courage, energy and laughter.

To Jacqui, who set me upon this transformative path – I'll never forget your faith.

To the rest of my family, especially my late father Professor Patrick Parks. Dad, I so wish you were still with us, yet I sense you are still among us. To my late mother, Sally O'Hara Parks, who passed on as I was completing this book. Mum, your love of poetry and theatre will forever inspire me. Mary, my incredibly special sister, and her family; my cherished brothers, Eddie and Geoff, and their families. Phil, Charlie, Chris and my worldwide circle of friends – you know who you are. Thank you all for the unwavering support and advice over the years. And to Gypsy, Whisky, Boopy and Tokyo – my *Kahu*.

To all the graceful leaders named in this book and especially the magic five who honoured me with in-depth interviews – Gillian, Hamida, Mohamed, Peter and Ugochi – I salute you.

To the countless individuals, teams and coaches who have taught me so much across the many cultures I've had the privilege to experience – my endless thanks. I've named several colleagues in various stories but here allow me to acknowledge the special support of Karen Mannan, Priya Ban, Geetu Gurung, Ahmed Al Mufty, Nian Gilyana, Leila Ensanzadeh, Kuenzang Wangmo, Namgay Dorji, Sreymach Than and Sopheng Prak.

To the Right Book Press team: Sue Richardson, Paul East, Beverley Glick, Andrew Chapman, Nick Redeyoff, Dawn Hoare and Natalia Fantetti – what a privilege to be guided by you all.

And to you, the reader – I hope that I have helped you to find your way into, or perhaps further into, graceful leadership. As Mahatma Gandhi once said, 'In a gentle way, you can shake the world.' Our world needs *you* now, more than ever.

About the leaders

Dr Mohamed Ag Ayoya of Mali is an assistant secretary-general of the United Nations. He is currently the deputy special representative of the secretary-general for the United Nations Multidimensional Integrated Stabilisation Mission in the Central African Republic (MINUSCA), resident coordinator of the United Nations system and humanitarian coordinator for the Central African Republic. Prior to his present position, Mohamed served in Afghanistan as the representative of UNICEF. He has also served as UNICEF representative in Somalia and South Sudan between 2019 and 2022, as well as in Guinea (2013–2016) and Zimbabwe (2016–2019). He played a critical role in leading UNICEF's response to the Ebola outbreak in Guinea, in child survival and development programmes in numerous countries and in managing complex and protracted emergencies, including Covid-19. Mohamed holds a medical degree from the School of Medicine and Pharmacy in Mali and a PhD in nutritional sciences from Cornell University in the United States. He is the author or co-author of more than 30 publications and has received various UNICEF awards acknowledging his leadership and achievements.

Ugochi Daniels is deputy director general of operations for the UN International Organisation for Migration (IOM). Prior to IOM, she was the chief of staff at the United Nations Relief and Works Agency for Palestine Refugees (UNRWA) covering Jordan, Lebanon, Syria and the Occupied Palestinian Territory. Between 2018 to 2020, Ugochi was the UN resident coordinator in the Islamic Republic of Iran. From 2013–2018, she was UNFPA's chief of the Humanitarian and Fragile Contexts Branch, covering more than 70 countries. Her stint at UNFPA also included assignments in the Philippines (country represent-ative, 2010–2013), Nepal (deputy representative, 2007–2010) and as deputy program manager for the Africa Youth Alliance

(2002–2007) covering Ghana, Tanzania, Botswana and Uganda. She also worked for the United States Agency for International Development (USAID) Mission in Nigeria (1999-2002). Ugochi is recognised as a UN (s)hero for her advocacy of women's health in humanitarian emergencies and for protecting human rights and promoting peace. She holds a bachelor's and master's in geography as well as a postgraduate diploma in information management for business decisions and is a Microsoft-certified systems engineer.

Peter Hawkins assumed the position of UNICEF representative to Yemen in November 2022. Before that, he was UNICEF's representative in Nigeria (May 2019–October 2022) and in Iraq (from September 2015 to April 2019). Prior to UNICEF, Peter worked with the UK's Department for International Development as head of profession for programme management (UK); team leader for human development (Ethiopia); group head for sub-national governance, conflict reduction and democracy, accountability and voice (Pakistan); deputy head for provincial reconstruction team (Afghanistan); and team leader for human development (Nigeria). Between 1985 and 2004, he served with Save the Children UK as regional director for East and Central Africa, regional director for South Asia, and emergency coordinator (all from Save's UK headquarters), as well as country director (Angola), deputy country director (Sri Lanka) and senior programme coordinator (Ethiopia). A British national, Peter holds an advanced degree in law (LLM) and a bachelor's in African language (Amharic) and law from the School of Oriental & African Studies (SOAS), University of London.

Hamida Lasseko is the former UNICEF representative in South Sudan, appointed in January 2021. She has extensive experience in diverse roles across multiple countries, often in volatile, uncertain and challenging environments. Before South Sudan, she served as UNICEF representative in Iraq, deputy representative in Syria, and held senior positions in Afghanistan, Somalia and Sri Lanka, leading complex humanitarian responses and development operations, including change management processes. Prior to her leadership positions, Hamida applied hands-on experience and skills delivering essential services to vulnerable populations; first as a national project officer based in Kigoma, Tanzania (1996–2001), and later as an emergency officer serving Burundian and Rwandese refugees in western parts of Tanzania (2001–2005). A Tanzanian national, she holds a master's in sociology from the Commonwealth Open University (United Kingdom) and an advanced diploma in nursing education from Muhimbili University College of Health Sciences (Tanzania).

Gillian Mellsop began her international development career in 1979 with New Zealand's Ministry of Foreign Affairs. In 1982, she joined the Australian Agency for International Development (AusAID) serving in Australian Missions in Bangladesh, India (also covering Nepal and Bhutan), Laos, the Pacific, Papua New Guinea, the Philippines, and lastly as director of AusAID's UN and Commonwealth Programme. Gillian joined UNICEF in April 2003 as representative in Suva, Fiji Islands, where she was responsible for the Pacific sub-regional programme covering 14 Pacific island countries. She then served as a representative with UNICEF in Nepal (2006–2011), in China (2011–2015) and Ethiopia (2015–2019). Since retiring, Gillian has acted as director of the Division of Human Resources (2021), representative in India (2022) and senior HR advisor in Afghanistan (2024). She holds a bachelor's in anthropology and history from the University of Auckland, a postgraduate diploma in community counselling from the University of Canberra and a master's in development management from the Australian National University.

About the author

A leader for UNICEF in the Kingdom of Cambodia, the Kingdom of Bhutan and the Islamic Republic of Iran, Will Parks also held senior UNICEF positions in the Republic of Iraq, the Federal Democratic Republic of Nepal and the Pacific Islands. He earlier worked for the Australian and UK Aid Agencies as well as the Secretariat of the Pacific Community and the World Health Organization. Will holds a PhD in public health and medical anthropology (University of Queensland), a master's in social anthropology (University of Durham) and a bachelor's in biology (University of Southampton). To date, he has authored and co-authored 36 publications, including books, book chapters and journal articles as well as presented at 40 conferences and international workshops. Will is also accredited with the International Coaching Federation. He can be contacted via LinkedIn: kh.linkedin.com/in/dr-will-parks-23149114 or email: parks_will@hotmail.com

EU Safety Representative: euComply OÜ Pärnu mnt 139b-14 11317 Tallinn
Estonia hello@eucompliancepartner.com +33 756 90241

www.ingramcontent.com/pod-product-compliance
Lightning Source LLC
Chambersburg PA
CBHW040141270326
41928CB00023B/3292